A FRAGILE SOCIAL FABRIC?

A Fragile Social Fabric?

Fairness, Trust, and Commitment in Canada

RAYMOND BRETON
NORBERT J. HARTMANN
JOS L. LENNARDS
PAUL REED

McGill-Queen's University Press
Montreal & Kingston · London · Ithaca

© McGill-Queen's University Press 2004
ISBN 0-7735-2576-9 (cloth)
ISBN 0-7735-2577-7 (paper)

Legal deposit first quarter 2004
Bibliothèque nationale du Québec

Printed in Canada on acid-free paper that is 100% ancient forest free
(100% post-consumer recycled), processed chlorine free.

McGill-Queen's University Press acknowledges the support of the
Canada Council for the Arts for our publishing program. We also
acknowledge the financial support of the Government of Canada
through the Book Publishing Industry Development Program (BPIDP)
for our publishing activities.

National Library of Canada Cataloguing in Publication

  A fragile social fabric : fairness, trust and commitment in Canada /
Raymond Breton ... [et al.].

Includes bibliographical references and index.
ISBN 0-7735-2576-9 (bnd)
ISBN 0-7735-2577-7 (pbk)

1. Social participation – Canada.   2. Social values – Canada.
3. Civil society – Canada.   4. Canada – Social conditions.
I. Breton, Raymond, 1931– .

FC97.F72 2003   306'.0971   C2003–902968–9
F1021.2.F72 2003

Typeset in 10/12 Sabon by True to Type

Contents

Preface

This study's goal is to enhance the debate about how to assess and promote the quality of societal life by drawing attention to the importance of a dimension that, in our opinion, has not been sufficiently emphasized. Our concern is to highlight the nature and importance of the social infrastructure and its basis in a civic covenant which defines what, as citizens, we can expect in our social relations, what we owe to each other, and what we owe to society. We believe that an exploration of the civic covenant in Canadian society is timely, because of the articulation and diffusion of a more narrow market view of what the health of a society entails.

Our audience is not primarily academic. Indeed, in addition to scholars, we seek to engage policy makers and the general public. We hope that our analysis is of interest to civil servants, researchers in public-policy institutes, journalists, social analysts, people active in non-governmental organizations, and advocacy groups concerned with pressing social issues.

This study began as part of a larger research initiative, "Individuals, Institutions and the Social Contract in Canada," directed by Paul Reed. Its data comes primarily from a Canada-wide representative survey which was conducted for us by the Environics Research Group. The construction of the interview schedule for the large-scale survey was based partly on the results of in-depth interviews, carried out in an earlier phase of the study, with a small sample of people of diverse backgrounds in Toronto, Montreal, Rivière-du-Loup, and Pembroke. The research reported in this manuscript was made possible by financial support provided by the Social Sciences and Humanities Research Council of Canada and by the Kahanoff Foundation; we gratefully acknowledge their assistance. For thoughtful suggestions that improved the analysis and its presentation, we wish to express our appreciation to Jeffrey Reitz, who read more than one version of the manuscript, and to James Giffen, Ron Gillis, Neil Nevitte, and Yaacov Glickman. Their critical comments and suggestions have been very useful. We also thank Michèle Wilkie for her valuable assistance in editing an earlier version of the manuscript; Donna Dasko, vice-president of Environics, for the facilitating role she played in the organization and execution of the survey; Laine Ruus, of the Data Library Service of the University of Toronto, for her assistance with the World Values Survey; and Curtis Fahey for the excellent final copy-editing. A special thank you to Erich Hartmann for the media searches, figures, and tables used throughout the book.

We realize that the scope of this study cannot do justice to phenomena as complex as the foundations of the social fabric and the dynamics of the social covenant. We are also conscious that, owing to the limitations of a cross-sectional study, we cannot trace changes over time. We believe that the main significance of this study derives from the new directions for research it suggests and from the expansion of the terms of the public-policy debate it proposes.

PART ONE
Assessing the Strength of the Social Fabric

I

Introduction

If the institutions of democracy and capitalism are to work properly, they must coexist with certain premodern cultural habits that ensure their proper functioning. Law, contract, and economic rationality provide a necessary but not sufficient basis for both the stability and prosperity of postindustrial societies; they must as well be leavened with reciprocity, moral obligation, duty toward community, and trust, which are based in habit rather than rational calculation. The latter are not anachronisms in a modern society but rather the sine qua non of the latter's success. (Francis Fukuyama, *Trust: The Social Virtues and the Creation of Prosperity*, 1995)

For a number of years, the Human Development Reports of the United Nations have ranked Canada as one of the countries with the highest quality of life in the world. This is a source of pride to many Canadians and an important theme in the feel-good talk by politicians and others about the state of our society.

But is this ranking sufficient? Does it tell the whole story or even an adequate one? The ranking is based on such indicators as economic performance (e.g., real GDP per capita), medical conditions such as life expectancy, and level of educational development. This is consistent with much of our preoccupations as a society. Indeed, we regularly assess the level of income, job creation, productivity, competitiveness, and health care. We attempt to probe the impact of globalization and free trade. We follow trends in the evolution of information technology and, recently, of "e-commerce." We are concerned with our educational institutions, but largely as economic enterprises, the focus being on how well our schools prepare the young to compete in the economy and how much university research contributes to the economy and to our international competitiveness. These concerns are quite legitimate. Some are indeed basic.

But what if people feel that they are not treated fairly; that they cannot trust one another and their political and business leaders? What if they find that their contribution to society is not recognized;

that they do not feel at home in their community or society or that they feel left behind in the evolution of economic and political institutions? What if they do not feel obligated to help others and contribute to the community because they see themselves primarily as consumers or, more generally, as private individuals pursuing their self-interest?

What would this say about the quality of their lives? And if significant numbers of people shared these perceptions, judgments, and experiences, what would it say about the state of our society, about the integrity of the social covenant that underlies the social order?

It is easily understood that, in order to function at all and to function effectively, our society depends on a material and technical infrastructure that includes electricity, roads, means of communication, the collection and diffusion of information, and so on. Our dependence on this infrastructure, which we usually take for granted, hits us when there is a major catastrophe like an ice storm, a temporary blackout, an even a malfunctioning of our telephone line.

It is perhaps less obvious that the society also relies on a *social and normative* infrastructure. Such an infrastructure consists in a set of taken-for-granted expectations based on common understandings, ideals, and normative standards. The infrastructure involves an *implicit covenant* that defines what individuals can expect from the society and what the society can expect from them: "Political community for the sake of provision, provision for the sake of community: the process works both ways, and that is perhaps its crucial feature."[1] This covenant is part of the *civic culture* of the society.

The covenant defines what individuals can count on when dealing with each other and with institutions and their agents. Membership in a society, if it is to be more than purely formal, entails social expectations such as full acceptance, respect, fair treatment and trust in dealings with others, and recognition of the contribution made to the community or society. These are based on ideals that people expect to see incorporated in public policies, in institutional structures, in business practices, and in the relations between individuals and the communities in which they live.

Similarly, the covenant defines what the society and its institutions can count on in terms of inputs and responses from individuals in the pursuit of the common good. They define what people are willing to do to support each other and sustain the collective capacity to cope with internal and external circumstances and problems. Thus, membership also entails obligations. It implies that members owe something to each other. The boundaries of membership identify those for whom one has a certain responsibility, those whose troubles one should worry about and feel some responsibility to alleviate. In addition, corresponding to the expectation of recognition for one's contribution to the community is the obligation to recognize one's debt to the community.

In short, the quality of life of individuals, the functioning of institutions, and the governance of the society depend on the state of the social and normative infrastructure. We will refer to this infrastructure as the social fabric. This expression is, of course, a metaphor, and one that is appropriate. Indeed, the *Webster New Collegiate Dictionary* defines a fabric as an "underlying structure" and "an arrangement of components in relation to each other." And among its synonyms, we find "foundation," which, in turn, can refer to pillar, backbone, anchor, and infrastructure. What we consider to be the constitutive elements of the social and normative infrastructure or social fabric are identified below.

Thus, while socio-economic indicators are essential to assess the state of a society, it is also vital to consider the extent to which people's expectations are met in other dimensions of their life experience and of their contribution to the society. This is not always explicitly recognized, for instance, by those, the prime minister among them, who cite the United Nations' high ranking of Canada as a reason why Quebec should stay in Canada. This is certainly one reason, but the continuing support for independence suggests that people can and do value something other than good socio-economic performance for their society.

The importance of counterbalancing the economic focus is forcefully voiced by Hugh Segal: "The Dow Jones Average, unemployment levels, and housing starts are indicators of but one variable: the economic one. It is compellingly important, but not the centre of life and society itself ... To make the economic components utterly and completely dominant is to deny the essence of what freedom and responsibility, combined, provide for the vast majority of our people."[2]

This book seeks to complement the economic assessments with an analysis of survey results pertaining to the state of the social fabric and to the social covenant of rights and obligations on which it is based – a covenant that concerns various dimensions of people's *social experience* in the society and of their *contribution* to it and that, as such, goes well beyond the dynamics of market transactions. Our focus is on community rather than on the economy. Such a focus is particularly relevant at a time when a pervasive *market culture* is progressively eroding the *civic culture* underlying the social covenant in contemporary western societies. This is not a primarily academic concern; it seems to be one shared by a strong majority of Canadians. Indeed, when asked their views about the problems faced by our society today,

- 90 per cent say *"that there are too many people preoccupied with what they can get out of system rather than with what they can contribute to the common good"*;
- 75 per cent say *"that a problem is that too many people will sacrifice their principles in order to get ahead economically"*;
- 83 per cent that *"there is too much concern for every group's fair share and not enough for the needs of the society as a whole"*; and
- 70 per cent say *that "there is less willingness to help those in need."*[3]

These perceptions and judgments clearly indicate a preoccupation with the damage that the unbridled pursuit of self-interest could eventually inflict on the social fabric. They address the dominance of the values that are inherent in the market *culture*. Canadians no doubt value a market *economy*, but they seem to fear that one of its cultural by-products may be the progressive erosion of the social fabric. These results, however, should not be interpreted to mean that Canadians do not perceive any willingness to contribute to the common good or to help those in need and no concern for the needs of the society as a whole. The statements to which most agree only say that there are too many people with certain attitudes and orientations.

Nevertheless, implicit in the statements is a rejection of the view of society as merely a mass of individuals trying to make a living and, if ambitious, achieve the highest standard of living possible. They question the conception of society as simply a set of individuals engaged in economic transactions as consumers of goods and services, as taxpayers "buying" services from governments, as entrepreneurs competing for markets, as employers or workers competing for profits and wages, in short, as rational actors trying to get the best possible deals for themselves.

Underlying these preoccupations is a conception of society as a set of interdependent people engaged in a multiplicity of different kinds of social relations and collective projects. In this conception of society, people live their lives not in isolation from one another but in relations of interdependence, not in a social vacuum but within social and institutional arrangements regulated by a set of social norms and expectations. Thus, there is a concern about the civic culture and about the state of the social arrangements within which various kinds of transactions and activities are carried out. This concern is not restricted to the average citizen; it is also one that inspires several lines of social analysis. Of course, the conceptual approach that informs the different analyses differ, but the underlying themes appear to be similar.

For instance, as is made clear in a recent study published by the Canadian Policy Research Networks, all analysis of the social fabric may be cast in the language of *social cohesion*. It addresses issues of belonging, inclusion/exclusion, participation, recognition, and legitimacy. One of its conclusions is the expression of a "concern about too enthusiastic an embrace of an agenda that fails to acknowledge continuing and legitimate claims for social justice and recognition."[4] Similarly, after widespread consultation with academics, business leaders, community and church representatives, and public servants, the Canadian Senate recently concluded that the country is failing to address the impact of various changes – globalization, technological, and economic – on the social cohesion of our society.[5]

Others see the decline of the strength of the social fabric as a decline in *social capital*. This kind of capital includes a particular type of resources, namely, those that reside in the organization of social relations and in the normative environment and not in finance and material inventories or in individuals (e.g., human capital). Social capital "inheres in the structure of relations between and among actors," in the norms and organization of the social units (e.g., families, groups, workplaces) to which individuals belong. Among its elements are several features of the social fabric such as trust, networks of mutual obligation, and norms seeking to prevent behaviour detrimental to other members or to the group as a whole or that compel beneficial action.[6] Like money, technology, and skills, social capital can enable individuals and communities to achieve their desired goals, whether these be economic, political, or sociocultural.

Judging from the conclusion reached by Jane Jenson, it seems that Robert Putnam's observations about American society are, at least to a certain extent, applicable to Canada: in recent decades, "citizens have become remarkably less civic, less politically engaged, less socially connected, less trusting, and less committed to the common good ... [they] "have dramatically less 'social capital' than they had even 30 years ago."[7] Angus Reid, who has been conducting polls for several years, agrees that "Canada's reserves of social capital" – by which he means trust, civility, and fairness – "are at risk of being quickly depleted by the mean-spirited individualism of the new economy and undermined by one-dimensional arguments that focus solely on the need for greater economic freedom."[8]

Communitarianism is still another approach to the analysis of the social fabric but several of its central observations are quite similar to those concerned with a decline of social capital or an erosion of social cohesion: the growing income gap in our society, the marginalization of certain categories of citizens, apathy in relation to political institutions and mechanisms, and various manifestations of a withdrawal from civic and communal engagement.[9] There is a sense that people feel less and less part of a larger order. There is "a worry that the individual lost something important along with the larger social and cosmic horizons of action ... [that] people no longer have a sense of higher purpose ... [that they] lost the broader view because they focus on their individual lives."[10]

Critiques of neo-liberalism attribute these tendencies to the growing dominance of market individualism in shaping the contemporary social, economic, and political order and its sustaining culture. To a large extent, neo-liberalism seeks to be all-encompassing. Its basic problem, critics argue, is to fail to make the crucial distinction between advocating markets for a well-functioning economy and attempting to organize the society and its institutions on the basis of market principles. It ignores the by-products of a sweeping market culture which, as John O'Neil points out, "imbalances rights and duties, aggravates private greed and public scarcity, and generates a fundamental confusion over what can be achieved on the level of self-interest and what is achievable through public association."[11]

These perceptions, analyses, and judgments, shared by social analysts, researchers, and citizens, indicate a certain cultural anxiety; they contain a worry that our culture is becoming too centred on the economic dimension of life, a fear that the view of society and its institutions as markets is disturbingly gaining ground. To the extent that this is so, it is a cultural orientation that will undermine the social fabric of our society if it remains uncorrected. An over-emphasis on the economic to the detriment of the social will make us ignore the social covenant and the culture of civic engagement on which the social, economic, and political system depends.

Of course, some of the connections between people entail economic transactions. But even economic transactions are based on a social infrastructure. They are partly shaped by family and friendship ties. They depend on a certain level of trust. They carry an expectation of fairness. They entail mutual obligations. In short, they depend on a social infrastructure and not only on a material and technical infrastructure that includes such elements as electricity, roads, means of communication, and mechanisms for the collection and diffusion of information.

When assessing the state of a society, it is therefore crucial that the society not be reduced to a marketplace with its material infrastructure. We need to take account of the quality of social relations among people and between individuals and the collectivities in which they live, quality being defined by the experience of fairness, recognition, trust, belonging, indebtedness, mutual obligations, and social contributions.

THE IMPACT OF SOCIAL TRANSFORMATIONS

The preoccupation of Canadians with the common good stems, in part, from the sometimes positive, sometimes disruptive transformations to which our society has been continually subjected for a number of decades. There has indeed been considerable demographic change, major transformations in social identities and aspirations, extensive economic restructuring, far-reaching technological innovations, and substantial policy initiatives. In such a context, it is not surprising that Canadians in general and social analysts in particular have started asking questions about the impact of these developments not only on the economy but also on institutions and social relations. The social fabric is always vulnerable, but it is especially so in periods of extensive and rapid change, as social analysts have frequently noted.[12]

Major transformations have taken place within the francophone population, especially in Quebec. Consider, for example, the Quiet Revolution, which involved or triggered major institutional changes: the shift in identity from "French Canadian" to "Québécois"; moves by the Quebec government and business to gain greater control over the economy; the independence movement; the language laws and their systematic attempt to define Quebec as a French-speaking society; the demand by Quebec for recognition as a "distinct society"; and the definition of Canada as a bilingual society and the related transformations of federal institutions through the Official Languages Act.

Partly as a reaction to the demands and gains of francophones, some non-British, non-French groups began to see themselves as part of a "Third Force," socially and politically, and to make their own claims for recognition. Fueling their growing socio-political consciousness was the increasing demographic weight of the "Third Force": from 20 per cent of the total population in 1941 to 42 per cent in 1996.[13] In response, federal and provincial governments adopted multicultural-ism policies. Grants were allocated to ethnic community organizations, and educational programs were modified to accommodate a number of ethnocultural groups.

Another important change has been the increase in the relative size of visible minorities: they constituted less than 3 per cent of the total population in 1961 and a little over 11 per cent in 1996 (a little over three million people).[14] In the process of becoming part of our society, members of visible minorities frequently have to deal with colour-based prejudice and discrimination, in addition to the difficulties that come with being immigrants[15] and with cultural differences. As a result, a number of issues have emerged, such as discrimination, treat-ment by the police, biases in educational programs, and employment equity.

Corresponding to these changing patterns has been a decline in the demographic weight of the British-origin population. In 1961, 44 per cent of the population was of British origin. In 1996 census counts were by single and multiple origins: 17 per cent declared British origins only (including combinations such as English and Irish) and 23 per cent declared British and another origin. Also, the "Canadian" origin selected by 19 per cent probably includes some with a British ancestry. Thus, the decline is both quantitive and, through a loss of salience in identity owing to multiple origins, qualitative. Many anglophones have experienced this demographic change, together with the claims and gains of other groups, as a progressive displacement from their traditional position of cultural and political dominance.

At the same time, native peoples have come to exert an impact on public institutions disproportionate to the size of their population (in 1991 the total aboriginal population enumerated in the census was only 1,002,670, a little less than 4 per cent of the total population). Beginning in the 1960s, major transformations have occurred not only in the aspirations of Native people but also in their conception of themselves. They have undergone a change in collective identity from Indians to Native peoples to First Nations. They have undertaken a rebuilding of their internal social and political organization, previously weakened by an historical experience as externally administered dependencies. This required the control of resources and of their own institutions. Thus emerged issues of land claims, fishing and logging rights, and benefits from the exploitation of natural resources and other forms of economic development. It also brought about demands to eliminate the traditional administrative dependency in favour of autonomy and self-government.

Tensions between ethnic, racial, and linguistic groups are quite common in contemporary societies, including Canada. Those tensions frequently result from the experience of perceived and/or real inequities: social exclusion, denial of equality of opportunity, or ranking as culturally inferior. Unfairness on the basis of ethnicity, race, language, or immigrant status can be a source of social tension and, as such, threatens the social fabric.

Women, too, have challenged the place they have traditionally held in society. This was partly triggered by their increasing presence in the labour force: from about 59 per cent in 1980 to 73 per cent in 1998. And, here again, society is confronted with issues of fairness in access to opportunities, pay equity, and recognition for contributions to society.

Our society has also experienced major technological changes which have permeated most domains of activity and which have been accompanied by an extensive restructuring of the economy. Among these have been free trade and the further integration of our economy in the continental and world systems, an increased concentration of economic power in large corporations, and changes in the occupational structure. There has been a growing emphasis on "flexibility": ease in hiring and firing, decreasing the power of unions, and the watering down of labour codes together with "downsizing" and "outsourcing." These changes are often presented as the result of globalization which "brings pressure to bear to change work practices, to raise productivity, and to lower wages."[16] Some occupational skills have declined in importance while others have gained; some have simply become redundant. Some jobs are stable while others are temporary. This is not to mean that the changes are automatic. Rather, they are responses to the perceived pressures of globalization, responses that usually involved a policy choice on the part of policy makers in governments or in the private sector.

Globalization, the introduction of new technologies, and the accompanying transformation in economic organization have a differential impact on different segments of workers. There are winners and losers in terms of income, career opportunities, social status, and socio-political influence. The distribution of income is characterized by growing inequalities. The skills and contributions to society of certain categories of workers are devalued while those of others are highly rated and even seen as key to the future of the society. Such phenomena as downsizing, computerization, and a diminished employer loyalty to employees increase the level of anxiety over unemployment. This can be the case among people with high as well medium and low levels of education.

To the extent that these phenomena produce frustration and social tension, they erode the social covenant. Those who see no chance of winning become alienated and marginalized, socially and economically – a result that is frequently referred to as "social exclusion." Such a situation is likely to be experienced as unfair and to generate a low sense of belonging, of trust, and of social commitment. Those whose contribution to society is devalued as well as those whose skills have become outmoded may feel alienated.

There have been important changes as well in the way the country is governed. For instance, there has been an increasing dominance of the executive over the legislative in policy making, at both the federal and provincial levels – a phenomenon not unique to Canada. This process of centralization has continued with a further shift of effective decision making from the cabinet to the prime minister (or premiers in the provinces).[17] Yet another significant political change has been the multiplication of citizens' and business groups to exert pressure on governments. Those already in existence have become better organized. "Over three-quarters of citizens' groups dealing with environmental, multicultural, native, and women's issues have been founded since 1960."[18] A similar expansion of business lobbies has also taken place. The expansion has generated a concern with "special interest groups" (a phrase frequently used to refer to groups that represent interests opposed to one's own and therefore with which one disagrees). This evolution was partly triggered by an increase in governmental activity. Indeed, in the course of the last three or four decades, governments in Canada – federal and provincial – acquired a more significant role in the economy, heath care, education, ethno-cultural relations, language, the environment, and cultural affairs than they had previously. Whatever the reason for the expansion of interest groups, however, the expansion itself may be what underlies, in part, the perception that there are too many people interested in their own advantage to the detriment of the common good.

There has also been an escalation of public-relations activities in order to sway public attitudes and opinions towards support for a particular policy position. For instance, the Canadian Public Relations Society has about 1,700 members and the Canadian chapter of the International Association of Business Communicators roughly 4,500.[19] The result may be an increasing sense on the part of citizens that they are being manipulated, something that could generate distrust of political and business leaders.

The greater familiarity with the political issues and processes (associated with increases in the level of education of the electorate) has been found to be the most important factor in the decline of deference to authority in Canada.[20] Together with this more critical attitude vis-à-vis authority, the changes in the system of governance and in the distribution of political influence may have affected the extent to which citizens trust leaders to consider the common good and the interests of citizens in policy making.

In the midst of all of this, profound cultural changes are occurring. Some of the basic polarities that have always been present in our culture seem to have resurfaced with intensity in recent years. On the one hand, individuals expect to be able to pursue their self-interest, their own goals, and their own aspirations with as few obstacles as possible. Thus, there can be a tendency to see collective and institutional requirements (e.g., paying taxes) as constraints and obstacles to be eliminated as much as possible.

On the other hand, individuals also count on institutions that function well, that provide collective goods and prevent collective harm. Underlying this expectation is a sense of shared interests and social interdependence. That is to say, in order to pursue their individual goals, individuals see themselves as depending, to a considerable degree, on means provided by the society and its institutions. Because of this, individual contributions to the collective good are considered important even though this may impose limitations on individual self-interest.

The tension between these two sets of expectations is not new in our society, nor is it peculiar to our society. It is present in all social groups and societies. What varies is the emphasis placed on each and the ways of coping with the tension between them. In Canada, there seems to have been, historically, a considerable emphasis on the quality of collective life and on the vitality of public institutions. However, in recent years, there seems to be an increasing emphasis on individualism. There seems to be a growing tendency for people to become more self-interested and less concerned with the well-being of others and with the common good. Canadians seem to feel that, more and more, they have to fend for themselves and that others should do the same. An extreme view is that those who are disadvantaged only have themselves to blame and should not expect anything from others.

The market culture places an emphasis on self-interest and self-reliance. This orientation may also be encouraged by the perception that governments are slowly pulling out of public programs and attempting to privatize the delivery of services. Such emphasis may discourage the recognition that we owe something to others and to the community. It may encourage a sense of self-worth derived from economic achievements and success rather than from contributions to the vitality of the society and of public institutions, and it may weaken the sense of indebtedness to society.

Another manifestation of the penetration of the market culture in our society is an increasing endorsement of the business framework as the main template for social relations and for the functioning of institutions: that all institutions should adopt the "business" model in which what counts is the bottom line.

In short, the country has been changing not only in the relative size of the groups that constitute it but also, and especially, in their identities and aspirations. The changes are among the factors that underlie the claims for institutional changes. These claims have triggered counter-movements fuelled by fears of a possible loss of economic advantages, status, or political power. They have involved controversies about what is fair and about ways of giving adequate recognition to the various groups. They have raised the level of distrust. In the process, some individuals may have been made to feel that they don't really belong here. The tensions may have lowered the level of social trust. They may also have led some people to feel differently about to whom they feel obligated.

In many ways, these changes – even if, in the long run, their effects are positive – act as a destabilizing force. They shake the social fabric; they challenge the social, political, economic, and moral order of the society. Some of the changes can potentially weaken the social fabric; others may strengthen it. Rarely, however, is their impact automatic or inevitable. It is important to respond to the changes and attempt to orient them in directions that will be beneficial for the society, that will exploit their potential advantages and prevent, reduce, and remedy the social damage they produce.[21]

DETERMINING THE STRENGTH OR FRAGILITY OF THE SOCIAL FABRIC

Given this context and the considerable concern among Canadians noted above, it is useful and timely to examine the strength of the social fabric of our society. This will be done by focusing on how Canadians seem to experience various elements of the social covenant; that is to say, on their *experience* with regard to what they can legitimately expect from the society and on the *contribution* that can be expected from them. Four types of experience seem to be particularly relevant, even basic in this connection.

- First, if individuals experience *fairness*, they are likely to develop an allegiance to the community and society that treats them so. In contrast, unfairness is likely to generate discontent and alienation. Fairness can generate bonds among individuals and across groups or categories of people, while unfairness is likely to bring about social tensions and fragmentation.

- Second, an adequate *recognition* of the contribution that individuals and groups make to the society is likely to strengthen their commitment to the society. Conversely, a lack of recognition and, worse, a demeaning of one's contribution is likely to generate alienation.
- Third, the fact that individuals can *trust* that others will not take advantage of them and that institutional leaders and agents will pursue the interest of the community is an indication of a certain robustness of the social fabric. The reverse is the case when distrust prevails.
- Fourth, a sense of *belonging* can result from experiences and social relations where people are made to feel at home in their community and society while the opposite is the case if they are made to feel like strangers or, worse, undesirable and unwanted.

We also need to explore the issue of an individual's contribution to society, which involves a sort of circular, self-reinforcing process. On the one hand, if individuals invest time, energy, and resources in the community and society, they will come to feel that these are their community and society. People contribute to make a community function well either by helping others or by contributing to community organizations and associations partly because they feel obligated to an entity that is one's own; partly because they do not want to be "free riders"; and partly because they feel indebted to it. On the other hand, contributing represents a commitment to the community since it is social reality that one is helping to maintain. It generates a sense of "social ownership." The following can then be taken as additional factors in generating social commitment and allegiance and, in turn, strengthening the social covenant.

- Fifth, in the way just explained, *contributions* to the functioning of the community and society strengthens the social fabric while their absence weakens it.
- Sixth, a sense of *indebtedness* to society – an appreciation on the part of individuals of what they receive from the community and society – similarly strengthens the social facric. Conversely, the absence of the sense that one owes something to society is an indication that there is something amiss in one's relationship with the society and thus denotes a weak commitment to it.
- Seventh, it is almost obvious that the sense of *social obligation* binds

people together by giving reality to the social covenant. Unreciprocated obligations or the absence of social obligations vis-à-vis others are indicative of a certain fragility in the social fabric.

These dimensions of the relationship between individuals and their society are important in determining the quality of life of individuals, the integrity of the social covenant, and the strength of the social fabric.

Generally, two approaches will be used for this diagnosis. First, the factors listed above will be taken as *indicators* of the strength of the social fabric and the underlying social covenant. Thus, following this approach, we could conclude that the higher the proportion of people who report a positive experience (e.g., fairness, recognition, social obligations), the stronger the social fabric. Conversely, the higher the proportion with negative experiences, the weaker the social cement that holds the community and society together.

Second, the analysis will attempt to identify *lines of fragmentation* or polarization between groups or categories of people. Such a situation would exist if some groups or segments of the population have positive while others have negative experiences along several of the social dimensions (e.g., unfair treatment, lack of recognition, not belonging) simultaneously. This type of social clustering of experience would reveal the existence of cleavages that could threaten the social covenant and the social fabric.

THE IMPORTANCE FOR PUBLIC POLICY

Such a diagnosis can be a significant ingredient in the public debate. In a liberal democracy such as ours, the social fabric and the quality of the social relations on which it depends should concern individual citizens and organized interest groups. But it should concern governments and other public institutions in a particular way since their policies, programs, and practices can affect not only the material conditions of life but also the quality of social relations. At an earlier period in our society's history, the church may have been the central guardian, preserving the civic culture and assuring the good functioning of the society. Today, however, even though churches still have a role, governmental institutions have the prime responsibility to strengthen the social fabric and to deal with threats to its integrity.

The conditions that impinge on the social fabric and the underlying social covenant are of political concern for three major reasons. First, to govern is to provide the conditions necessary for citizens to pursue and achieve what they value for themselves and their families, for their communities, and society, since, as Francis Fukuyama points out, a society requires certain socio-cultural habits in order to function well. Central among those are fairness, recognition of each other's social contributions, trust, and conditions that support belonging, social obligations, and contributions.[22] These are the *social and normative foundations* that *enable* the society to function. As such, they are clearly a major component of governance.

Second, the socio-cultural habits embedded in the social fabric define what people can take for granted in dealing with each other and with their institutions. As such, they reduce social and material costs because, to the extent that they are lacking, organizational mechanisms must be set up to guarantee them (e.g., to monitor those who cannot be trusted; to police those who, because they are treated unfairly, may become resentful and uncooperative; and so on). Thus, a nurturing of socio-cultural habits is an effective way of assuring the good functioning of the society and of its institutions.

Third, the state of the civil society is a valuable policy objective not only because of its role with regard to the functioning of the society but also because it enhances the quality of life for individuals. Indeed, beyond the material needs for a comfortable existence, people need to feel that they belong, that they can trust others and be treated fairly. The possibility of a social contribution to the community and society – either through work, communal activities, or financial inputs – that is satisfying and recognized can also nurture a sense of identification with the community and society. All these are important ingredients of the quality of life.

WHAT WE ADDRESS

Before proceeding with the social diagnosis based on our survey results, we will present findings on Canadians' perceptions and judgments of their society. This is done in the next chapter.

The two diagnostic approaches mentioned above are used for the presentation of the survey results. Using a number of social indicators, the first part of this presentation examines five dimensions that we consider critical for the strength of the social fabric. Specifically, Chapter 3 deals with the *fairness* of the society and the ways in which different categories of people are treated. Chapter 4 attempts to assess the extent to which different groups or categories of people are satisfied with the *recognition* they receive for their contribution to society. Chapter 5 is concerned with the level of *horizontal trust*, that is, trust in social transactions. It deals with the extent to which respondents are afraid others will take advantage of them. Whether Canadians feel that institutional elites can or cannot be trusted to give priority to the public interest is addressed in Chapter 6, which focuses on *vertical trust*. Chapter 7 deals with the strength of *belonging* and asks if there are Canadians who, for one reason or another, feel that they do not fully belong.

The next three chapters deal with the commitment of individuals to the society and to their fellow citizens. The willingness of people to recognize their *indebtedness* to the society is examined in Chapter 8, followed by an analysis of *social obligation* in Chapter 9 and, in Chapter 10, the extent of *contributions* to the community as manifested by helping others either individually or through communal activities. Based on the dimensions considered, Chapter 11 presents some conclusions about the condition of the social fabric.

An analysis of the condition of the social fabric based on the degree of social *fragmentation* between segments of our society is carried out in the next section. Chapters 12 to 15 examine four lines of possible fragmentation in our society: gender, ethnicity and race, social class, and provinces. Implications for the strength of the social fabric are presented in Chapter 16.

In the final chapter (17), we will review our major finding and formulate an overall diagnosis with regard to the social fabric of our society. Also, since the 1995–98 World Values Survey includes items identical or similar to the ones included in our study, the results for those items will be presented for selected countries and regions of the world. By providing benchmarks against which some of our results can be assessed, the comparisons complement the diagnosis. Finally, we will identify some policy issues that are suggested by the findings.[23]

The analysis to be presented is based on the results of a countrywide survey carried out in 1997.[24] The survey data consists of experiences and judgments reported by a sample of 2,014 respondents. The study does not attempt to provide "objective" indicators of the various components of the social fabric. Rather, it deals with the perceptions, experiences, and attitudes of Canadians. Such subjective data are as relevant, if not more so, than objective indicators when dealing with the quality of social relations on which the social fabric is based.

Our work also draws on in-depth interviews conducted with a sample of sixty-four Canadians from two small towns and two large cities in Ontario and Quebec. Comments and observations made in these discussions are incorporated throughout our analysis for descriptive, analytical, and illustrative purposes.[25]

WHAT THIS BOOK IS NOT

It is also important to note what this work does not set out to do. These comments are not offered as an apology; rather, they provide the context for the contribution we hope to make.

First and foremost, this is not an academic treatise. While informed by a rich variety of theoretical traditions, it does not set out to prove the relative interpretive value of one approach over another. Academic debate about the validity of competing schema is not our goal. Nor do we attempt to provide a causal analysis of the determinants of fairness, trust, and social commitment. Rather, our goal is to provide an overall diagnosis of the health or robustness of the social fabric of our society using dimensions based on sociological theory.

Also, since our goal is to paint a picture of everyday Canadians' experience with key dimensions of the social fabric, to document the ways in which different social groupings encounter them and to raise questions for ongoing research and public-policy debate, our statistical analysis is descriptive rather than inferential.[26] Basic data are provided for each of the indicators so that readers have access to the finding for themselves and can devise alternate interpretations. For ease of presentation, the majority of the findings are presented in graphic form wherever possible.

Like any study, our research has limitations. First, we would have liked to present far more comparative data for Canada and other countries than we do. Indeed, our analysis would have benefited considerably from such an approach. Unfortunately, there are only a few studies that allow us to compare, in a systematic way, the present situation with an earlier era or that in other societies. We hope that the data we present will set a baseline to permit future comparative analyses. Second, a longitudinal study would also have been highly valuable. Indeed, over-time data would have allowed the identification of trends and made it possible to establish how certain patterns of beliefs, values, and behaviour develop and change in a society.

Finally, we note that our work relies heavily on the subjective interpretation of Canadians in all walks of life. We do not argue that these perceptions are descriptions or explanations of what is actually going on in contemporary society. We do not claim objective accuracy for our subjective data. Rather, we believe that people's perceptions of their own experiences, either as individuals or as members of particular social groups or categories, their beliefs about what their society should be and about what is wrong with it, and their social attitudes and predispositions are significant components of social reality.

Studying such phenomena does not replace studies of objective factors, it complements them. In short, we believe, as W.I. Thomas so forcefully argues, that if phenomena are perceived as real, they are real in their consequences for behaviour, whether they are in fact real or not.

2

What Matters? Canadians'
Observations on the Good Society

Community building will be our salvation in the new millennium. Strong communities are where it all starts; places to which people can point with pride as a reflection of their values, their sense of belonging, their ability to do great things together. (Carole Goar, "Canada: a continuing act of will," *Toronto Star*, 1 January 2000)

The social fabric is a social construct and therefore a potentially fragile creation. It requires strong bonds among individuals and between individuals and the groups to which they belong. Creating and sustaining this fabric requires a significant investment of economic, social, and cultural capital. Participation must provide for the basic necessities. Social relationships and institutional arrangements must be both fair and perceived to be fair. Members must contribute to communal life and feel valued for the contributions they make. Trust between individuals and among social groups is fundamental.

But these are far more than theoretical constructs; they are issues about which Canadians are deeply concerned. Daily conversation, informal observations, media commentaries, and formally structured research studies all point to the same conclusion. A cohesive society and the cement that holds it together matter to all of us. In other words, Canadians seem to see the quality of their individual and communal life as dependent, at least in part, on the state of the social fabric.

The importance of cohesive communities and inclusive social structures infused the observations made by respondents during the in-depth interviews conducted as part of the study. For example, we asked, "*What do you remember and like about where you grew up*"? Although the answer was frequently cast in terms of physical characteristics and conveniences, it was more often phrased in terms of the social climate of the neighbourhood. Answers such as the following were commonplace:

"It was a cohesive community ... we looked after each other." (Pembroke, Ont.)

"My neighbourhood was a friendly place ... folks helped each other out ... we watched out for each other ... gave an encouraging word ... lent a hand." (Toronto, Ont)

When we probed the values most Canadians hold in common, the emphasis on the quality of the social fabric and its building blocks surfaced even more forcefully. For one respondent who grew up in the east end of Toronto, the emphasis on collective action and concern is perhaps our most defining characteristic. According to her, the value that most Canadians hold in common is "community. We differ from the Americans in that we care far more for those things collectively ... we look for more general equity ... we are more tolerant of government involvement." Another, living in Montreal, noted that what unites our social order is "people who are involved with one another, who care for one another. There has to be a recognition of interrelationship and interdependency for it to be a society." As a Toronto respondent put it, "Canada stands for civility ... being kind to other people, getting along ... doing good turns, that sort of thing." For another, "contribution to the common good, participating in community ..." is the characteristic most important for society to function well.

Respondents were also clear that the essential building blocks of the cohesive society form an integral part of the Canadian value structure. Fairness and a sense of obligation play prominently in their observations:

"fairness is the basis of society. If people don't think they have a fair chance they will not do as well as they could. You will not invest as much in society if you don't feel part of it." (Burlington, Ont.)

"I think everybody has to be responsible for everybody else. I don't see how we could live without being responsible for each other." (North York, Ont.)

Another respondent (Grimsby, Ont.), who lived through the Great Depression, put it even more forcefully: "as Canadians we do not owe anything to each other – I don't know who said that, but they should be shot or put out of the country!"

Freeloaders are seen as a great threat to the strength of the social fabric. Time after time, Canadians from small towns and large cities noted that what makes things worse for society and its institutions is "people who take advantage of the system" or "people who have that 'you owe me attitude'" or "people who bleed the system." Mutual obligation is considered a key factor in the structure of the social fabric.

The importance of commitment to the quality of collective life emerged even more clearly from our survey sample. In our study we asked for respondents' views on twelve conditions that could facilitate or hinder the functioning of society and its institutions.[1] Issues were grouped to measure five major dimensions:

- individual versus collective orientation;
- perceptions of fairness of the system;
- public trust;
- economic performance; and
- social integration.

Our analysis shows that the perceived strength of commitment to the social covenant strongly influences how effectively Canadians believe contemporary society functions and thus the degree of social cohesion we can expect.

"THE TROUBLE WITH CANADIAN SOCIETY"

The majority of Canadians believe that the level of commitment to the common good, the performance and fairness of the economic system, the behaviour of our business and political elite, and the level of social fragmentation all matter. This is true regardless of age, gender, race, social class, and, with only one exception, the region of the country in which one lives.

What we see as problems tells us much about what we value. Our apprehensions mirror our beliefs. While there is agreement that failure to honour the basic elements of the social covenant weakens the prospect of a healthy society, there is also significant variation in the level of perceived risk for society associated with the different issues. If we use the percentage of Canadians who agree that the issue is a source of difficulty as an indicator of our concerns, an interesting picture of our value structure emerges (Table 1).

Canadians are of one accord. Pursuit of self-interest rather than concern for the common good is seen as the most significant threat to a well-functioning society. Fully 90 per cent of Canadians believe that a preoccupation with what one can get from the system, rather than what one can contribute, is a source of problems in our society. The next highest levels of agreement about sources of problems for society see these problems as deriving from the lack of trust in those responsi-

Table 1   Perceived Problems Faced by Canadian Society

Rank	Trouble with Our Society Is:	Percent Agree
1	People preoccupied with what they can get out of system rather than contribution to common good	90.4
2	Public trust weakened by behaviour of people in positions of public responsibility and leadership	88.3
3	People who expect to get something for nothing	87.9
4	Too much concern with every group's fair share rather than needs of society as whole	83.3
5	Two sets of rules: one for those who have money and one for those who don't	79.7
6	Too many people sacrificing principles to get ahead economically	75.3
7	Public trust weakened by behaviour of people who manage business corporations	73.9
8	Declining standard of living	73.2
9	Less willingness to help those in need	71.0
10	Less concern with fairness and social justice	65.2
11	Decline in tolerance for people who are different	61.0
12	Ethnic, cultural, or racial diversity is too much encouraged	57.2

ble for ensuring the public good, from the fact that too many people expect to get something for nothing, and from an undue concern for the interests of one's group rather than for societal needs. These issues are believed to be important regardless of the situation in which individuals find themselves. Preoccupation with oneself rather than with collective well-being is the most frequently cited threat to a healthy Canada by both sexes, by all age groups, by all social classes, and in all regions of the country.

The importance we attach to a collective orientation as a condition of a healthy, cohesive society comes into even sharper focus when Canadians' intensity of concern is taken into account. Respondents to our survey indicated the degree to which each of the items presented in Table 1 contributed to "problems for society" on a four-point scale ranging from strongly agree to strongly disagree. Only four issues emerged where more than 40 per cent of respondents "strongly agree" that the item is a potential source of trouble in Canadian society (Table 2).

Three of the four items relate directly to interest in, and /or contribution to, the common good. Violations of the communal interest are the issues over which Canadians are most deeply concerned.

Table 2   Intensity of Concern with the Problems Faced by Canadian Society

Rank	Trouble with Our Society Is:	Percent Strongly Agree
1	Two sets of rules: one for those who have money and one for those who don't	43.2
2	Public trust weakened by behaviour of people in positions of public responsibility and leadership	42.2
3	People who expect to get something for nothing	41.6
4	People preoccupied with what they can get out of system rather than contribution to common good	41.1
5	Too much concern with every group's fair share rather than needs of society as whole	29.1
6	Public trust weakened by behaviour of people who manage business corporations	27.0
7	Declining standard of living	26.7
8	Too many people sacrificing principles to get ahead economically	24.3
9	Less willingness to help those in need	24.3
10	Ethnic, cultural, or racial diversity is too much encouraged	24.0
11	Less concern with fairness and social justice	23.2
12	Decline in tolerance for people who are different	17.5

The importance of collective interest stands in interesting contrast to Canadians' views on the effect of economic performance and our actual treatment of each other. While important, the latter are generally seen as less significant threats to the functioning of Canadian society than our value orientations. The decline in the standard of living is perceived as problematic by three-quarters of all Canadians. It ranks eighth among the twelve issues sampled – significantly behind indicators of acting in the common interest. It is also below the perceived impact of unfair advantage for the monied class (fifth), sacrificing principles for personal gain (sixth), and the behaviour of the business elite (seventh).

There are, however, interesting variations on the perceived role of deficiencies in our economic system. As one would expect from the differential distribution of opportunity across the country, the greatest difference over what is seen as a declining standard of living occurs along regional lines.

• The issue is regarded as most problematic, in both absolute and relative terms, by those in the Atlantic provinces. There, 85 per cent of respondents believe it to be a source of problems in Canadian society. They rank it fifth of twelve items in importance.

- Québécois are close behind: over 81 per cent of them consider the issue an important contributor and rank it sixth in overall impact.
- In Ontario, the issue takes on lesser importance; for residents of that province, it ranks eighth.
- Among western Canadians, the level of concern over the issue drops even further, to ninth spot, and is shared by 68 per cent of the respondents. From this region, Manitobans most often see economic decline as a source of difficulty.

The issue is also of somewhat greater concern to people aged twenty-five to fifty-four (seventh) than younger or older Canadians (ninth). As expected, upper-class Canadians are the least concerned about the impact of this issue and lower-class Canadians the most.[2]

However, the picture is not entirely bleak. There are features of our community life that most respondents did not identify as threats to the "good society": the willingness to help those in need, the concern for fairness and social justice, the degree of tolerance for those different from ourselves, and the encouragement of ethnic, cultural, or racial diversity. These items, which relate to how we actually treat each other in everyday life, consistently rank as the least-frequently mentioned threats to societal well-being (that is, ranks nine to twelve). The positive assessments of most respondents indicate that there is, in some regards, a concern for the common good and the social covenant in our society.

Once again, there is little difference between men and women, most age groups and almost all social classes and regions of the country. The sole exception is that the decline in the willingness to help is seen as slightly more of an issue among those eighteen to twenty-four years of age (seventh) and upper-class Canadians (eighth). These are also the items, as we noted in Table 2, with which Canadians express the least intensity of concern.

As we noted in the opening chapter, diversity is at the heart of the Canadian experiment. A vast geography, a multiplicity of ethnic and racial groups, a plethora of communities scattered in disparate regions, and a diversity of languages and cultures have combined to make ours a most complex nation. And we continue to become more diverse. By 1996, immigrants comprised 17.4 per cent of our population, significantly up from 15 per cent in 1950. And the number of countries and cultures constituting our population grows ever broader. Given the nature of Canadian society, the potential for assigning blame for social ills to our emphasis on diversity and to the level of intolerance is high.

Yet, compared to other factors, these are the two least often cited sources of "the problem with Canadian society." Moreover, the emphasis on diversity is the only measure to which less than half of any segment of the population ascribes cause.[3] The decline in tolerance is also least frequently cited as a strong source of societal problems. It is much as John Ralston Saul has noted: "If there is a characteristic proper to Canadians, it is that we have not rigorously set out to eliminate differences. Our nationalism exists on a spectrum from the impossibly generous idea that all people belong to all communities, to the inclusive and negative opposite in which each of us is limited to a single community ... Our more realistic and indeed real attitude is that we belong to several communities and do so at several levels ... The idea of belonging to multiple communities makes practical sense in a decentralized federation built upon three cultural foundations."[4]

Although the translation of the idea of diversity into a policy of multiculturalism clearly continues to make a portion of the population uncomfortable, it is an idea around which we have learned to build a society and cultivate the values and perceptions to support it. Indeed, results from the World Values Survey show that "Canadians appear to be more tolerant, or rather less intolerant, than most Europeans and Americans."[5] The good society is believed to be far less threatened by our differences than by our willingness to put our interest above that of others.

A NATION OF PRACTICAL IDEALISTS

Canadians are concerned with the state of the social fabric. Trust, fairness, mutual recognition, and a sense of obligation are seen as crucial in determining the quality of the social relationships on which it depends.

Most of us believe that there is a broad range of issues which have the potential to pose threats to the "good society." The commitment to our collective well-being, however, is seen as the most threatening to our social well-being. This concern far outweighs matters related to our material well-being. Contemporary problems are seen to stem more from a belief that too many of us are concerned with what we can get for ourselves than from a decline in the standard of living, decreasing tolerance, or increasing social diversity. Our apprehensions suggest an unwelcome shift in the balance between rights and obligations.

It may well be that the concern with issues of self-interest stems from the value shift that Canadians observe around them. As Neil Nevitte notes, such a shift is reflected in "attitudes to 'civil permissiveness,' the idea that people will 'free ride' at public expense, or put their own interests before the public welfare if they think they can get away with

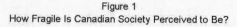

Figure 1
How Fragile Is Canadian Society Perceived to Be?

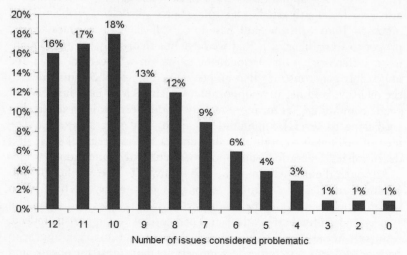

Perceived Fragility	Number of Issues	Percentage of Sample
Little	0–4	6%
Moderate	5–8	30%
High	5–12	64%

it."[6] He found that such permissiveness is higher in Canada than in most European countries and is significantly higher than in the United States. Fully 44 per cent of Canadians believe that some form of "freeloading" or putting one's interest before the public welfare is acceptable at some time. Figures for the United States and Europe are 32.7 per cent and 37.9 per cent. And the rate has grown over time.

Far too many of us are perceived to be driven by what we can expect to get rather than by what is due to our fellow citizens and what we owe to society. It is well expressed in the observation that "everywhere we have been forgetting the value of community, of public investment and reducing our commitment to it ... There is much these days – lack of selflessness and solidarity, lack of courtesy and respect – to break the ties that bind us."[7]

If we take the number of problems with the society as an indicator of fragility, our data also permit us to develop a picture of how fragile Canadians actually view their society to be. In the simplest terms, respondents can be ranked by the number of issues that they believe to be sources of "problems with society." The scores can then be categorized as low, medium, or high on a "fragility index." It is important to note that the respondents themselves may not think in terms of fragility; rather, it is our way of exploring the significance of their responses. The results are presented in Figure 1.

For the majority of Canadians, perceived threats to our society occur in constellations. Only 5 per cent believe that our society is threatened by four or less of the twelve items examined. Another 30 per cent agree that there are between five and eight issues with which we should be concerned. Nearly 65 per cent of Canadians reported concern with almost all of the indicators of our commitment to the common good, the integrity of the moral order, social commitment, and confidence in public institutions. For most, the potential for fragility is high.

As noted earlier, what we see as problems tells us much about what we value. Our apprehensions truly mirror our beliefs. Our data suggest that Canadians care passionately about the common good but are concerned that our pursuit of self-interest threatens its attainment. We are, however, more satisfied with the outcome of how we actually treat each other than our suspicions about our individualistic attitudes would suggest. We are, at heart, a nation of practical idealists. While we perceive promise, we also believe that there is potential for fragility. The ways in which the basic building blocks of the social covenant – trust, fairness, a sense of belonging and obligation – affect the strength of our social fabric form the core of our analysis.

3

Fairness in Canadian Society

In justice as fairness, social unity is understood by starting with the conception of society as a system of cooperation between free and equal persons. Social unity and the allegiance of citizens to their common institutions are not found on their all affirming the same conception of the good, but on their publicly accepting a political conception of justice to regulate the basic structure of society. (John Rawls, *Justice as Fairness*, 1993)

Fairness is an issue that comes up regularly in a variety of circumstances. The distribution of company benefits between shareholders and employees, the growing gap between those at the top of the income distribution and others, tax dodging by well-off companies and individuals, and the administration of public programs are but a few examples. The Ontario ombudsman has declared that "there has been a shift from an emphasis on fairness in the delivery of services that governed the public service in the early part of the decade to the businesslike, bottom-line values being espoused today."[1] Fairness is part of the demand for compensation for perceived injustices incurred by many groups of Canadians. Such groups include those who have been victims of the tainted-blood transfusions and the over five thousand people in Ontario "who have taken their case in the past year to the Social Benefits Tribunal after their disability claims were rejected."[2]

Some see a fairness issue in the decreased ability of governments to do things:[3] "I think the sense that our society is fair is generally widespread right now. I think it's harder to believe if you are poor. Economic factors will make it harder to believe. The government debt reduces the ability for the government to do things and I think the government does have a role to play in people's well-being. And globalization, Free Trade, those are restrictions on government" (Toronto, Ont.).

There is quite a widespread perception of unfairness in the justice system. This perception may be based, for instance, on news about the wrongful imprisonment of individuals. An international survey conducted in 1992 by Angus Reid[4] found that 64 per cent of Canadians *disagree* (almost half of them strongly) that "everyone – no matter who they are – is treated the same by the justice system in Canada."[5]

Fairness also underlies the debates over the socio-economic and technological changes that have been taking place in recent years. This is largely because these changes do not affect everyone in the same way. Some gain, some lose. As a result, questions are asked about the degree of fairness of the social distribution of the gains flowing from socio-economic and technological change, as well as about the costs of this kind of economic transformation.

For some, the introduction of new technologies and organizational changes represent better career opportunities, a higher income, greater social influence, and gains in prestige and self-esteem. For others, it means the opposite: the loss of a job, a move to a lower paying job, a disrupted career, a decline in social standing, and, possibly, a sense of social marginality and a lower self-image.

Some benefit from globalization because their personal talents, skills, and resources allow them to respond with relative ease to the requirements of international trade, to the global movements of capital, or to shifts in production from one part of the world to another. These include the owners of capital, workers in the financial sector, high-technology professionals, and technicians. But there are those whose resources do not allow them such mobility. They bear the costs of the declining opportunities that result from technological change, downsizing, and outsourcing. Moreover, in many cases, the skills and personal resources of these people make them unable to take advantage of new opportunities.

The uneven distribution of benefits and costs is also shown by the way earnings have risen and declined in the last several years: "In the early 1970s, average earnings tended to rise in tandem – the rich were getting richer but the poor were getting richer as well ... Between 1973 and 1989, real earnings of men in the middle quintile grew by a modest 1.4 percent. But the earnings of men in the bottom quintile declined by 16.3 percent while men in the upper quintile saw their earnings rise by 7.9 percent ... The disparity among women working full-time full-year is if anything even larger than among men."[6]

This pattern continued in the 1990s.[7] As a result, inequality in before-tax family income increased overall from 1980 to 1997. The coefficient of inequality rose from a little above .37 in 1980 to .42 in 1997.[8] The share of the total income received by the 20 per cent of families at the bottom of the income-distribution scale declined from 6.3 per cent in 1980 to 6.1 per cent in 1996; the share of those in the top quintile rose from 38.3 per cent to 40.6 per cent.

The UN's Committee on Human Development may place Canada near the top in terms of overall quality of life, but another UN committee (on Economic, Social and Cultural Rights) finds great faults in our society: growing homelessness; a dramatic increase in food banks; a "gross disparity" between the condition of aboriginal peoples and that of other Canadians; and reduction in the level of protection and support (unemployment insurance and social assistance) for those most affected by downsizing, technological changes, and globalization.

Between 1986 and 1995, there have been a large number of strikes in Canada: each year, 292 days have been lost per 1,000 workers because of strikes. This is no doubt partly related to the fact that, in eleven of the fifteen years between 1982 and 1996, the annual change in the level of inflation has been higher than the average wage settlement. The strikes indicate that workers want to keep up with increases in the cost of living.

In short, there are people who reap a large share of the benefits of change while others bear a large share of the costs. Such a situation may well be perceived as unfair. This would be especially so if those who bear the negative consequences of change are not adequately compensated, if the burden they have to bear for "progress" is not even recognized, if they are blamed for not trying hard enough to deal with the problems the changes have imposed on them, or if the protection and assistance that government programs could provide are reduced or eliminated. In short, those who see no chances of winning in the changing circumstances, and especially those who feel that they are blamed for the losses they are experiencing as a result of economic changes, may well become alienated and resentful. They are likely to experience their lot as unfair. A circular feedback is possible here: those who are alienated and resentful for whatever reason may become pessimistic and see themselves as having no chance of winning.

In such contexts, it is not only those who are disadvantaged who may be concerned with the fairness of the distribution of gains and losses. Indeed, the more the gains and losses are unequally distributed, the more the question "Is that fair?" comes up in public debates. There is concern among those whose lives are disrupted and impoverished. But among many others, too, there is concern about the strength of the social fabric because, judged as unfair, a substantially unequal distribution of gains and losses can generate resentment and social tension.

Fairness is one of the basic yardsticks against which the effects of social changes are assessed. It is also a standard in the assessment of laws and regulations, government policies and programs, political influence, business practices, job opportunities, and the administration of justice. "That's not fair!" is a definitive condemnation of a state of affairs in any domain of life.

Fairness is an important pillar of social cohesion. The sense of being treated fairly, of being given a fair chance, does much to determine the degree of attachment to the institutions, the communities, and the society in which people live their lives. Fair treatment nourishes loyalty to the society and makes people more willing to contribute to its functioning. In contrast, unfairness is socially destructive. The feeling that others are taking advantage of us, that a particular division of responsibilities is inequitable, or that rules and practices with regard to hiring, wages, and promotions are biased tends to generate anger, social tension, and conflict. There is also resentment when some groups are seen as differentially advantaged by the "rules of the game," by public policies, by the decisions of public authorities, or by employers.

As already noted, social changes do not have an equal impact on all segments of the population. But, even if the impact is unequal, it is not necessarily experienced as unfair. People live constantly with differences in life conditions. And they generally accept such differences. They are also willing to accept the fact that socio-economic conditions and changes do not affect everyone in the same way. In short, it is not inequalities as such that can generate resentment and social tension. Rather, it is the perception of unfairness that constitutes a possible threat to social cohesion. The competition for scarce resources (such as jobs) can lead to anger and conflict if it is perceived as biased in favour of workers against others.

In a study of Quebec francophones in the labour force, it was found that competition for jobs "has a significant effect on support for separation only when the competition is perceived as unfair."[9] If people see the system as being against them or, at best, as making no place for them, they will want out. If they perceive the rules of the game as stacked against them, they will seek to quit and establish a system in which they have more control over the allocation of resources. In some instances, it may take the form of political separation. In others, the withdrawal is social: people simply give up trying. In still others, they rebel in one way or another. However the resentment is expressed, such outcomes can undermine the social fabric. It is therefore important to find out how Canadians assess the fairness of their society.

In this chapter, the perceptions and experiences of Canadians with regard to fairness are examined at three levels. First, what is their overall judgment of the fairness of our society? Second, do they feel that, personally, they are treated fairly in our society? Third, do they experience fairness or unfairness as members of particular groups or social categories (e.g., as women or as members of an ethnic or racial minority)?

FAIRNESS:
THE OVERALL ASSESSMENT OF CANADIANS

Do all Canadians experience fairness or unfairness to the same degree? The publicly expressed grievances and the controversies over certain public policies in recent years suggest that there is an uneasiness among a number of Canadians about the equity of the distribution of resources or the way institutions treat people. Different kinds of people have been involved in these controversies but particularly women, linguistic, ethnic and visible minorities, Native peoples, the poor and the middle class, and people in "have" as well as in "have not" provinces (but for different reasons). Fairness has been an issue underlying much of the controversies over public policies. As one of the respondents from Toronto put it, "people have to believe the society is fair. What you find now is that a whole bunch of people on a whole range of issues don't feel that things are fair. They feel that there are biases, that they never can win."

The concerns have been partly about the degree of *equity* in the way people are treated in our society. Do visible minorities have the same opportunities as others with the same qualifications? Are women payed in proportion to their skills, merits and contributions? Are those "downsized" adequately compensated for the harm inflicted on them by technological change and economic restructuring? There have also been issues concerning the *impartiality* of public policies and programs and about the decisions of judges, police officers, and of those who run public agencies and programs. Are they affected by prejudice and stereotypes about different categories of people as defined by gender, race, ethnicity, sexual orientation, religion, or physical traits? Finally, questions have been raised about the degree of *equality* in the distribution of societal resources. Even though inequalities are generally accepted in our society, the growing gap between the top and bottom 5, 10, or 20 per cent in the income-distribution scale has been a source of concern. So have been the differences between the gains of shareholders in comparison to those of employees. Many see these gaps as unacceptably large and thus unfair.

Overall, it seems that Canadians make a more negative than positive assessment of the fairness of our society[10] (Figure 2). In fact, most Canadians *do not* feel that their society is basically fair: only 38 per cent say that it is fair for most people while 43 per cent say that it is fair for some and 18 per cent for only a few. Such a widespread perception suggests a potentially severe social and political problem.

In addition, two-thirds of Canadians feel that they themselves are personally experiencing unfairness.[11] For them, the inequity experi-

Figure 2a
Perception of Fairness of Canadian Society

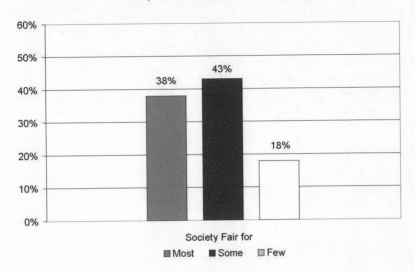

Society Fair for
■ Most   ■ Some   ▨ Few

Figure 2b
Perception of Fairness of Personal Treatment

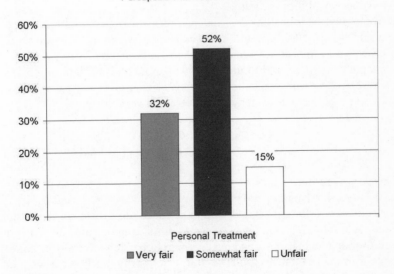

Personal Treatment
■ Very fair   ■ Somewhat fair   ☐ Unfair

enced does not appear to be major; 52 per cent say they are treated somewhat fairly. But a non-negligible proportion – 15 per cent – consider that their ill treatment is severe. Only 32 per cent say they are being treated very fairly in this society.

These two judgments are related: those who personally experience fairness tend to think that the society is basically fair while the opposite is the case for those who experience unfairness in their personal lives. This is not surprising. But there are about a third who are fairly treated but consider that the society is fair for only a few. These are people who recognize their own essentially privileged situation. There are some, on the other hand, who experience unfairness but feel that our society is fair for most. That is to say, they seem to consider themselves exceptions in a basically fair society. But they are exceptions: only 7 per cent think this way.

GROUP-SPECIFIC EXPERIENCES OF UNFAIRNESS

Respondents were asked about job opportunities for members of their own gender and of their own cultural, ethnic, or racial group (Figure 3a). They were also asked if their social class is treated fairly (Figure 3b).[12]

The overall results are as follows:

- About one in three feel that they have *fewer* job opportunities than have members of the other gender. About one in four feel that they have *more* job opportunities.
- About one in four consider that members of their own ethnic, cultural, or racial background have *fewer* opportunities than people of other backgrounds. On the other hand, about one in five say that people of their background have *more* opportunities than others.
- Close to one-third feel that their social class is not treated fairly. Only 15 per cent consider that it is treated very fairly.

MULTIPLE JEOPARDY:
THE CUMULATION OF DISADVANTAGES

The perceived experience of unfairness, as we have seen, is unevenly distributed in terms of gender, ethnicity, social class, and region. But it is not always different people who experience unfairness on these different bases. In fact, some experience a cumulation of unfairness, a sort of multiple jeopardy. For instance, women in particular ethnic or racial categories may be in situations of double jeopardy. Or being a woman in a certain social class and a particular ethnic or racial category may mean triple disadvantage.

In our sample, only 29 per cent claim no unfair treatment because of their gender, ethnicity, social class, or region of the country in which they live. Slightly over one-third say that they experience unfairness on

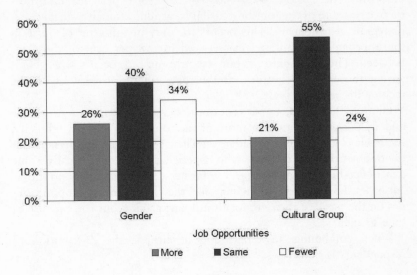

Figure 3a
Perceived Fairness in Job Opportunities

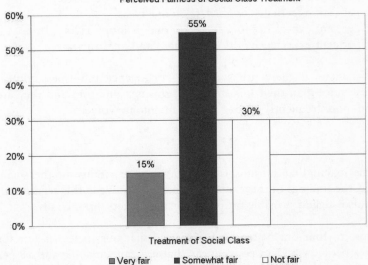

Figure 3b
Perceived Fairness of Social Class Treatment

the basis of one of these factors. The remainder (37 per cent) find themselves in "multiple jeopardy," with almost one half of them claiming disadvantage on all four grounds.

There appears to be a lower, a middle, and an upper class with regard to multiple jeopardy. It is class identification that makes the most difference: in the lower class, 57 per cent experience unfairness on two or more of the four bases (that is, gender, ethnicity, social class, or region of residence). This occurs for only one-quarter of those in the upper-middle or upper classes and for 38 per cent of those in-between. The same pattern, but less pronounced, occurs when comparing those at the bottom, at the top, and the in-between in the income-distribution scale.[13]

On the other hand, 34 per cent of the sample feel *advantaged* on one and 13 per cent on two or more of the four bases (gender, ethnicity, social class, or region of residence). Their social distribution is about the opposite of that of those who experience unfairness. Finally, some experience both advantages and unfairness, but presumably on different bases. For example, some may feel they have more job opportunities on the basis of their ethnocultural background but less because of their gender.

When combining advantage and unfairness, the distribution of respondents is as follows:

- 13 per cent experience *neither* advantages nor unfairness.
- 16 per cent experience *advantages* on one or more bases.
- 15 per cent experience *unfairness* on one basis.
- 25 per cent experience *unfairness* on two or more bases.
- 31 per cent experience *both* advantages and unfairness.

Of course, if there are some who experience unfairness, others receive more than their fair share, but this is a minority and they are found more frequently among men than among women.

HIGHLIGHTS

To the extent that fairness is essential for the vitality of the social fabric, the findings of this chapter are partly positive in this regard, but they also suggest possible problems for our society. Specifically:

- Close to four out of ten Canadians say that our society is fair for most people while 43 per cent say that it is fair for some and 18 per cent for only a few. Although this assessment is partly positive, it reveals a fairly severe evaluation of our society. Indeed, Canadians seem to be more negative than positive in their assessment of the fairness of our society.
- About one-third feel that they are themselves treated very fairly in this society. Again, the assessment is somewhat more negative than

positive. However, for most, the inequity experienced does not appear to be major: half say that they are treated somewhat fairly. Only 15 per cent consider that the unfairness they experience is severe.

- About one-third feel that they are subjected to unfair treatment because of their gender; about one in four think themselves unfairly treated because of their ethnicity or race; and another third believe that they are the victims of unfair treatment because of their social class or the province in which they reside.

- More than one-third experience unfairness for more than one of these reasons; they are victims of multiple jeopardy.

Other surveys provide evidence that support these findings even if the questions asked are somewhat different from ours. One survey, conducted in 1987, dealt with the distribution of life chances. It found that 57 per cent of Canadians basically agreed that "one of the big problems in this country is that we don't give everyone an equal chance." In addition, 71 per cent agreed that, "if people were treated more equally in this country, we would have many fewer problems."[14] A related result comes from an international Angus Reid survey. Respondents were asked whether "in this country, getting ahead is more a matter of who you know, not how hard you work." Two out of three Canadians said that this is indeed the case.[15]

Other analyses relate unfairness to the fact that some people are seen as paying a disproportionate share of the costs of economic restructuring and technological change while others are receiving a disproportionate portion of the benefits. This situation is seen as unfair because it is unbalanced but also because those who benefit tend to be those who are already relatively well-off while the losers tend to be found among those in the lower echelons of the socio-economic scale. This strikes many as being profoundly unfair.

Associated with this is the perception of Canadians that "corporations are becoming more irresponsible," something that Angus Reid relates to the corporate sector's "obsession with maximizing shareholder values to the detriment of employee and community interests."[16] This obsession can easily be perceived as an unfair distribution of resources.

4

Recognition of Contribution
to Society

Satisfaction of the self-esteem need leads to feelings of self-confidence, worth
... of being useful and necessary in the world. But thwarting of these needs produces feelings of inferiority, of weakness, and of helplessness. (Abraham H.
Maslow, *Motivation and Personality*, 1954)

Our identity is partly shaped by recognition or its absence, often by *mis*recognition of others, and so a person or group of people can suffer real damage,
real distortion, if the people or society around them mirror back to them a con-
fining or demeaning or contemptible picture of themselves. (Charles Taylor,
The Politics of Recognition, 1992)

Money and material security are not all that matters to people, even if
they are in difficult economic situations. They also want recognition
and appreciation for what they contribute to the communities to which
they belong and for what their community contributes to society.
Whatever the community in which people are involved – place of
work, local organizations and associations, church, political party, and
the society at large – they expect that whatever they contribute to its
functioning will be recognized and appreciated.

Public awards are regularly given to individuals for their contribution to the society, the community, or to a particular cause and organization. Contributions can be acknowledged with material rewards:
an increase in salary, a promotion, a prize, or a gift. Symbolic means
are also used, such as plaques, monuments, awards, and public
speeches that honour individuals or groups for their contributions.
There are general awards such as nominations to the Order of Canada.
But there are also awards in fields such as literature, cinema, and
science. These clearly show the importance of social recognition for the
achievements of individuals.

Some awards, although perhaps not as many, are given to groups and communities. The United Nations gives them to countries. In Canada, awards are given to communities. For instance, the Ontario Trillium Foundation gives Caring Communities Awards to communities that look for and find creative, local solutions to their problems. The Alberta Wild Rose Foundation provides assistance to community groups. Another example is provided by students in a west-end community of Toronto who, with their teacher, produced a book that acknowledges the reality of neighbourhood life while capturing the determination and compassion of a community working to change its circumstances. The students were honoured by Lieutenant Governor Hilary Weston. The ceremony *recognized the countless volunteer hours that they have poured into community-development projects.*[1]

Underlying the expectation of recognition are the dynamics of reciprocity in social exchanges. Just as it is expected that help to others, gifts, and expressions of friendship will be reciprocated, so there is an expectation that social contributions will be recognized for their value to others and to the community.

Recognition is a dimension of fairness. If others do not recognize what an individual or a category of individuals contributes to the group, they are, so to speak, being unfair. They fail to acknowledge the efforts and resources invested in the collective good. We previously dealt with fairness as equity; here, attention is on fairness as reciprocity.[2] Both are important for individual well-being, self-esteem, and motivation. Both are part of the cement that holds the community or society together.

In this study the concern is with recognition of the contribution to society and not with identities or distinctive cultural attributes as such. In day-to-day life, these two aspects of recognition are no doubt related since they represent two dimensions of the relationship of individuals and groups to the society. Indeed, recognizing a social contribution is tantamount to recognizing a particular attribute or socio-cultural resource of an individual or group. However, recognizing a distinct group identity does not necessarily mean that the group's contribution to society is also recognized. In fact, the recognition could even be negative in the sense that the group is seen as a burden on society. In the present survey, we focus on the *positive recognition* of the "contribution" to society.

A group that is perceived as being a burden on society, as trying to extort the maximum from the rest of society without making an appropriate contribution, could be seen as having a distinct identity but this evaluation is negative. Thus, dissatisfaction with the recognition received may refer to a recognition that is negative, even degrading, rather than to a failure to be recognized. Sometimes, the negative evaluation may be justified. But frequently, it is based on stereotypes that are degrading and that fail to recognize the efforts of the individuals and groups involved. The west-end Toronto students mentioned above said that stereotypes are far more damaging than many of the economic hardships they might endure: "It is so hard to be slapped with the label poor," they explained.[3]

Some members of professional or occupational groups see their work as superior to that of others. They make disparaging remarks about certain fields of activity being largely useless for the society. Some believe that particular fields of study in colleges and universities should be eliminated. Frequently, however, it is not that there is negative labelling, but rather that efforts go unrecognized. For example, in the Black community, "there are numerous organizations supported by a host of volunteers that work to motivate and recognize the work of many brilliant and wholesome black youths *who are not portrayed in the media*. Those organizations will, no doubt, continue with the scholarships, awards, workshops, heritage programs and so on that they have been doing unsung for decades."[4]

Recognition has been an element in many of the claims made by various groups in recent decades. Women who raise children, immigrants, visible minorities, long-established ethnocultural communities, workers in occupations with little status in the "new economy," or people in dire financial situations struggling to manage their lives — all insist that their contribution to the community and society be recognized. In fact, it can be argued that, to a certain extent, a number of policy initiatives and institutional changes were made in response to claims for recognition as well as fairness. Some groups have been seeking recognition of their identities. Frequently, even though the claims were expressed in terms of respect and dignity, what was also sought was an acknowledgment of their contribution to the society.

Recognition of their social contribution is important to individuals because it is an element in the maintenance and/or reinforcement of their self-esteem or self-worth. Recognition is the opposite of being unappreciated, of being defined as socially insignificant, of being seen as contributing little or nothing to the community, or, worse, of being perceived as a social burden and thus despised. (It could, however, be argued that being ignored is worse than being seen as a burden.) Recognition goes beyond simple acceptance. It involves appreciation for what one brings to the community and society even if it is only one's efforts to deal with the hardships encountered as a result of poor health, loss of employment, or other difficult circumstances. Recognition is a powerful force in shaping one's self-image.

Communities, organizations, and societies depend for their vitality and effective functioning on different kinds of inputs from their members. A lack of recognition tends to discourage individuals from contributing even their fair share, let alone anything beyond that. Unappreciated contributions of time, effort, or money tend to erode the sense of personal responsibility for the common enterprise. Individuals may retreat from social commitment and future contributions. Disappointment and disillusionment may set in, and may even lead to rejection of the organization, the community or the society as a whole. As a consequence, the vitality of the community and its social fabric can suffer.

As with fairness, recognition can apply to individuals or to the groups and social categories to which they are affiliated. Both are critical since the self-esteem of individuals derives not only from the appreciation of their own contributions but also from the recognition accorded to the social groups or categories to which they belong and with which they identify. Canadians feel good when people in other countries admire some positive feature of our society. People feel proud when the work of their professional group is praised; they feel bad when the opposite takes place.

In our assessment of fairness or unfairness, we found that people compare the way their own and other groups are treated. Similarly, they reach conclusions on the adequacy of the recognition received in part by comparing it to what they perceive is granted to other groups. Because the assessment is comparative, a perceived inadequacy can generate social resentment and trigger tensions between groups. It can lead people to ignore or dismiss their interdependence on others. Such reactions, if frequent, can weaken the social fabric.

HOW SATISFIED ARE CANADIANS
WITH THE RECOGNITION RECEIVED?

In measuring satisfaction with the recognition of social contributions, this study focuses on groups, not on individuals.[5] We chose this focus because we were limited in the number of questions we could ask and, more important, because we felt that the recognition of the contribution of groups or social categories is more crucial to the health of the social fabric. Three groups or categories are considered: people of the same gender; of the same ethnic, cultural, or social background; and of the same level of education and training.

Are Canadians satisfied with the recognition that the social groups and categories to which they belong receive for their contribution to society? Do they feel that they are receiving more, less, or about the same recognition as they did a few years ago?[6] The percentages

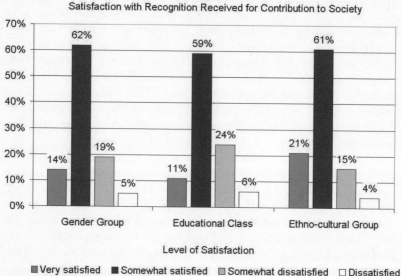

Figure 4
Satisfaction with Recognition Received for Contribution to Society

expressing satisfaction and dissatisfaction with the recognition their group receives for its contribution to society are shown in Figure 4 for each of the three groups or categories.

As can be seen, in none of the three instances does *very high* satisfaction exceed one in five respondents. The proportion of *very* satisfied is the highest with regard to the contribution of the ethnic, cultural, or racial group (21 per cent), followed by the satisfaction with the gender group's contribution (14 per cent). The lowest is in the case of the educational class (11 per cent). However, a strong majority are *somewhat* satisfied: between 59 and 62 per cent. Thus, the total who are satisfied varies between 70 and 81 per cent.

Another way of describing the overall assessment is to count the number of people who express satisfaction or dissatisfaction with the recognition received for the contribution of one, two, or all three of the social groups or categories to which they belong. These results appear in Figure 5.

It can be seen that a majority are satisfied with the recognition that all three social groups or categories receive for their contribution to society.

There is also a substantial degree of dissatisfaction. About one in five Canadians is dissatisfied with the recognition received by two or three of the groups to which they belong – gender, ethnic group, or educational class. About one in four are dissatisfied with the recognition

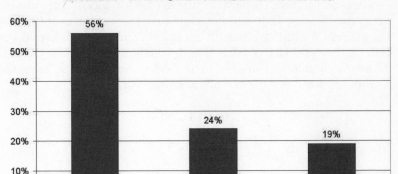

Figure 5
Dissatisfaction with Recognition for Group Contribution to Society

received in only one area. Adding these two categories together, we find that close to half of the sample are frustrated to some degree with the recognition received for the societal contribution of at least one of the groups or social categories to which they belong.

If we wanted to emphasize satisfaction, we could say that 80 per cent are entirely satisfied in relation to *two or three* social memberships. However, if we wanted to underscore the level of dissatisfaction, we could say that as many as 44 per cent are dissatisfied in relation to *at least one* of their social memberships.

These results are comparable to those of Reginald Bibby, who found, in a recent survey, that 33 per cent are concerned "a great deal" or "quite a bit" with the lack of recognition they receive "for the things they do." This is essentially the same as the 30 per cent in our survey in connection with the contribution of people of the same educational class. The reader should note, however, that there is a difference in the wording of the questions in the two surveys. Bibby's question is cast in terms of personal concerns, ours in terms of group concerns. Yet both surveys reveal a similar proportion of Canadians concerned in one way or another with the recognition they receive for what they do or contribute.

Experiencing a lack of recognition is experiencing a lack of fairness. The two are related in the sense that a number of people feel that they are not treated fairly and are also dissatisfied with the recognition received by the group(s) to which they belong. But many experience either unfairness or a lack of recognition. Only 23 per cent of the sample say they that they are treated very fairly and are also satisfied with the recognition received by the groups or social categories to which they belong. That is to say, more than three-quarters of Canadians express dissatisfaction with regard to fairness, recognition, or both. In short, the lack of fairness and the failure to recognize the contributions of different groups to the collective enterprise have the potential to weaken the social fabric of our society.

HIGHLIGHTS

To recapitulate:

- Overall, the level of satisfaction with the recognition received for the contribution made by different groups to society is fairly high. This is the case with regard to the contribution of all three social categories: gender, cultural, ethnic, or racial group or people at the same level of education or training.
- The level of satisfaction with recognition is higher than with the degree of fairness. Indeed, we saw in the previous chapter that the majority of Canadians express some dissatisfaction with the fairness of our society and of the way they are personally treated.
- However, the level of dissatisfaction is not negligible: more than two in five express some dissatisfaction with the recognition of the contribution of at least one of the social segments to which they belong.
- Dissatisfaction with the social recognition received is more frequent among persons with particular levels of education than among members of the gender or ethnocultural categories.

5

Trust in Social Relationships

Our boundless interdependence and mutual vulnerability in societies is fascinating. To a large extent we cope with complexity, ambiguity, and risk because we trust each other. Life is a boundless set of social interactions made possible by trust between and among people. (Trudy Govier, *Social Trust and Human Communities,* 1997)

Trust is a central attribute of the social relations that constitute the social fabric. It is an expectation based on beliefs and feelings about other people's motivations and future behaviour. "When we trust, we take risks and are vulnerable. There are no guarantees, and it would be an indication of lack of trust to look for them ... We feel that we can rely or depend on the other, even though there is always some possibility that he or she will act in unexpected ways, or even betray us."[1]

Without trust, it would be difficult to function effectively in the extensive networks of interdependence in which we are involved. It would be difficult to cope with our vulnerabilities in dealing with others. We need to know what to expect from them and from the institutions with which we interact. We also need to have some assurance that others will not take advantage of us even if it is to their advantage to do so. Thus, trust is not a given of nature. It is something that is achieved over time. There are favourable as well as detrimental circumstances in the building and the maintenance of social trust. And, sometimes, the situations in which such trust is important are the same ones that make sustaining it difficult.

Rapid and extensive social and economic change may be a factor in this difficulty. Most of the contexts in which people function evolve in more or less drastic ways: work, religion, politics, health care, education, entertainment, economic organization, and the demographic environment. Such changes can bring about social dislocations. They can upset some of the established patterns of social expectations. For instance, the experience of upward or downward mobility, of being a gainer or a loser in the restructuring of the economy, and of being advantaged or disadvantaged by changes in government policies may all raise the level of anxiety among people about their situation relative to that of others.

In such instances, social trust is crucial for individuals and for the functioning of organizations, communities, and the society in general. Yet it can be undermined by the disruption of customary social expectations or the creation of situations where no such expectations have yet been established. It is precisely when a strong social fabric is needed that it risks being eroded by the shocks of drastic transformations. In addition, although the market economy cannot function effectively without trust, it generates conditions and a cultural climate that tend to erode social trust. Indeed, in a market culture, individuals are expected to be concerned above all with their own interests and to get "the best deal" possible in their transactions with others or with institutions. The expectation that others are pursuing their self-interest makes their behaviour somewhat predictable. However, it offers no guarantee that one's own interest will be respected. This fosters the attitude that one should be careful about trusting others.

Trust is an important resource for individuals. It helps them to cope with complexity, ambiguity, and uncertainty. It increases predictability. Of course, trust can be risky; to be too trustful may expose us to harm. Some degree of distrust, at least in initial encounters with other individuals and with organizations and their agents, is no doubt sensible. But if distrust becomes intense and generalized, it complicates social interaction and exchanges. It leads to social, legal, and organizational measures to control the behaviour of those whose intentions are suspect. It may also lead people to isolate themselves from each other, socially and geographically (as, for example, in separate organizations, clubs, or neighbourhoods).

The more people are interdependent, the more trust is necessary. Not much can be achieved in organizations or in personal relationships without being dependent on the actions of others and thus having to trust them. When we drive, for example, we have to rely not only on those who manufactured the car but also on mechanics and on other drivers on the road. We are involved in complex systems of interdependence for food, health care, education, housing, and so on. In order to operate in day-to-day life, we need to feel that most people are trustworthy. It is a fundamental element in social and economic relationships. Today, in spite of the emphasis on individual self-realization and self-reliance, the degree of interdependence is extremely high. Because of this, the social fabric depends heavily on social trust.

The present study focuses on one dimension of trust, namely, the confidence that others will not take advantage of us. It seeks to assess the extent to which Canadians feel they experience such trust in their social relationships, the extent to which they feel they live in a trustful social environment. To address this question, we asked our respondents to tell us how they assess level of trust, first, as a general social expectation, and, second, in particular types of social relationships (e.g., with family, friends, co-workers).

THE OVERALL LEVEL OF SOCIAL TRUST

"Individuals should be careful about trusting others since there are too many people who only seek to benefit themselves."

A stunning 82 per cent of Canadians agree with this statement. Almost as many women (80 per cent) as men (84 per cent) do so. This is in line with a 1995 survey which found that 75 per cent said that "one cannot be too careful in dealing with people."[2]

Perhaps some agree because they do not want to appear gullible. But it is doubtful that many have this attitude since 88 per cent of the respondents also think that one of the problems faced by our society is that "there are too many people who expect to get something for nothing."[3] In addition, one third of the respondents agreed *strongly* with the statement that individuals should be careful about trusting others. At worst, this result indicates a low level of trust in others. At best, it suggests an ambivalence about what can be expected in dealing with others.

In conditions of change and in a culture of self-interest and self-reliance, trust can be difficult to establish. As already noted, in such conditions people become preoccupied with their niche in a socio-economic order in transformation, with their status in the community, with their influence and that of others on economic, social, and political issues and policies. Unfortunately, our survey does not allow us to assess the extent to which such preoccupations exist.

However, we found that 46 per cent say that *"these days, they are so hard-pressed to take care of their own needs that they worry less about the needs of others."* A 1997 survey found that 71 per cent of Canadians agree that "people who are overly honest in our society are often taken advantage of" (the percentage agreeing was 78 in the 1995 survey mentioned above).[4] Such perceptions, while perhaps understandable in periods of change, are not conducive to the building of social trust. On the contrary, they nurture the feeling that one *"should be careful about trusting others since there are too many people who only seek to benefit themselves."*

Indeed, trust tends to be associated with the perception that people value integrity in their relationships with others and with society. Conversely, distrust is associated with the view that self-interest dominates in social transactions among people. In this sense, the carefulness that most Canadians express about their transactions with others may be related to their perceptions that the ethical standards of Canadians have declined in recent years. There may be a connection with the finding of a recent survey that 52 per cent think that such deterioration of standards has taken place among average Canadians.[5] In our survey, we find that suspicion or distrust in social relationships is also associated with views about acceptable behaviour in social transactions. Specifically,

- those who feel strongly that *"only agreements that are written and signed need to be honoured; that verbal agreements don't matter"* are much more likely to be distrustful than those who strongly disagree with this view (56 per cent compared to 34 per cent);
- those who strongly agree that *"being honest makes it more likely that you will not come out ahead"* are much more likely to be distrustful than those who strongly disagree with this view (67 per cent compared to 35 per cent);
- those who strongly agree that *"promises are just made to get people to do things for you and don't always have to be kept"* are much more likely to be distrustful than those who strongly disagree with this view (76 per cent compared to 35 per cent); and
- those who strongly agree that *"everything is relative, and there just aren't any definite rules to live by"* are much more likely to be distrustful than those who strongly disagree with this view (63 per cent compared to 36 per cent).

The perception that others are focused on their self-interest may lead people to be cautious in their social relations. For instance, we found that three-quarters of Canadians think that *"too many people will sacrifice their principles in order to get ahead economically"*; 88 per cent feel that *"there are too many people who expect to get something for nothing"*; and 81 per cent think that *"in our society, there are two sets of rules: one for those who have money and one for everyone else."* These assessments of the moral climate in our society are related to the level of trust or distrust. Indeed, those who strongly agree with the following statements are more likely to be distrustful than those who disagree:

- *"Too many will sacrifice their principles to get ahead economically"* (51 per cent compared to 36 per cent).

- *"There are too many people who expect to get something for nothing"* (49 per cent compared to 20 per cent).
- *"In our society, there are two sets of rules: one for those who have money and one for everyone else"* (48 per cent compared to 23 per cent).

In short, the high level of distrust or suspicion revealed by our survey should not be too surprising given the substantial and rapid social changes that have taken place in recent decades, including the growing predominance of the "market" culture which values self-reliance and the pursuit of self-interest.

TRUST IN DIFFERENT SOCIAL RELATIONSHIPS

People are involved in different types of social relationships. First, they relate to each other as individuals when they interact, for example, with family members, friends, and co-workers. They also deal with institutions such as governments and their agencies, churches, media, businesses, banks and investments brokers, charitable organizations, or recreational and athletic associations. Thus, we can talk about two types of trust: horizontal[6] and vertical. The second will be considered in the next chapter.

Horizontal trust can be interpersonal, such as when people trust or distrust particular individuals. But relationships can also be between individuals and categories of people such as members of particular ethnic, racial, religious, or political groups. In addition, they can be ranked in terms of intimacy or closeness, as follows:

- relationships with family members and friends;
- relationships with *co-workers;*
- relationships within ethnocultural boundaries; and
- relationships across belief and moral boundaries, that is, with people who have different political or religious beliefs or moral values.

Figure 6 shows the percentages of those who trust *a lot*, or *not at all*, that they will not be taken advantage of in each of the four types of relationships.

Several observations can be made on these findings:

- First, the percentage who indicate a lot of trust declines steeply and rapidly: from 79 to 5 per cent. The degree of trust is quite high in family relationships but declines rapidly in other interpersonal relationships: 79 per cent to 59 per cent and 30 per cent, respectively,

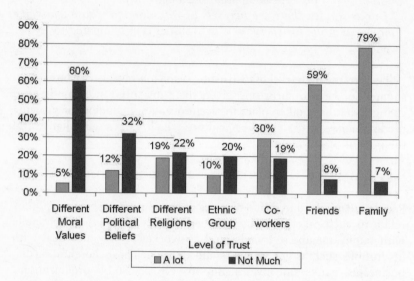

Figure 6
Whom Do Canadians Trust?

express a lot of trust for family, friends, and co-workers. This quite pronounced decline is observed in all social categories – defined in terms of gender, of socio-economic status as defined by level of income and education, of class self-identification, and of region.

- Second, the closer the social relationship, the higher the incidence of trust or the lower the level of distrust. Thus, almost four out of five express a very high level of trust in their family while only 5 per cent express such trust in people whose values are other than their own.
- Third, even though the level of trust is high in family relationships, about one in five respondents express some degree of distrust (14 per cent somewhat and 7 per cent not at all). This may be low compared to what occurs in other types of relationships, but it is not negligible.
- Fourth, respondents are more likely than *categories of people* to be very trustful in their relations with *particular individuals*. Specifically, the percentage who express a lot of trust in family members, friends, and co-workers never goes below 30 while it never exceeds 19 in relation to members of ethnic, cultural, or racial groups or to people with different religious and political beliefs or moral values.
- Fifth, the level of trust *within* cultural, ethnic, or racial collectivities is relatively low. This is somewhat surprising. We expected that cultural, ethnic, or racial identities would be a basis of social trust, that people would strongly trust those who have the same background as their own. But we find that only one in ten say that they trust

members of their own group "a lot" (This will be explored further in Chapter 12.)

- Finally, there is considerable distrust across boundaries of beliefs and values, whether these are religious, political, or moral. That is to say, few people trust those whom they see as ideological, religious, or moral "strangers."

Surprisingly, there is not much difference by religious affiliation in this regard, especially when different political beliefs and moral values are concerned. Whether one is Protestant, Catholic, member of another church, or without a religious affiliation, the level of distrust is about the same. In the case of religious beliefs, there is also little variation, except that the level of distrust is lower among Protestants than among the others.

It may be that, when values and beliefs are involved, the lack of trust is partly based on the fact that the motives of those who differ are unknown and, as a result, their behaviour is unpredictable. Such a perception engenders suspicion. But it may be that the motives and the related social and political agenda are known. When this is the case, distrust is based on the fear that those with different values and beliefs will attempt to impose their preferences on others and/or on the rest of the society or will promote policies that would change valued features of our public institutions. Given the intense public debates on various issues such as health care, education, privatization, welfare, and abortion – debates that most of the time reflect profound ideological differences – it is not surprising that the level of distrust across differences in moral values and political beliefs is quite high.

Thus differences in values and beliefs can act as social boundaries that prevent the emergence of trust. In order to be effective and stable, relationships with strangers require a lot of trust, yet it seems more difficult to build trust in such relationships. This is significant given the high degree of social and cultural diversity in the Canadian population.

Trust is different from tolerance. Canadians are fairly tolerant in their acceptance of people who are different from themselves and their own self-image. But tolerance may be primarily a reasoned attitude, an attitude derived from humanitarian or religious principles, or an attitude seen as a prerequisite for peace and order. This is perhaps the reason why it is generally higher among the more educated.

Tolerance, a "live and let live" attitude, may exist without people interacting with each other. This is not the case with trust. Indeed, trust is relevant when there is social exchange or competition either between individuals or groups. In the case of groups, the exchange or competition takes place through their leaders or representatives. Trust is needed, for example, when groups who differ in their moral, ideological, or religious principles compete over particular public policies. But we find that the level of trust across such differences is fairly low in our society.

HIGHLIGHTS

To summarize:

- a strong majority of Canadians hesitate to trust others because there are too many out there who only seek to benefit themselves;
- the level of trust is high among friends and co-workers;
- there appears to be much distrust of people with different beliefs and values, indicating a substantial social split along those lines; and
- the level of trust *within* cultural, ethnic, or racial collectivities is relatively low.

6

Trust in Institutional Leaders

"Where have all the leaders gone?" "How elites have lost the faith of the general public." "Judge blames lawyers' behaviour for low confidence in legal system." "Culture du secret à Ottawa." "How can there be accountability without responsibility?" "Public relations: A new class of professional influence peddlers, most of them former journalists and political aides, is manipulating public attitudes about everything from the Persian Gulf war to Garth Drabinsky. That they do this in almost complete secrecy holds disturbing implications for democracy in the Information Age."

The above are samples of headlines, titles, and subtitles recently found in newspapers. Some survey results indicate that critical views of institutional leaders expressed by newspaper editors and columnists are also shared by many in the general public. The results also indicate that Canadians have become more critical in recent years. For instance, an analysis of election studies since 1965 and of the World Values Surveys since the early 1980s show a decline in the level of trust in the federal government. However, such a trend in attitudes vis-à-vis governments is not peculiar to Canada, it is also observed in other Western industrial states.[1]

In addition, Allan Gregg and Michael Posner found that "in the early 1980s, most Canadians described politicians as hardworking (70 per cent), principled (63 per cent), and competent (57 per cent). And 51 per cent said they held somewhat (or very) favourable feelings towards politicians. But, by March 1990, that faith had dramatically eroded. Then, 57 per cent of respondents said that politicians are unprincipled; 81 per cent said that politicians are more concerned with making money than helping people; and only 32 per cent said that they hold "generally favourable views" about politicians.[2]

Although views of business leaders are more favourable, assessments of their chief characteristics have also declined through the 1980s. In 1990 "only a slim majority thought [they] were principled; and 37 per cent said they were incompetent. Most Canadians agree with the statement that 'people who run corporations don't really care about people like me.'"[3] While not as pronounced as for government, trust in "major companies" has also fallen between 1981 and 1990, a trend that is not observed in the United States. The recent spate of corporate scandals involving Enron, World Com, Johnson and Johnson, and Hydro One serve to fuel these perceptions.

Such critical perceptions and judgments suggest a serious problem of trust in institutions and those who run them, a problem that may have considerable implications for the cohesion of a society. Indeed, the social fabric depends on, among other things, the institutional matrix of the society. This is because much of the economic, social, cultural, and political life of a society takes place in or through its institutions. The social fabric rests not only on the quality of the horizontal relationships among members but also on the tenor of the vertical transactions between them and their institutions and leaders.[4] Both are critical.

Vertical relationships are those that take place between individuals and institutional authorities and agents such as employers, businessmen, and politicians. In such instances, we can speak of vertical or institutional trust.

As previously noted, social cohesion is based on the strength of the attachment and loyalty that individual members have to their society. This includes its institutions. Attachment and loyalty to institutions depend on the quality of the relationships with them which, in turn, is defined in part by the degree of trust in those who hold positions of power and authority in them.

Trust involves expectations about the behaviour of others. Some of these expectations are based on perceptions of technical competence. That is to say, we can have confidence in the doctor, the hospital, the accountant, the mechanic, the politician, or the government ministry because we feel that they know what they are doing and have the required competence and resources. This kind of trust is critical in defining the quality of the relationship with institutions and their authorities.

But there is another kind of trust: moral trust. It is based on expectations that people will meet their moral obligations, act responsibly, and not take advantage of others. It is the confidence that they will consider your interest as well as their own in dealing with you, or, perhaps more critically, that they will not act against your interest even if it is in their own to do so. In other words, this trust involves the belief that others will consider your point of view and situation, that they will not cheat you nor try to take advantage of you. It is with moral trust that we are concerned in this study.

In addition, much of the relationships between groups or social categories with different interests are mediated by institutional leaders. The quality of the mediation usually affects the level of vertical trust. For instance, distrust is certain to rise if institutional policies are seen as favouring one group over another: the interests of employers over those of workers, the interests of one region over those of another, the interests of one social class over those of another, the interests of landlords over those of tenants, and so on. Such perceived behaviour not only generates distrust of institutional authorities, it also fuels distrust among social groups or categories and creates tensions among them. These negative experiences risk weakening the social fabric.

Conversely, to the extent that it exists, trust buttresses the legitimacy of institutions and their authorities. Indeed, people will more readily accept institutional policies and practices if they can see that these have been designed for the benefit of the community or society; that power and authority have been used for the common good; that the statements of public authorities are believable – in short, when they are seen as trustworthy. Otherwise, citizens become cynical and lose respect for the institution and/or for those who run it.

Our survey reveals that the level of trust in institutional authorities[5] is not very high in our society (Figure 7). It is even lower than what Gregg and Posner found in 1990 (see above). Very few Canadians are highly confident that businessmen and politicians, both federal and provincial, *will not* take advantage of them.

Of the four categories, employers enjoy the highest level of trust, with only 24 per cent declaring little or no confidence at all in them. Distrust is much higher in the three other categories: about half (47 per cent) express little or no trust in businessmen and about two-thirds in provincial and federal politicians (67 and 71 per cent, respectively).

It was seen above that the experience of fairness or unfairness is associated with the level of general social trust. Distrust of politicians and businessmen is associated with

- a personal experience of unfairness;
- the feeling that the social class to which one belongs is not treated fairly; and

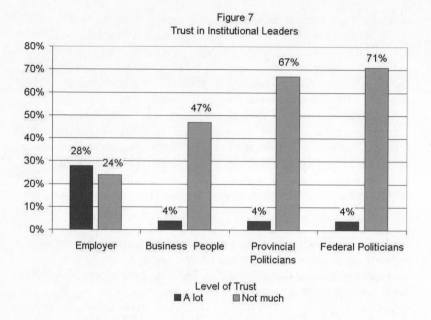

Figure 7
Trust in Institutional Leaders

- the perception that one's province is getting less than its fair share of
  federal government programs.

These findings are consistent with the results of research which has suggested that "when citizens are evaluating government leaders or institutions, *justice is actually a more important influence than is the level of
outcomes received.* In other words, citizens act as naive philosophers in
evaluating government, judging its actions against abstract criteria of
fairness. The major implication of these results for the study of dissatisfaction is in the recognition that citizen evaluations of political authorities are based upon judgments about the justice of the actions of government institutions and of the decisions of government leaders."[6] This
statement, we believe, can also be applied to the actions and decisions
of businessmen and corporate decision makers.

Trust is required primarily when the goals, aspirations, or interests
of people diverge. Indeed, when two parties have the same interest with
regard to a particular matter, trust is less important since, by pursuing
its interest, the other also pursues its own. Trust becomes critical when
interests differ.

Thus, the low level of trust in relation to institutional authorities
may be due to the perception that they are more concerned with profit
and power than with the interests of citizens. Or, more precisely, that

Table 3   Priorities of General Public and Decision Makers

Priorities	Rank Assigned by General Public	Rank Assigned by Decision Makers
Competitiveness	20	1
Excellence	18	5
Prosperity	19	8
Minimal Government	22	3
Integrity	4	2
Liberty	1	7
Individual Rights	5	15
Collective Rights	10	18
Equality for All Regions	7	20
Clean Environment	2	10
Healthy Population	3	9

Source: Ekos Research Associates, *Rethinking Government '94. An Overview and Synthesis* (Ottawa: Ekos Research Associates 1995).

when their interests and those of citizens differ, they will tend to chose in favour of their own. To the extent that such a judgment exists, suspicion will reign. There will be a tendency to feel that institutional authorities are not to be entirely trusted to take other people's interests into account in their decisions.

The actual or perceived divergences in interest may be more frequent in vertical than in most horizontal relationships. Or it may be that in vertical relationships, it is easier for people, especially those who control or can manipulate the media, to conceal their true interests. Advertising and public relations may influence people but frequently may leave the impression that all has not been revealed, that the exercise was aimed partly at concealing something. There is also the fact that much of the decision making by businessmen, corporations, and politicians is carried out behind closed doors. A high degree of secrecy tends to make people suspicious.

Elites and citizens may also differ in what they define as problematic and important. A recent survey by Ekos Research Associates, for instance, has shown that there is a gap between the priorities of decision makers and the general public (Table 3).[7]

Two of the three items placed at the top of the scale by elites and decision makers are located at the bottom for the general public: competitiveness and minimal government. Also, the Ekos report notes that governmental as well as non-governmental elites agree on these priorities. This kind of findings suggest that, at least in part, elites and citizens favour different political agendas.

More serious from the point of view of trust is the perception by an important proportion of respondents that governmental elites are inordinately influenced by the lobbies of powerful interests, that they serve the interests of national and transnational corporations and of the wealthy rather than those of citizens and of the society as a whole. These perceptions have been documented in a 1998 survey. (Graves and Reed, 1998). Only 18 per cent of Canadians feel that the general public interest is the main concern of governments in their decision making. On the other hand, almost four out of five think that what matters in those decisions are the interests of large corporations (32 per cent), of politicians and their friends (28 per cent) or of special-interest groups (19 per cent). This judgment is made of both federal and provincial decision makers.[8]

Corresponding to these views is the perception of a decline in the responsiveness of governments. A 1992 survey found that three out of four Canadians felt that "governments here are becoming somewhat or much less responsive to the needs of your own community."[9] This view is related to the sense of political efficacy. It makes sense to assume that responsiveness on the part of governments and the feeling that one has some influence on them would tend to go together. Such is the conclusion suggested by a study in Alberta which indicated that greater feelings of political efficacy increase the confidence of citizens in their government.[10]

Along the same lines, the distrust of politicians and businessmen is also associated with the view that there are two sets of rules in our society, one for those with money and one for everyone else. In the words of one of our respondents (Pembroke, Ont.), "what is the *most* important for a society to function well is that there be easily understandable rules that apply in the same way to everyone." But in Canada today, "the rules don't apply to everyone." The situation will not change in the future "unless the people revolt." Depending on the situation, who you are or how much money you have, the rules do change. Judges can be bought, policemen can be bought, I think about anybody can be bought so, if you've got a lot of money you are not going to fall into the justice system. What happens to you depends on who you are – they talk about our Constitution but to me, it's kind of flexible ... "

The difference in the level of distrust between those who do and those who do not have this perception of the prevailing rules is substantial: a difference of twenty-five percentage points. This difference is observed in relation to businessmen and to both federal and provincial politicians. It is smaller in the case of employers: only 14 per cent.

Another facet of the issue is the growing disjunction between accountability and responsibility. Jeffrey Simpson writes that, in recent years, there have been several instances of serious hesitation or refusal on the part of government officials to assume responsibility (e.g., the Somalia, tainted-blood, and Airbus matters). He argues that "the notion of accountability must somehow be tied to accepting responsibility, because if that link is broken, then accountability becomes a hollow concept."[11]

These perceptions and judgments may be due to the public visibility of corporate and government behaviour. Although the decision-making process is shrouded in secrecy, information about the outcomes of some decisions and about the way they were made eventually becomes known to the public. The role of the media is important in this regard. But the media can also have a corrosive effect insofar as they focus on the negative in government actions to the point that the positive recedes to a distant background in the public consciousness.

The level of education can also be critical in changing citizen-state relations. Indeed, more educated citizens tend to have a better understanding of issues and of the mechanisms of decision making. Their level of political engagement is also likely to be greater.[12] This results in an awareness of political realities which, as Neil Nevitte found, turns out to be the most important factor in accounting for the decline of deference to authority in Canada.[13]

Many Canadians also think that government officials and business managers are themselves generating distrust. Indeed, there is strong agreement with the propositions that *"public trust is being weakened by the behaviour of people in positions of public responsibility and leadership"* (42 per cent strongly agree and 46 per cent agree – a total of 88 per cent) and *"by the behaviour of people who manage business corporations"* (27 per cent strongly agree and 47 per cent agree – a total of 74 per cent), leaving only 9 per cent and 21 per cent who disagree with the first and second statement, respectively.

One of our respondents (Toronto, Ont.) says that what is involved is "a complex interaction of incentives and opportunities": "There are some people in Canada who are taking unfair advantage of public programs and services, but not because people are cheating welfare. I think it is a complex interaction of incentives and opportunities. It is not just poor people. There are groups that are very adept at getting grants. The system of redistribution is very complex; a systematic way of buying off people, so I think government is really at fault. The money is used politically. Politicians know the outcomes (they are not as stated). Politicians use that money to buy votes, ineffective ways too, the system is fundamentally corrupt. There are many who are culpable."

This view is strongly related to the assessment that respondents make of the trustworthiness of both federal and provincial politicians. Among those who strongly agree that the erosion of public trust is due to the detrimental behaviour of public leaders, about four in five say that they trust politicians little or not at all. In contrast, less than half (46 per cent) express a high level of distrust if they think that public trust is not weakened by the behaviour of public leaders.

A similar relationship exists between the view that "public trust is weakened by the behaviour of people who manage business corporations" and the level of trust in businessmen: 62 per cent of those who strongly agree express little or no trust in businessmen compared to 35 per cent of those who disagree with this view, a difference of twenty-seven percentage points. With regard to employers, the percentages are 31 and 14, a difference of seventeen points.

Other authors have suggested a link between the behaviour of authorities and the level of trust or distrust. For instance, an Angus Reid survey conducted in 1996 found that "60 per cent of Canadians feel that corporations are becoming more irresponsible – an obsession with maximizing shareholder values to the detriment of employee and community interests."[14] Peter Newman expressed a similar view in quite strong language:

Canadian soldiers, who once claimed their own beach in Normandy and treated their captured wounded as well as their own, now forced recruits to choke on their own faeces, paraded their bigotry before home cameras and committed atrocities against the very people they were sworn to protect ... Hockey and baseball stars became businessmen first, celebrities second and role models for a nation's youth hardly at all. Priests lusted for choir boys' bodies instead of their souls; teachers sharpened their skills as trade unionists while their students struggled with maths and reading skills; Greenpeace activists turned into money-collectors; politicians became a separate class that advanced its own interests, not those of the voters; auditors fixed books; experts turned out to be fools; lawyers went to jail; diplomats cheated; the Red Cross's carelessness killed."[15]

There are two aspects to these observations. First, the problem exists in virtually all institutional sectors. Second, it is through institutional practices that institutional authorities lose their credibility and authority. One can question the choice of illustrations selected by Newman, but our survey results seem to indicate that many Canadians agree with his basic argument.

The Graves and Reed 1998 survey mentioned above also indicates that "a plurality (49 per cent) believe that the ethical standards of both the federal government and business have declined in the past decade." In short, the behaviour of politicians and businessmen, while not entirely responsible for the distrust that exists of them in the population, seems to play an important role.

HIGHLIGHTS

To summarize:
- The results indicate a substantial gap *between elites and the general public.* Of the four categories of people in positions of power and authority, employers benefit from the highest level of trust, since only 24 per cent declare little or no confidence at all in them. Distrust of businessmen is higher (47 per cent) and still higher for politicians, both provincial (67 per cent) and federal (71 per cent).
- A commonly held view among Canadians is that this elite-public dichotomy is due, in part, to the behaviour of those in positions of authority, whether in government or in business.
- There is a concern that the policies crafted by governments or by corporations and other business organizations may not be in the public's interest but rather in those of the decision makers themselves and their allies.

7

Belonging in Community and Society

Social cohesion is a set of social processes that help instill in individuals the sense of belonging to the same community and the feeling that they are recognized as members of that community. (Commissariat Général du Plan, France, 1998)

But varied as such particulars may be, I do believe it is possible to say that in all cases, the function of basic group identity has to do most crucially with two key ingredients in every individual's personality and life experience: his sense of belonging and the quality of his self-esteem. (Harold R. Isaacs, *Basic Group Identity*, 1974)

Feeling like an outsider is painful. This is true in any place where one expects to belong, to feel at home: the workplace, the neighbourhood, the church, the town or city, or the country.

It can happen to immigrants when they are not considered to be fully Canadian. About three out of ten Canadians think that immigrants cannot expect to be considered as fully Canadian as those who were born and raised here. It is also a feeling that can be instilled when the public discourse includes distinctions between those who are *pure laine* and those who are not.

It can happen to Black persons who are asked what country they come from when their families have been in Canada for generations; to those who do not speak the language of the majority or who speak it with an accent; to immigrants who criticize some of our ways and are told to go back "home," that is, to their country of origin.

It can also happen to people who move from small towns to large cities, or to anyone moving to another city or neighbourhood. It is sometimes said that established residents are somewhat cool to newcomers, that it takes a lot of time to become fully accepted in the town or neighbourhood. Suburban developments bring people from the city to surrounding towns. In his discussion of this phenomenon, Dale quotes a new resident of an old town who observes that "some of these old towns, they're very cliquish, and it takes a while to break that down" and goes on to note that "this coolness towards newcomers was so pronounced that for years a kind of caste existed that separated old-stock villagers and the first new wave of suburbanites."[1]

It can happen to those who disagree with some of the orthodox views in their religious congregation; to those who feel that they cannot openly express their views on certain issues; to those who have a lifestyle different from that of the surrounding majority. And it can happen to those who are socially defined as "losers" or failures in their community, or to those who are defined as "special-interest groups" in contrast to those who are presumed to belong, namely the taxpayers.

Identifying with an organization, a community, or a society is difficult if, for one reason or another, one feels like an outsider. Indeed, feeling at home implies a certain identification with the community or society, a sense of being an integral part of that community. Authentic membership implies that some of the elements that define the individual's personal identity are also among those that define the collective identity of the community or society. Thus, the more pluralist the collective identity, the more encompassing it is of people who vary in their individual identities, the more different kinds of people are likely to feel at home in the society.

The distinction between formal and authentic membership is fundamental. One can be a formal member without feeling at home in the group, community, or society. The sense of belonging goes beyond formal or legal inclusion. It goes beyond the formal rights of citizenship, although such rights do constitute an essential basis on which the sense of belonging can develop.

Mutual social acceptance means that members cannot conceive of their community or society without fully accepting each other whatever social, economic, or cultural differences exist among them. In contrast, individuals or groups are excluded when they are judged not to possess certain desirable characteristics or when their behaviour is judged to be "non-Canadian." The result for those so targeted is that they feel as strangers, that they do not belong.

Belonging provides individuals with an anchorage for their personal identity and self-esteem. Because of this, it constitutes a critical factor in their psychological well-being. In addition, being socially integrated is a resource that individuals can use in the pursuit of personal and social goals. It is a resource in the sense that, through it, individuals can obtain socio-emotional support, social approval, contacts, and valuable information. It is so basic that it is a social expectation that comes automatically with being a member of a group, community, or society. Indeed, the opposite is estrangement, a feeling akin to that of being a stranger.

The sense of belonging is particularly important in societies, such as our own, that are highly differentiated along such dimensions as socio-economic position, cultural background, moral values, political philosophy, and sexual orientation. In such contexts, it can be tempting for some to define the collective identity in terms of their own preferences and to see the "others" as not having the "right stuff" and therefore as second-class citizens or even as outsiders.

Nurturing the sense of belonging is partly a matter of accepting differences among members of the community. Canadians are generally quite tolerant. Yet many have a problem with differences. Consider, for example, the following findings:

- About three out of ten Canadians (29 per cent) think that immigrants cannot expect to be considered as fully Canadian as those who were born and raised here.
- One in three Canadians (34 per cent) does not approve of people with ideas and lifestyles that differ significantly from what is generally accepted.
- About the same proportion (36 per cent) believe that to be gay or lesbian is unacceptable.
- Fully 86 per cent feel that ethnic, cultural, and racial groups should try as much as possible to blend into Canadian society.
- Three out of four Canadians (76 per cent) think that the ideal society is one in which people are sufficiently similar to feel at home with one another.
- There is considerable distrust of people who are different in terms of religious, political, and moral beliefs and values.

Given such attitudes about social differences, we can expect that a certain number of Canadians may not feel entirely at home in our society. These attitudes may not be expressed openly, but this does not mean that their sting is not felt. We will consider this feeling of being at home in both the local community and in the society as a whole.[2]

FEELING AT HOME IN THE LOCAL COMMUNITY

We do find that, even though a solid majority of Canadians (57 per cent) feel very much at home in the community where they live, about

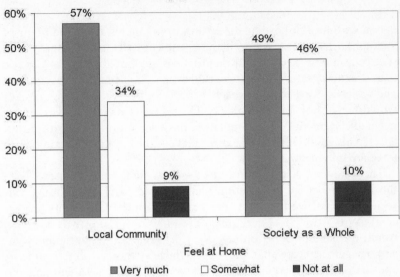

Figure 8
Sense of Belonging in Different Types of Communities

one third (34 per cent) feel somewhat at home and one in ten feel a little or not at all at home (Figure 8). As could be expected, people who live in small communities (less than 5,000) are more likely to feel that they *very much* belong than those in large metropolitan areas: 65 per cent compared to 51 per cent. However, the percentage who feel like strangers, that is to say, who feel a little or not at all at home, is about the same, regardless of the size of the community (about 9 per cent). The difference between small and large communities is a matter of intensity, a strong as opposed to a moderate sense of belonging.

Marital and family situations are also relevant for feeling at home in the community. First, the divorced are the least likely to feel very much at home in the community where they live (44 per cent). They are followed by the singles (50 per cent), the separated (56 per cent), and the married (61 per cent). Being divorced, single, and, to a lesser extent, separated are conditions that appear to marginalize some in the sense that they become more socially isolated than married people. It may be that in certain social milieu there is still a stigma attached to a marital breakdown. But, whatever the reason, the divorced feel less at home in the community where they live than those who are married.

FEELING AT HOME
IN THE SOCIETY AS A WHOLE

Perhaps a more important dimension of belonging from the point of view of societal functioning is the sentiment of being at home in the society as a whole. Given all the qualities attributed to life in Canada (e.g., freedom, safety, tolerance, the virtual absence of severe conflicts and violence), one would expect that a large proportion of Canadians would feel at home in this society. However, we have seen that a non-negligible segment of the population have some problems with differences. This would lead us to expect that a significant proportion do not feel they fully belong.

The following distribution can be seen as somewhat consistent with the co-existence of these somewhat contradictory attitudes in our society. Indeed, we find that less than half of the respondents (44 per cent) say that they feel very much at home in the society as a whole. About the same proportion (46 per cent) say that they feel somewhat and 10 per cent say that they feel a little or not at all at home. It appears that many experience social conditions that are alienating and lead them to feel more or less estranged from their society.[3] Unfortunately, we do not have any information on whether or not respondents have been made to feel unaccepted because they are in some way different. We have, however, their assessment of the existing degree of tolerance in our society. This will be considered in relation to the sense of belonging as well as their experience of unfairness, lack of recognition for the contribution to society, and distrust.[4]

THE TOLERANCE OF DIFFERENCES
IN OUR SOCIETY

More than six out of ten Canadians (64 per cent) believe that "*tolerance for people who are different from ourselves is declining in our society.*" Close to two out of ten strongly agree that this is the case and only 4 per cent strongly disagree with this assessment. Among those who feel tolerance is declining, some may have personally experienced intolerance.

This may account in part for the fact that the sense of belonging is associated with this perception of the evolution of social attitudes. Close to six out of ten (57 per cent) of those who are quite convinced that tolerance is declining feel somewhat or not at all at home in this society compared to less than four out of ten among those who strongly disagree with this evaluation.

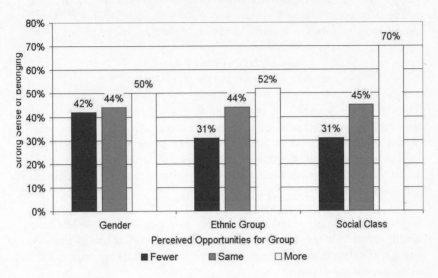

Figure 9
Strong Sense of Belonging by Job Opportunities

FAIRNESS

The experience of fairness is also associated with the feeling of being at home in the society. This is not surprising. Only 30 per cent of those who say they are personally treated unfairly in this society feel at home compared to 65 per cent of those who feel they are treated very fairly, a difference of thirty-five percentage points.

Similar results are obtained when we consider the perceived fairness experienced by the social groups or categories to which the respondent belongs. Those who perceive a fair distribution of job opportunities by gender, a fair distribution of job opportunities across cultural, ethnic, or racial lines, and a fair treatment of people of one's social class are more likely to feel at home in the society than those who perceive unfairness in these connections (Figure 9).

Of the three, it is the treatment of one's social class that matters the most. Indeed, there is a difference of forty percentage points between those who perceive a high and those who perceive a low degree of fairness in the treatment of their social class. In contrast, the differences in percentage points are roughly eight and twenty with fairness of job opportunities by gender and by ethnicity or race.

It should be noted that there is practically no relationship between the feeling of being at home and the perceived fairness of federal programs for one's province. This is somewhat unexpected since public debates suggest that feelings of alienation and even of secession develop in areas where people feel cheated in the allocation of national resources. Obviously, other factors are at work in the emergence of such feelings.

RECOGNITION OF
THE CONTRIBUTION TO SOCIETY

The enjoyment of social recognition of one's contribution to society has implications for the strength of social identification. It would seem that it is difficult to identify with a society when we perceive that it fails to appreciate our contribution to it. The negative impact would be worse if the perception is that the recognition is not only inadequate but declining.

The survey does show that both satisfaction with the recognition received and the perceived direction of change in the degree of recognition matter for the sense of belonging. It shows that this is the case for the contribution of the respondent's ethnocultural group, gender and educational class:

- 70 per cent of those who are very satisfied with the recognition received by members of their *own cultural, ethnic, or racial group* feel very much at home in this society, compared to only 25 per cent of those who are dissatisfied *and* think that there is less recognition than a few years ago, a difference of forty-five percentage points.
- 74 per cent of those who are very satisfied with the recognition received by members of their *own educational category* feel very much at home in this society, compared to only 26 per cent of those who are dissatisfied *and* think that there is less recognition than a few years ago, a difference of forty-eight percentage points.
- 70 per cent of those who are very satisfied with the recognition received by *people of the same gender* feel very much at home in this society, compared to only 32 per cent of those who are dissatisfied *and* think that there is less recognition than a few years ago, a difference of thirty-eight percentage points.

In all three instances, the association between the recognition of social contributions and the sense of belonging to society is quite strong.

SOCIAL TRUST AND SENSE OF CONTROL

There are different ways in which the social context can be unfriendly. There can be intolerance, unfairness and lack of appreciation for a

Figure 10
Sense of Belonging Decreases with Cumulation of Social Disadvantage

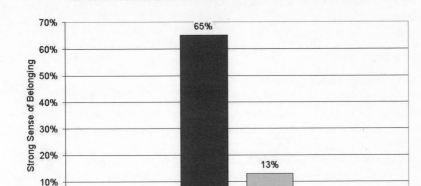

person's contribution to society. But the social context can also be "user friendly" in the sense that it instills in its members the confidence that others will not take advantage of them for their own benefit. On the other hand, it can be "user unfriendly" by emphasizing self-interest so much that people come to fear that many cannot be trusted because they are out to get the maximum benefit for themselves even to the detriment of others. Thus, as expected, we find that trust is associated with the sense of being at home in the society: 57 per cent of the trustful compared to 41 per cent of the distrustful feel very much at home in our society.

Finally, the social context can be favourable or unfavourable in terms of the possibilities it offers its members to manage their lives.[5] If people feel that what they do has no effect on the way their lives turn out, they will tend not to feel as much at home in the society as those who feel in control. And this is what we find: the percentage who feel a strong sense of belonging increases steadily from those with a low to a moderate to a high sense of control over their lives: 23, 39, and 55 percent, respectively, a total increase of thirty-two percentage points.

These four factors – tolerance, fairness, recognition, and sense of control – have a cumulative impact on the sense of belonging. This can be observed by comparing the percentage of those who feel a strong sense of belonging and experience disadvantage in none of these regards to the percentage of those who have a weak sense of belonging and whose experience is negative on all four dimensions.

As Figure 10 demonstrates, the difference is substantial. Cumulative disadvantage leads to a fivefold decrease in a strong sense of belonging to society.

HIGHLIGHTS

Our principal findings, then, are as follows:

- A majority of Canadians (57 per cent) feel very much at home in the community where they live; about one-third feel somewhat and only one in ten feel a little or not at all at home there.
- Close to half of the respondents feel very much at home in the larger society. About the same proportion say that they feel somewhat and 10 per cent say that they feel a little or not at all at home. Thus, the percentage who feel highly integrated is higher at the level of the local community – the level that is closer to them – than that of the larger society.
- Few respondents (only about one in ten) feel they belong little or not at all at both levels.
- Positively related to the sense of being at home in this society are four assessments: that tolerance of differences is *not* declining; that one is being treated fairly; that one's contributions are receiving adequate recognition; and that one is in control over the outcome of one's own life.

8

Indebtedness to Society

Generosity of spirit is thus the ability to acknowledge an interconnectedness –
one's 'debt to society' – that binds one to others whether one wants to accept
it or not. (Robert Bellah et al., *Habits of the Heart*, 1985)

How much of our material and social situation in life can we justifi-
ably attribute to our own efforts and how much to circumstances of
birth and to the resources that are or are not available to us in our
community and society? How dependent are we on publicly provided
services such as education, health care, and a variety of other services?
Is the role of the resources we draw upon in the construction of our
lives acknowledged?

In other words, to what degree do we recognize the extent to which
we depend on others, directly or indirectly, and on a collectively provided infrastructure of services? It is obvious that, by ourselves, we
cannot survive let alone organize a satisfying and fulfilling life. Nor can
we form a personal identity, since such an identity is inevitably derived
from group memberships.

Interdependence is a fundamental characteristic of human life. Membership in a community or society implies the recognition of this interdependence. It implies acknowledging that one's individual condition
is dependent, in part, on others and on the quality and vitality of the
community and its institutions. To the extent that this is recognized,
community members will almost spontaneously see its moral implications, namely, that they owe something in return. They will feel that
they ought to do their part to maintain the social organization on
which depends the quality of life – their own and that of other
members.

Some individuals may not acknowledge this interdependence or may
underestimate it. They may emphasize their ingenuity and hard work,

discounting the role played by their family and by the various institutions that provided them with opportunities and resources for the construction of their lives. This is perhaps more likely among those who achieve some degree of success. In a culture of individualism and self-reliance, individuals tend to give considerable weight to their own motivation and efforts and discount the benefits received from sources over which they have no control. Such benefits include the parents' education and income, the extensiveness of the educational system, the availability of assistance for higher education, the state of the economy when entering the labour force, and so on.

But to the extent that people recognize their dependence on others and on societal resources, they will feel the need to reciprocate in response to their indebtedness for what they have received. There are, of course, many ways in which people can reciprocate, such as the payment of taxes, contribution through an occupation, community activities, and financial contributions.[1] Some may be unable to give something back, beyond the acknowledgment of their indebtedness. But this acknowledgment has in itself an important social and symbolic value. Socially, the recognition of a debt lubricates social relations. Symbolically, it affirms the reality and significance of social interdependence. It thus strengthens the social fabric.

Respondents in our survey were asked if they agree or disagree that "*everyone owes something to society and should try to give something back.*" Most agree – fully 83 per cent – while only 17 per cent disagree. There appears to be a common feeling that a person's relation to society implies reciprocity, a sense of indebtedness for what has been and continues to be received from others and from the society. Still, close to one in five Canadians do not hold this position. And there is a variation in the intensity of indebtedness: only about a third (31 per cent) feel strongly about it while 52 per cent are more moderate in this regard.

INDEBTEDNESS AND CONCEPTIONS OF THE RELATIONSHIP OF THE INDIVIDUAL TO SOCIETY

The view that everyone is indebted to society and, accordingly, should give something back is part of larger perspectives concerning the relationship of individuals to society. On the one hand, the feeling of indebtedness is part of a collectivity oriented approach which leads to a concern for the well-being of others. Thus, those who strongly agree that everyone is indebted to society are less likely than those who disagree to believe that "*the needs of individuals are the responsibility of themselves and their families and not of the community."* Following the same social logic, they are also more likely to reject the view that *"the best way to be a good member of the community is to mind your own business and not bother other people."*

The sense of indebtedness is also associated with what individuals consider as most important for a society to function well and with what they see as their most important social obligation as a member of society. Specifically, it is associated with the view *"that people give up some of their personal advantages for the common good"* and with the view that the most important social obligation is *"to always consider the common good in your decisions and actions."*

On the other hand, a self-oriented approach to the society does not include the view that everyone is obligated to society. Rather, it is based on the principle that individuals can best contribute to society by pursuing their own goals and aspirations to the best of their abilities. The idea is that each person has a certain potential defined by their physical energy, talents, and bundle of resources – social, psychological, and material. Accordingly, the best way for people to contribute to society is to develop that potential and to pursue goals that allow them to make the most of it. It is also to "mind your own business" and not interfere in other people's lives, rather, the obligation is to focus on your own goals and aspirations.

In short, in contrast to those who are collectivity-oriented, there are many who see life as a personal rather than a social project – a project concerned with the development of one's potential rather than one that locates the personal project in the context of the common good. This self-orientation seems to lead individuals to see themselves as "self-made" and therefore as having little or no obligation to society.

Our survey shows that those who reject the idea that everyone owes something to society are more likely to think that what is most important for a society to function well is *"that individuals independently pursue their own goals"* and to see their most important social obligation as *"pursuing your own goals and aspirations to the best of your abilities."*

Individuals who do not feel socially indebted are more likely than others to agree that *"the needs of individuals are the responsibility of themselves and their families and not of the community"* (69 per cent compared to 52 per cent); to admire the most *"people who go their own way without worrying about what others think"* (as opposed to *"people who learn to fit in and get along with others"*); and to accept the view that *"the best way to be a good member of the community is to mind your own business and not bother other people."* However, this orientation seems to characterize a fairly small percentage of Canadians. Most seem to give some importance both to their own self-realization and to the common good.

Since the sense of social indebtedness is related to values, such as justice, which are proclaimed by religions, it can be expected that the feeling of obligation to society will be related to the degree of self-assessed religiosity. This is indeed the case: a strong sense of indebtedness to society and the view that one ought to give something in return are 19 per cent more likely among those who declare themselves very religious (45 per cent) than among those who say they are not (26 per cent).

But there are also differences by religious affiliation: Catholics (26 per cent) are less likely than are Protestants (37 per cent) or members of other religious groups (40 per cent) to agree that everyone owes something to society. Those with no religion are close to Catholics in this regard (30 per cent). However, there is no difference between Catholics and Protestants who are very religious;[2] the difference exists only among those who are fairly or not very religious.

INDEBTEDNESS AND
THE EXPERIENCE IN SOCIETY

The sense of social indebtedness is associated with age. The longer people benefit from society and its institutions, the more they are likely to feel indebted: four out of ten of those fifty-five years of age and over compared with two out of ten of thoseaged eighteen to twenty-five feel strongly that all owe something to society, a difference of nineteen per-centage points.

It may also be that, with age, people become increasingly aware of how much their condition in life depends on other people and on the community and society in which they live. This may be accompanied with a change in the frame of reference that individuals use to assess their life situation. It may be that the young tend to feel indebted to their families rather than to society. With age and experience, the frame of reference broadens to include the social and institutional context.

The *nature* of the experience in society also matters for the sense of indebtedness. For instance, those who see our society as fair for only a few and especially those who personally experience unfairness are less likely than those whose perception and experience are positive to think that everyone owes something to society and should try to give something back (Figure 11).

People who think that our society is fair for only a few are two and a half times more likely than those who think it is fair for most people

Figure 11a
Perceived Societal Unfairness Decreases Sense That We All Owe to
Society

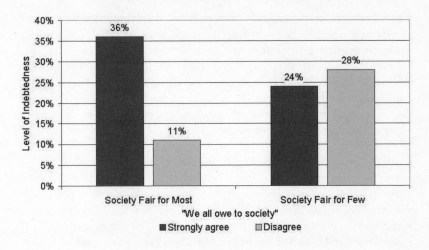

Figure 11b
Sense That We All Owe to Society Decreases with
Unfair Personal Treatment

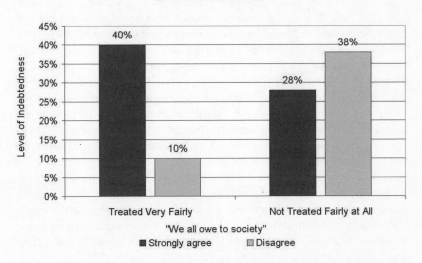

to *disagree* about everyone's indebtedness to society (28 per cent compared to 11 per cent). The difference is even more pronounced with fairness of personal treatment: 38 per cent compared to 10 per cent.

INDEBTEDNESS AMONG
THOSE WHO ARE TREATED UNFAIRLY

There are some respondents – 10 per cent of the sample – who say they are treated unfairly but nevertheless think that everyone owes something to society and should try to give something back. They are "deviant" cases in the sense that they do not follow the pattern described above. What is even more paradoxical is that they tend, in comparison with the rest of the sample, to be found among the more disadvantaged in a number of respects. Specifically, they are more likely to be found among those who

- are in the lower echelons of the socio-economic hierarchy;
- are unemployed;
- are in situations evolving negatively or poorly rather than positively;
- experience unfairness on one, two, or three bases;
- have less sense of control over the way their lives turn out;
- are dissatisfied with the number of friends they have; and
- do not feel at home where they work, where they live, and in the broader society.

We can only speculate as to the reasons for this seemingly paradoxical situation. It may be because people who are disadvantaged and nevertheless feel indebted to society compare their lot with those who are still more disadvantaged than they are and, as a result, feel that they are relatively lucky. In other words, disadvantaged people can observe in concrete ways that there are varying degrees of disadvantage while those in higher echelons tend to see the lower echelons of society largely as a homogeneous lot. People in the middle echelons of the social hierarchy who feel unfairly treated may be comparing themselves with those who are better off and, as a result, feel cheated rather than indebted in relation to society.

In addition, people who are disadvantaged by a low income, unemployment, or some other unfavourable condition may be more frequently the recipients of various kinds of assistance from government agencies or community organizations. This assistance could be something for which they would feel grateful and which would make them feel indebted to society and its institutions.

LACK OF A SENSE OF INDEBTEDNESS
AMONG THOSE WHO ARE TREATED FAIRLY

There are also respondents who are treated fairly yet do not agree that all owe something to society and should give something back. There are only 12 per cent in this category, but it is nevertheless intriguing to identify their social characteristics. Contrary to those who feel unfairly treated yet think that all owe something to society, these respondents are scattered more randomly in the population. There are little or no variations among categories of gender, level of education, income, class self-identification, region, community size, cultural, ethnic, racial affiliation, financial situation, and satisfaction with the recognition of the contribution to society.

There are variations among people in different occupational levels and fields. Generally, the more highly skilled the occupation, the less frequent is the type who feels treated fairly and has no sense of social indebtedness. As far as fields of occupational activity are concerned, the financial sector (banking, investment, insurance) stands out with 19 per cent of this type. In contrast, public administration and education include few such types (3 per cent and 5 per cent, respectively).

Religious affiliation and religiosity also make a difference. Almost no one (2 per cent) in "other religions" are in this group, compared to about 12 per cent among Catholics, Protestants, and those with no religion. In addition, there are fewer cases among those who say they are very religious (6 per cent) than among the not very religious (13 per cent). This suggests that a value orientation may underlie the attitude of those who feel fairly treated but lack a sense of social indebtedness. The same conclusion is suggested by the relationship between this view and what is considered most important for a society to function well. Among those who think that what is most important is that individuals independently pursue their own goals, 18 per cent do not agree that all are socially indebted even if fairly treated. The lowest percentage (8 per cent) is among those who think that what is most important is that people give up some of their personal advantages for the common good.

HIGHLIGHTS

To summarize:

- Although only about one-third feel *strongly* about it, most Canadians believe that everyone owes something to society and should try to give something back. Close to one in five does not share this view.
- The sense of indebtedness is related to age, that is, to the extent of experience in the community and society.
- It is also related to the assessment of the fairness of our society and the sense of being personally treated fairly or unfairly.
- People who think that "minding your own business" is the best way

to be a good member of the community and that the most important social obligation is "*to pursue your own goals and aspirations to the best of your abilities*" are less likely to feel socially indebted than those who do not share this view.

9

The Obligation to Help Others

He is not a citizen who is not disposed to respect the laws and obey the civil magistrate; and he is certainly not a good citizen who does not wish to promote, by every means in his power, the welfare of the whole society of his fellow-citizens ... The wise and virtuous man is at all times willing that his own private interest should be sacrificed to the public interest of his own particular order or society. (Adam Smith, *The Theory of Moral Sentiments*, 1853)

In the in-depth interviews we carried out before undertaking the survey, we asked respondents if they thought that there was less compassion in our society today than a few years ago, if it was true that compassion increasingly takes a back seat to the wish to look after one's own interest. Several agreed that this was indeed the case:

"We are in a society where it is each for himself. People are very little concerned with others. We are in a phase in which individuals think of themselves, are centred on themselves, are concerned little for others, the environment, and of the generation that will follow." (Montreal, Que.)

"Yes, there is less compassion. If you ask somebody for a dollar, they'll tell you to get a job." (Pembroke, Ont.)

"I sit around and wonder why I am so darn insensitive myself. Really, you go to the office and you barely know the people there and you barely talk to the people there and if there is an event they rush off home and yet when I reflect on social programs and willingness to pay taxes I would be very unique among my peers. Most people would be keen to avoid them. They are not looking at the end result. They are thinking about mismanagement, they are thinking about a hit to their pocketbook or things they could do with this money themselves." (Toronto, Ont.)

But many also said that they could not see such a pattern, that compassion and the willingness to help others was as strong as before:

"No, I don't think this is the case. There is a lot of compassion. People are very generous if we explain the needs to them. They are generous with their time, money, material goods ... " (Montreal, Que.)

"No, people respond more than before ... For example, a poor mother brought me some money for Easter for someone in need, a child who had cancer and had to be hospitalized and whose parents were poor. This mother was able to say that she had enough to help others. This is beautiful on the part of someone who is poor, disadvantaged. People are able to be very generous and they show it." (Rivière-du-Loup, Que.)

"In fact politicians have forgotten about compassion for others in the fight for power ...   At the social level, people have compassion for one another. Fundraising campaigns for Centraide [Quebec's equivalent of the United Way] do give results ... " (Montreal, Que.)

"I don't think so. I think a lot of people are stuck right now in their own worries, their own troubles, but on the whole I think it's fine. At least in my world." (Pembroke, Ont.)

Which of the two assessments do the survey results support? Do they show that both have some validity? These questions are explored in this and the next chapter by looking at the extent to which Canadians feel obligated to help others and the extent to which they contribute to people in their communities.

The previous chapter on indebtedness to society was concerned with the obligation to give something in return for what one receives, that is, with the social obligations that stem from the norm of reciprocity. However, one can also feel the obligation to help others because "giving something for nothing" is morally and socially desirable and even required on the part of "good" members of any kind of community.

Justice, the principle that people should receive what is rightfully theirs, that they be treated fairly and receive the recognition that is their due, is an important element of the social fabric. But beyond this basic requirement, there is the recognition that some members of the community may still have much less than they either need or can legitimately aspire to have, and that they are thus entitled to some help.

Underlying helping behaviour is the belief that more than strict justice is required in social relationships and for the functioning of groups and institutions. There is the idea that the needs and legitimate aspirations of those who do not have the resources to meet them should also be taken into account. The norm of reciprocity, whereby people and communities receive their due, needs to be supplemented with the norm of beneficence which requires that people give others such help as they need.[1]

A community and a society can be seen as a network of mutual obligations, of "generalized reciprocity and civic solidarity."[2] In the forceful words of Michael Walzer:

Membership is important because of what members of a political community owe to one another and to no one else, or to no one else to the same degree ... This claim might be reversed: communal provision is important because it teaches us the value of membership ... Political community for the sake of provision, provision for the sake of community: the process works both ways, and that is perhaps its crucial feature ... There has never been a political community that did not provide, or try to provide, or claim to provide, for the needs of its members as its members understood those needs ... "[3]

Networks of obligation and reciprocity can take many different forms. Only some are dealt with in this study. The next chapter will consider involvement in communal activities and financial contributions to different organizations and causes. Here, the focus is on the extent to which people feel obligated to help others. Two questions are addressed. First, to what extent do respondents feel obligated to help others? Second, what are the "social boundaries" of obligation, that is to say, do people feel obligated to help only others like themselves or do they extend their responsibility beyond those social boundaries?

THE STRENGTH OF THE OBLIGATION
TO HELP OTHERS

How strongly do people feel about helping "*family, friends, people in the same boat as I am in life, people from my ethnic, cultural, or racial background,* and *any person in society who needs help?*" Figure 12 shows that, generally, Canadians do feel an obligation to help others. No respondents feel unobligated to help people in all five social categories; almost half feel either a "very strong" or a "moderately strong" obligation to help *all five* kinds of people. Among them, 10 percent feel a "very strong" obligation.

The sense of obligation does not apply equally to all types of social relationships:

• Family commands the highest level of obligation and friends the next

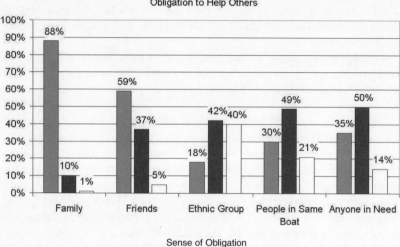

Figure 12
Obligation to Help Others

highest: 88 and 59 per cent express a "very strong" obligation to help them.

- More than a third express a very strong obligation to help anyone in need and only 14 per cent express a weak obligation to these people or none at all.
- Only 18 per cent declare a very strong obligation to help people of the same ethnic, cultural, or racial background and four in ten declare a weak obligation to these people or none at all.

This finding is surprising in view of the multicultural definition of Canadian society. Indeed, if ethnic attachments are valued, one would think that this would carry a strong sense of mutual obligation. But this does not seem to be the case. On the contrary, the obligation to help anyone in need is considerably stronger than the obligation defined along ethnic lines.

VALUE ORIENTATIONS

It was seen earlier that other elements of membership, such as social indebtedness, are associated with certain conceptions and values concerning the relationship of individuals to the community. This is also the case with the obligation to help others. For instance, those who disagree with the statement that *"the needs of individuals are the responsibility of themselves and their families and not of the community"* are more likely than those who agree with it to feel an obligation to help others. (The exception here is help to family, which is very high whether one agrees with this statement or not.) In addition, those who attach a lot of importance to encouraging children to be concerned with others are much more likely to have a strong sense of obligation to help all the five categories of people mentioned.

The particular church to which one belongs does not seem to matter with regard to the sense of obligation to help. But the degree of self-assessed religiosity does, at least for certain types of social relationships. Specifically, the more religious are more likely than the less religious to feel a strong sense of obligation to help "people in the same boat," people of the same ethnocultural or racial background, and, especially, anyone who needs help. As already indicated, the concern for others is part of the values and norms of virtually all religions. What matters is how seriously those precepts are taken by church members.

In the family relationships, the degree of religiosity does not matter. The obligation to help, which is quite strong, is based on primary, long-nurtured social bonding.

THE SOCIAL BOUNDARIES OF OBLIGATION

It seems that, for many, the sense of obligation applies only to certain kinds of people. In their case, the norm of beneficence does not seem to extend beyond particular social boundaries. It applies to family and friends, for instance, but not to wider social circles; to people known personally, but not to "strangers"; to people who are like them, but not to those who are different in some regard.

The question asked in the survey begins with a restricted circle of social relations (family and friends) and moves to more inclusive social boundaries (people "in the same boat" as I am in life and people from my ethnocultural or racial background). It ends with an all-inclusive, universalistic category (any person in society who needs help).[4]

The percentages of those who feel a *very strong* obligation to help show a "curvilinear" pattern. It is very high in the case of family (88 per cent). It then decreases as we move to more inclusive social boundaries: 59 per cent for friends; 30 per cent "for people in the same boat"; 18 per cent for people from the same ethnic, cultural, or racial background. However, it increases to 36 per cent for the most inclusive category, any person who needs help. The pattern is the reverse with the percentages of those whose sense of obligation is "not very strong" or "not strong at all."

It is important to emphasize that, beyond the personal relations of family and friends, it is the universalistic obligation to help that is the most prevalent. This is not the case for the majority, but nevertheless it is held by more than a third of Canadians. In addition, only 14 percent declare a weak obligation to help anyone in need, compared with 21 percent for "people in the same boat" as they are in life and 40 percent for people from the same ethnic, cultural, or racial background.

In the following analysis, the respondent's orientation is deemed "universalistic" if the sense of obligation to help anyone in need is stronger than the obligation to two or more of the four specific categories of persons. Such people constitute 25 per cent of the sample.

The survey results show that the predominance of universalistic over particularistic social obligations is part of a certain orientation to society. Specifically, it denotes an openness to diversity, an acceptance of differences as indicated by an agreement or disagreement (depending on the item) with the following statements. We can expect the responses to these statements to be associated with universalistic over particularistic social obligations. (The difference in percentage points in universalistic orientation between those who strongly agree and those who strongly disagree is shown in parentheses for each item.)

1 "I do not approve of people with ideas and lifestyles that differ significantly from what is generally accepted" (11 per cent).
2 "The ideal society is one in which people are sufficiently similar to feel at home with one another" (10 per cent).
3 "I find that to be gay or lesbian is acceptable" (10 per cent).
4 "Immigrants cannot expect to be considered as fully Canadian as those who were born and raised here" (19 per cent).
5 "Ethnic, cultural, and racial groups should try as much as possible to blend into Canadian society" (3 per cent).
6 "People have to stay attached to their own ethnic, cultural, or racial group because it is *only* there that they can count on being fully accepted" (16 per cent).
7 "There is nothing wrong with giving advantages to people from the same ethnic, cultural or racial group as yourself" (16 per cent).[5]
8 My ethnic, cultural, or racial background is very important to me (7 per cent).[6]

The reaction to the statements that indicate an acceptance of diversity show a higher percentage with universalistic social obligations (1, 2, 3). Conversely, with the responses that suggest a preference for cultural or moral conformity, particularistic social obligations predominate (4, 5). The same is the case with the statements that indicate an "in-group" orientation (6, 7, 8).

One of the respondents (Toronto, Ont.) in the in-depth interviews mentioned a reluctance to help strangers because of a concern for personal security: "I'm a little nervous of helping a stranger now because of the society now. If I hear of a family [in need], I prefer to donate anonymously. I think Canadians are compassionate, but society has changed, there is more concern about security. I wouldn't stop now for a car with a flat tire."

A universalistic orientation to social obligations is also associated with the sense of fairness. This is so both for the perception of the fairness of the society and for the personal experience of fairness: among those who feel that they are being treated very fairly, about three out of ten show a universalistic orientation to social obligations. In contrast, this occurs in only about one in ten among those not treated fairly at all.

Protestants, Catholics, and those with no religion do not differ in the degree of universalism (between 24 per cent and 27 per cent). The percentage is a little lower among those who belong to other churches (19 per cent). Earlier, it was observed that religiosity increases the propensity to feel obligated to help others while religious affiliation does not. Here we find that it is not related to the propensity to help anyone in need over people with whom one has some sort of social relationship.

The social boundaries of obligation are significant with regard to the strength of the social fabric. Indeed, at the extreme, if all networks of reciprocity were self-contained within certain social boundaries, there would be considerable cohesion, but at the same time the society would be highly fragmented. Cohesion would exist within, but not across, social boundaries. However, it is impossible to imagine a society in which social obligations would totally disregard the boundaries of family, friendship, and mutual interest. A strong social fabric is based on a combination of both close and distant social ties and social obligations.

HIGHLIGHTS

By way of summary:

- Almost all feel some obligation to help at least one type of person.
- About half of the respondents express either a very strong or a moderately strong obligation to help all the five different kinds of people considered in this study: family, friends, people "in the same boat,"

people from the same ethnocultural or racial background, and anyone who needs help.

- About one in three have a strong universalistic sense of obligation, that is, the obligation to help anyone in need.
- A universalistic sense of obligation is associated with the acceptance of diversity and an "out-group" orientation. A preference for cultural or moral conformity and an "in-group" orientation tend to accompany particularistic social obligations. It is also related to the experience of fairness and a sense of personal security.

10

Contributions to Community and Society

It may be expected that the moral code of any relatively stable social system will contain a principal component that requires men to do more than conform with the norm of reciprocity. [This component, the norm of beneficence] requires men to give others such help as they *need*. Rather than making help contingent upon past benefits received or future benefits expected, the norm of beneficence calls upon men to aid others without thought of what they have done or can do for them, and solely in terms of a need imputed to the potential recipient ... In short, to give something for nothing. (Alvin W. Gouldner, *The Importance of Something for Nothing*, 1973)

The previous two chapters considered people's views about indebtedness to society and the sense of obligation to help others. This chapter will focus on the actual contributions to community and society, as declared by the respondents themselves. Three kinds of contributions will be considered: activities through an organization,[1] informal help,[2] and donations.[3] These can be referred to as *communal contributions* since they are inputs into different dimensions of the social fabric of the community and society.

It should be noted that people can contribute to society in other ways as well, for instance, by paying taxes, through their jobs, and by being concerned with public matters and participating in public debates over issues. Because our study, like any study, is necessarily limited, we have not been able to include these types of contributions in our analysis.

We have chosen to focus on communal contributions because they are both voluntary in nature (in contrast with taxes, for example) and directly related to the vitality of community life. Indeed, members of a community or society do not deal with their interdependence only through exchanges in the marketplace and through delegating the task of providing collective goods to public institutions. They also do so through communal organizations and associations. Interdependence, then, is interpreted here as the voluntary cooperation whereby individuals contribute resources for collective projects and/or actively participate in the organization necessary for their realization.[4] As Alexis de Tocqueville noted long ago: "When the members of a community are forced to attend to public affairs, they are necessarily drawn from the circle of their own interests and snatched at times from self-observation. As soon as a man begins to treat of public affairs in public, he begins to perceive that he is not so independent of his fellow men as he had imagined, and that in order to obtain their support he must often tend them his co-operation."[5]

Contributing is one of the duties of membership or citizenship. In the city states of antiquity, these kinds of activities were called "liturgy," that is, "duty performed by the people" and consisted of "services aimed to lighten the public burden of the polis. The citizens performed these services voluntarily, i.e., from their own resources, in a planned sequence to satisfy certain public needs." Doing liturgy was regarded as "an honorable duty rather than as burdensome or alienated forced labour."[6] Liturgies were the ancient world's equivalent of communal contribution.

Two questions are dealt with in the following analysis. First, to what extent do Canadians engage in communal activity? Second, do they feel that they contribute as much as they should? These questions will be considered in relation to the attitudes examined previously with regard to the obligation to reciprocate, namely, indebtedness to society and the obligation to help others. Communal contributions will also be related to the way people experience society: in terms of fairness, recognition of the contribution to society, trust, and the sense of belonging. We can expect that people whose experience of the society is positive in these regards will be more likely to contribute to the community.

THE EXTENT OF COMMUNAL CONTRIBUTIONS

The majority of Canadians contribute to community life in one way or another (Figure 13).

A little over half of the sample have engaged in activities through an organization in the last twelve months while more than three-fourths have helped others informally or have made donations. However, people contribute through formal activities and informal help on a more regular basis than through donations. When contributions are made, 50 per cent make donations less than once a month, compared

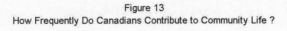

Figure 13
How Frequently Do Canadians Contribute to Community Life ?

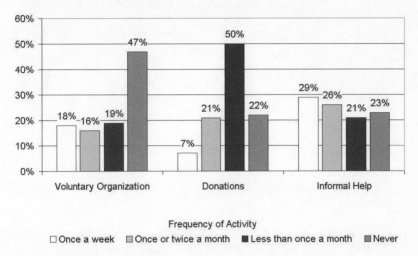

Frequency of Activity

□ Once a week ▨ Once or twice a month ■ Less than once a month ▨ Never

to 19 per cent and 21 per cent for the other two types of communal contributions.

Are the three types of contributions substitutes for one another? For a significant proportion of Canadians, this does not appear to be the case. Since there is a high percentage of respondents who contribute in each of the three different ways, there is a fairly strong correlation among them:[7] there is a significant proportion of people who engage in two and even three of the different types of communal contributions.

As can be seen in Table 4, 42 per cent make the three types of communal contributions, although not necessarily at the same frequency in all three. Another 32 per cent engage in two of the three types of contributions. Of those, it is the "informal help and donations" combination that is the most frequent: about two-thirds of the 32 percent, that is, 21 percent.

People who are involved only in activities through an organization are quite rare – only nine respondents (0.5 per cent of the sample). The proportion who provide only informal help or make only donations is about the same in each case: 8 and 10 per cent. Finally, only 7 per cent of the sample engage in no activity and make no donations.

With 74 per cent of the sample involved in two or three of the communal contributions, we can conclude that, generally, one type of contribution is not a substitute for another. That is to say, engaging in one is not a way of avoiding the other forms of contributions, since people

Table 4   Involvement in Types of Communal Contributions

Type of Involvement			Per cent Involved
Helped an Organization	Informal Help	Donations	
Yes	Yes	Yes	42
Yes	Yes	No	6
Yes	No	Yes	5
No	Yes	Yes	21
Yes	No	No	1
No	Yes	No	8
No	No	Yes	10
No	No	No	7

tend to combine two and quite frequently three of the different kinds of contributions. This is important since there exists a stereotype of financial donors as people who do not want to get directly involved, as individuals who would rather give money and stay socially aloof. In fact, just 10 per cent only make donations and do not engage in either formal or informal communal activities.

Another way of looking at the level of communal involvement is to consider the frequency of the three types of contributions. A very high level of involvement can be defined as carrying out the activity at least once a week. By that standard, 40 per cent show a very high level of involvement in at least one type of activity. This is rather remarkable. Among them, about a third are highly involved in more than one type of activity.

It may be argued that it is misleading to include donations in this measure, since it probably includes people who give at church every Sunday, something that may indicate little in terms of communal involvement. However, even if donations are not included in the measure, the level of very high involvement is not altered: 37 per cent are highly involved (that is, at least once a week) in one of the activities (other than donations). Of these, 11 per cent are highly involved in both formal activities and informal help.

CONTRIBUTIONS AND SOCIAL OBLIGATIONS

Most Canadians contribute some of their time, energies, and money to community organizations or to social causes. Yet many feel that they are not contributing as much as they should. Indeed, when asked whether *"you help as much as you think you should either through an organization or on your own,* more than a third reply in the negative. About one-third feel that they do not donate as much as they should, either to a religious (33 per cent) or to a non-religious (32 per cent) organization.

Not surprisingly, those who do not help on their own or through an organization are the most likely to feel that their social contribution is inadequate, while those who help frequently are the most likely to feel that they are helping as much as they should. Specifically, with regard to the view that they are not helping as much as they should, there is a difference of more than 35 percentage points between those who help others every week and those who do not help at all.

A similar pattern is observed with regard to financial donations, either to religious or non-religious organizations: the more frequent the giving, the more likely is the feeling of meeting one's own standards. Yet about one in four of those who give every week are not satisfied and feel they should give more.

A number of attitudes and social experiences considered in previous chapters are relevant in the present context. In particular:

- the feeling of indebtedness, that is, the obligation to give to society something in return for what is received;
- the obligation to help others; and
- the nature of the respondent's social experience in terms of fairness, recognition, trust, and belonging.

Do these attitudes and social experiences translate into social contributions such as activities in community organizations, informal help to others, and donations? To answer this question, involvement in the three types of activities was grouped together to form a single measure of communal contribution. Respondents were then classified as frequent contributors, infrequent contributors, or non-contributors.

As could be expected, being a frequent contributor is associated with the sense of indebtedness to society and with the feeling of obligation to help others (Figure 14).

Such attitudes and contributory activities seem to go together, although not to the same extent with all types of social obligations. (There is one exception: whether people feel obligated or not to help those of the same ethno-cultural or racial background as themselves, they are about equally likely to contribute socially.)

A strong sense of social indebtedness also increases the likelihood of being a frequent contributor. Nearly half of those who feel they owe a great deal to society are frequent contributors to communal life. Only

Figure 14
Frequent Contribution Increases with Sense of Social Obligation

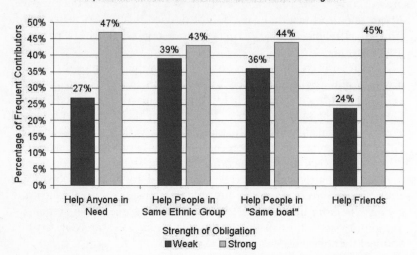

a third of those with a weak sense of social obligation fall into the frequent-contributor category. In addition, fairness, social trust, and a sense of belonging seem to lead people to contribute to the community and society while negative experiences in these regards appear to deflate such motivations. There is about a fifteen-percentage-point difference in the likelihood of being a frequent contributor between those with very positive and those with very negative experiences in these areas.

With social recognition, the relationship is more complex: recognition of the contribution of one's ethnocultural group or of one's educational class is positively related to contributory behaviour; recognition received for the social contribution of those of one's gender, however, is negatively related to social contributions. Those who are satisfied are somewhat less likely to be frequent contributors than those who are dissatisfied. This is the case among both women and men.

Some respondents, however, may feel that they have met in some other way their obligations vis-à-vis their community and society. For instance, some may feel that *"as long as one pays one's taxes, it is not necessary to support community organizations and activities."* About one in five Canadians feel this way (only 5 per cent strongly). This is not a negligible proportion, but it is nevertheless a small minority. The overwhelming majority do not think that paying taxes exempts them from their communal responsibilities[8]. But insofar as this attitude exists, it is related to community involvement. Indeed, only one in four of those who agree that it is through taxes that they make their contribution to the community and society make communal contributions, compared to about half of those who strongly disagree with this view.

It was seen earlier that religiosity but not religious affiliation is related to the sense of social obligation. With regard to communal contributions, we find that both are important. Protestants are more likely to be frequent contributors than respondents in any of the other religious categories: about half of them compared to about a third of Catholics and members of other churches and 38 per cent of those without a religious affiliation.

The difference between Catholics and Protestants may be due to differences in the organizational structure of the churches and in their ethic. Specifically, it may be that, to a greater extent than the Catholic church, the Protestant churches have structures that allow individual enterprise and an ethic that emphasizes individual initiative. However, this interpretation is quite tentative.

In spite of these variations in contributory behaviour, members of the different religions are about equally likely to feel that they ought to help or give more than they do. The variations are relatively small and show no systematic pattern.

The level of contributory behaviour is positively associated with the self-assessed degree of religiosity. Those who say they are very religious are more likely (51 per cent) to contribute than those who say they are fairly religious (41 per cent). The least likely are those who say they are not very religious (35 per cent). Religiosity suggests that the individual has internalized certain beliefs, values, and norms. And given the importance of altruism in Judeo-Christian religions, it is possible to suppose that it has some impact on those for whom religion is important. The phenomenon may, however, be more general. It has been noted that "the norm of beneficence is commonly and cross-culturally associated ... with supernatural sanctioning." The norm is complied with not only because of the perceived needs of others, but also because of conformity to the expectations of one's God.[9] Thus, those who are religious can be expected to be more involved in other-oriented behaviour than those who are less religious.

CONTRIBUTIONS
AND THE SENSE OF BELONGING

The sense of belonging and social involvement seem to go together, at least to a certain extent. Helping others through an organization and the sense of belonging are related. This connection is also indicated by the relationship between religiosity and belonging, if we assume that the very religious are more involved in their local church than the less religious.[10]

These are probably two-way relationships. Those who feel at home in and presumably identify with their community may be more likely to become involved in community organizations. And those who become involved probably come to feel that the community is really theirs, since they are contributing actively to its life and, as a result, feel increasingly at home in it.

The relationship may also operate through friends and acquaintances. This is suggested by the existence of a strong connection between satisfaction with the number of friends and community integration: 71 per cent of those who are satisfied with the number of their friends feel very much at home in their community. This is much higher than the 39 and 25 per cent observed among those who are somewhat satisfied and dissatisfied. People may become involved in community activities through friends, relatives, or acquaintances. A recent survey of volunteering in Canada found that about 10 per cent of volunteers became involved because they were asked by a friend or relative outside the organization and 44 per cent by someone within in the organization. The survey also found that 22 per cent volunteered because their friends did so.[11] It is also possible that some people became active in community organizations in order to make friends.

HIGHLIGHTS

In summary:

- The majority of Canadians contribute in one way or another.
- Many contribute in more than one way: for them, the different types of contribution are not substitutes for each other.
- Many feel that they do not contribute as much as they should while a minority feels that contributing through taxes is sufficient.
- Those whose experience in the society is positive – in terms of fairness, recognition, trust, and belonging – are more likely to make contributions than those whose experience is negative.

It seems that many Canadians behave according to a sort of social exchange between themselves and the different communities in which they construct and live their lives: their town or city, their province, and their country as a whole. To a certain extent, the social logic of interdependence appears to shape the attitudes and orient the actions of Canadians in relation to their communities and society.

Communal contributions are partly self-interested, but they are also driven by certain norms and expectations that are part of the codes of membership in our society. And this is socially fruitful. Indeed, "a prescriptive norm within a collectivity that constitute an especially important form of social capital is the norm that one should forgo self-interest and act in the interests of the collectivity. A norm of this sort, reinforced by social support, status, honour, and other rewards, is the social capital that builds young nations"[12] and, it can be added, other social groups and communities as well. In other words, by contributing, Canadians help to maintain or reinforce the social fabric of our society.

11

Conclusion: Strength and Fragility of the Social Fabric

In spite of the individualistic component of our culture, then, there is a fairly high degree of social commitment among Canadians. This social commitment is expressed in the recognition that we all owe something to society, in the feeling of obligation to help others, and in various kinds of communal investments. We found the following:

Indebtedness. Most Canadians feel that everyone owes something to society and should try to give something back; only one in six do not share this sentiment.

Social obligations. Almost all feel some obligation to help at least one type of person and about half express either a very strong or a moderately strong obligation to help all the five different kinds of people considered in this study. Also, about a third feel reveal a universalistic orientation: the obligation to help anyone in need rather than only those with whom they feel connected.

Communal contributions. The majority of Canadians contribute in one way or another and many feel they do not contribute as much as they should. Only a small minority, however, feel that contributing through taxes is sufficient. Those whose experience in the society is positive – in terms of fairness, recognition, trust, and belonging – tend to make social contributions.

Such social commitment and investments suggest a fairly strong social fabric.

Although our barometric readings lean towards the positive, there is a worrisome negative indicator: the relative strength of social obligations that do not go beyond particular social circles. As already indicated, if the sense of obligation were self-contained within certain social boundaries, there would be a lot of cohesion, but at the same time the society would be highly fragmented. The fabric of the society requires that social obligations extend beyond immediate social circles. If they tend to remain within and not cross social boundaries, the situation is potentially detrimental to the vitality of the social fabric.

In addition, it has been seen that Canadians value fairness but are not satisfied with the level of fairness experienced in either their personal lives or in the country's social structures. We believe that trust is critical, but we also acknowledge that there are groups who feel that trust is not extended to them and are unwilling to extend it to others. Recognition for the contributions made as individuals or members of social groups is important to all of us, but not all groups believe that they are accorded what they are due. Many believe that they benefit differentially from Canadian society and have a varied sense of attachment to it. The overall findings in these regards are as follows:

Fairness. Close to four out of ten Canadians say that our society is fair for most people while 43 per cent say that it is fair for some and 18 per cent for only a few. Although this assessment is partly positive, it reveals a fairly severe evaluation of our society. Indeed, Canadians seem to be more negative than positive in their assessment of the fairness of our society.

Recognition. Overall, members of the different groups or social categories considered (gender, cultural, ethnic, or racial group, or people at the same level of education or training) feel that the level of satisfaction with the recognition they receive for their social contribution is quite high. Yet more than two out of five express some dissatisfaction as members of at least one of the social segments to which they belong.

Horizontal trust. A strong majority of Canadians hesitate to trust others, fearing that too many seek to benefit only themselves. As far as trust in particular social relationships is concerned, there seems to be *a substantial social split between people with different beliefs and values.* However, there is a high level of trust among friends and co-workers.

Vertical trust. There is a substantial social split here, as far as trust is concerned, *between elites and the general public.* A commonly held view is that this split is partly due to the behaviour of those in positions of authority, whether in government or in business.

Belonging. Overall, a majority of Canadians feel very much at home in the community where they live and a little less than half feel very much at home in the larger society. Only about one in ten feel a little or not at all at home in either their community or the larger society. Insofar as there is a sense of alienation, it seems to be associated with negative experiences with regard to fairness, recognition, and control over one's life. It also appears to be related to the perception that the tolerance of differences is declining in our society.

What do these findings tell us about the social fabric of our society? Is it strong? It is difficult, indeed impossible, to give a quantitative answer to such a question, but, based on the assessments and experiences of Canadians, the conclusion certainly cannot be overwhelmingly positive and optimistic. Nor can it be outrightly negative and pessimistic. It is somewhere in-between. The situation is not quite the same on all the dimensions: on some of them, the barometer is more on the negative than on the positive side; on others, it is the opposite. But it seems to us that these findings suggest that we should be seriously concerned with all of them. Some of the implications of these results will be discussed after considering how the perceptions and experiences vary by gender, ethnicity or race, social class, and province of residence.

But first we will examine how Canadians themselves view the situation. Do they believe that the present state of affairs affects our ability to build a healthy society? To what extent are loss of trust in our business and political elite perceived to hinder the functioning of Canadian society? Is pursuit of self-interest believed to be a threat to the social fabric? What role do Canadians believe lack of reciprocity, "freeloading," and decline in compassion play in undermining social relations and institutional systems? How do such factors compare to the impact of a decline in the standard of living, rising intolerance, and heightened interest-group politics?

PERCEPTIONS OF THREATS TO OUR SOCIETY

Perceptions of what constitute major threats to our society occur in two major clusters. One pertains to the values, attitudes, and beliefs of individuals; the other to the consequences of their behaviour. These relate mainly to our commitment to the common good. What can put this commitment in jeopardy are values and attitudes such as the expectation of getting something for nothing, the preoccupation with self-interest, and the willingness to sacrifice principle for personal gain. The proportion of Canadians who see these as threats to our society is quite high:

- 86 per cent agree (42 strongly) that there are too many people who expect to get something for nothing;
- 90 per cent feel (41 strongly) that there are too many people preoccupied with what they can get out of the system rather than with what they can contribute to the common good; and

- 75 per cent agree (24 strongly) that too many will sacrifice their principles in order to get ahead economically.

The commitment to the common good can also be weakened by behaviour that reflects a decreased willingness to help those in need, less concern with fairness and social justice than in the past, and a decline in tolerance for those who are different. Many Canadians seem to think that this is happening in our society today:

- 71 per cent feel (24 strongly) that there is less willingness to help those in need;
- 65 per cent agree (23 strongly) that people today are less concerned with fairness and social justice than they were a few years ago; and
- 60 per cent feel (17 strongly) that tolerance for people who are different is declining in our society.

It seems that Canadians perceive possible weaknesses in the social fabric of our society similar to those revealed by the survey results presented in this study with regard to the perception of fairness, the sense of obligation, and contributory behaviour In fact, on some points, there seems to be more widespread concern than what the survey results would warrant.

THE IMPACT OF LIFE EXPERIENCES
ON SOCIAL PERCEPTIONS AND ASSESSMENTS

The perceptions of specific issues considered problematic for the social fabric occur in different constellations and are, to a large extent, shaped by the interaction between our perceptions and evaluations of social situations and the way in which we personally experience social life. The impact of life experiences on whether specific issues are considered a threat is best illustrated by the profile of those who believe that *"people today are less concerned with fairness and social justice than they were a few years ago"* (Figure 15).

Although a significant proportion of all Canadians believe that a decline in fairness and social justice is an issue, the extent of agreement is significantly affected by experience. The more positive one's personal treatment, the less frequent the perception that people are less concerned with fairness and social justice than previously. Issues related to the erosion of public trust further demonstrate this relationship:

- The weakening of trust in public officials is associated with the perceived fairness of the share of federal-government money received by

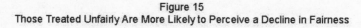

Figure 15
Those Treated Unfairly Are More Likely to Perceive a Decline in Fairness

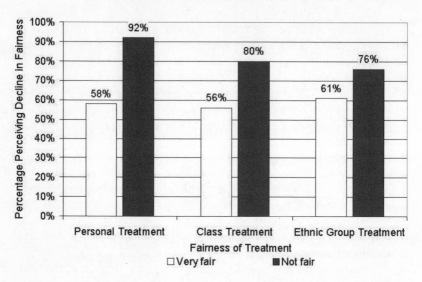

the province. Slightly over 78 per cent of those who believe their province gets more than its fair share of federal-government money believe that the behaviour of public officials contributes to a decline in public trust and confidence. For those who feel that their province is getting less than its fair share, the figure rises dramatically to 94 percent.

• Trust in corporate officials is related to the level of satisfaction with family financial status. Just under 75 per cent of those who are very satisfied with their families' financial status believe that *"public trust is being weakened by the behaviour of people who manage business corporations."* The figure rises to nearly 88 per cent of those expressing dissatisfaction with their financial lot.

What people subjectively experience in their everyday lives clearly makes a difference for their assessments of the society and its leadership.

The view that *"tolerance for people who are different from ourselves is declining in our society"* also depends on the basis of our identity, as reflected in what we consider important to transmit to our children. Specifically, the perception of a decline in tolerance is more likely if one considers it important to teach children loyalty to the traditions to one's ethnic, cultural, or racial group than if this is seen as secondary.

Figure 16
Attitudes Affecting Perceived Decline in Tolerance

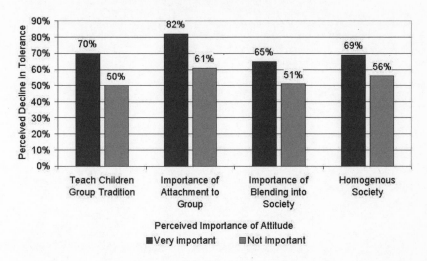

The perception that tolerance for diversity is waning is also more likely among those who attach great of importance to their ethnic, cultural, or racial background and among those who believe that assimilation and social homogeneity are the preferred state of affairs for a society (Figure 16).

Social recognition for the contribution of one's group matters as well. Those who believe that their group does not receive appropriate recognition are far more likely to see a decline in tolerance. Three-quarters of those who believe that their ethnic, racial, or cultural group are receiving less recognition suggest that tolerance is on the decline. Only slightly more than half of those who see recognition increasing hold the same view. Furthermore, being very satisfied with the level of recognition received decreases the perception of a decline in tolerance from 67 per cent to 51 per cent.

In short, the threats to the fabric of our society perceived by Canadians are similar to the weaknesses revealed by the survey results presented in this study. Also, the perceptions of specific dimensions considered problematic are notably shaped by the interaction between our values and the way in which we personally experience social life.

PART TWO

Identifying Lines of
Social Fragmentation

The Experience of Women and Men

The status of women and men is as much an issue of power and privilege as is the status of people of different races and social classes. (Judith Lorber, *Paradoxes of Gender*, 1994, 284)

It is quite clear from casual observation in day-to-day life that women and men are not treated the same way in our society. This is the case with regard to employment, in the workplace, in the care of children, in public life, and in the distribution of domestic chores. Of course, differential treatment is not necessarily experienced as unsatisfactory. But there is not only differential treatment, there is also gender discrimination and inequality. And these have been and, although perhaps to a lesser degree, continue to be fundamental characteristics of the social and economic organization of domestic life, of community organizations, including church and schools, and of economic, political, and cultural institutions.

Through social and political movements in recent decades, women have challenged the place they have traditionally held in society in these various domains of activity. Such movements indicate a certain dissatisfaction with their roles, prerogatives, and responsibilities in society. They have placed on the public agenda issues of employment opportunities, promotions in business and professional organizations, and pay equity. They have confronted the obstacles to their equality with men in society, such as the stereotypes about their expected domestic and social roles, the "old boys networks" that act as barriers to their progress, and the cultural biases built into school curricula.

Thus, it is important to ask if women and men are satisfied with their present situation and with its evolution in recent years. Do they feel that they have fewer opportunities to participate in the economy than men have? Are they more likely than men to experience unfairness? Do they feel that their contribution to society is adequately recognized?

Similar questions could be asked about the experience of men. In particular, do men feel displaced or potentially disadvantaged as a result of the claims of the women's movement and the gains that have been achieved by women in recent decades, either in the labour market, in politics, or in socio-cultural life?

This chapter presents a few findings that could shed some light on these questions. The results may help to assess the extent to which the social fabric could be strengthened by dealing with the alienating experiences of women and, in some instances, of men as well. In other words, is our society potentially fragmented along gender lines? We will explore this question in terms of the issues dealt with in the first part of the book.

Overall, it seems that there is relatively little such fragmentation. There are few differences between women and men with regard to trust, social and institutional; the sense of belonging to the local community and to the society; social indebtedness; obligations to help others, and involvement in communal activities. There are exceptions to this general picture, ones that suggest a somewhat greater sense of social commitment among women than among men. For instance, women are a little more likely to feel obligated to help close friends or "any person in need." They also tend to be more active in community organizations. The difference is eight percentage points between women and men for each of these three items. Although not negligible, such a difference does not suggest drastically divergent experiences among men and women in their relationship with the communities in which they live. What does set them apart to a greater extent, however, is their experience with regard to fairness and the recognition received for their contribution to the society.

FAIRNESS

The pattern of perceptions and judgments expressed by both women and men is essentially the same as the one observed for the population as a whole: they are equally likely to consider the society as fair for most (about four out of ten) and to report a very fair personal treatment (about three out of ten). When asked about opportunities for jobs and promotions, however, the responses of women differ significantly from those of men (Figure 17).

Indeed, 53 per cent of women feel that they have fewer opportunities than men have. This is so whether they are gainfully employed or not. A good proportion of men make the same assessment of their own relative advantage in the labour market: 40 per cent say that they have

Figure 17
Perceived Job Opportunities by Gender

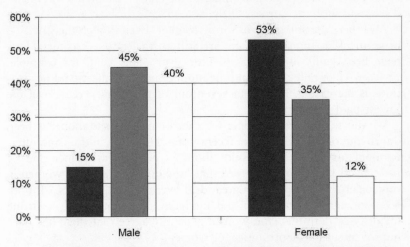

■ Less than Opposite Sex ■ Same as Opposite Sex □ More than Opposite Sex

more opportunities than women. In contrast, only 15 per cent of men feel that they have fewer opportunities than women.

In addition, we saw earlier that people can experience unfairness because of their gender, ethnicity, social class, or the region in which they live. In the sample as a whole, it was seen that 34 per cent experience unfairness on one basis, 23 per cent on two, and 14 per cent on three or more. Thus, 37 per cent experience unfairness on a combination of two or more of their social affiliations. However, the percentage is ten points higher among women than among men (42 and 32 per cent, respectively).

Such findings are not surprising in light of the protests and demands made by different groups of women over the last few decades. Before then, most women may not have compared their situation with that of men. They were not in the labour force or, if they were, they were concentrated in all-female occupations. Such circumstances did not lead to social comparisons. However, important changes in social consciousness were triggered by a major increase in labour-force participation, frequently in traditionally male occupations. Forty years ago, three-quarters of women did not work for pay; now nearly three-quarters of them do.[1]

This and other changes in the cultural climate led to the emergence of the feminist movement which, in turn, challenged the dominance of men in many areas of life. In the socio-economic domain, there were protests against barriers and demands for equal opportunity and for equal pay for work of equal value. These clearly are manifestations of discontent with the fairness of the system.

And there are still grounds for discontent. Even though the situation of women has improved, there are still obstacles to overcome. There have been gains in earnings (a little over 6 per cent, for example, between 1980 and 1996), and the number in the highest-paid occupations is increasing. But about seven out of ten women remain in the lowest-paid occupations.

We did not ask respondents whether or not the situation has been improving or deteriorating in recent years. However, in the 1992 international survey by Angus Reid, about 45 per cent of women and 55 per cent of men *strongly* agreed that "the opportunities for women in this society have improved a great deal over the past 20 years." If both levels of agreement (strong and moderate) are considered, a strong majority of both men and women generally agree that there has been improvement in opportunities for women.[2]

As we have just noted, 15 per cent of men feel that they have fewer opportunities than women. This is not a large percentage. Even so, some may find it surprising that this is the perception of as many as 15 per cent. But in fact it is not that unusual when we consider, for example, that men who have entered the labour market recently earn poorer wages than those who entered the labour market in the 1960s. This pattern is found among high school- and university-educated male workers alike. It did not occur among female workers.[3]

Another factor that is perhaps of significance here is that, in one-quarter of dual-income families, wives are earning more than their husbands. Yet it should also be noted that, even when women are the primary wage-earners, their earnings still lag significantly behind those of men in similar situations. It is not because their incomes increased considerably that women became the primary earners but mainly because men were losing their jobs. Either way, many men probably suffer from the comparison.

RECOGNITION OF THE SOCIETAL CONTRIBUTION

Traditionally, when most women were not in the paid labour force, their work was generally thought to be less important than that of men, for many, it was not even considered critical for the well-being and development of the society. Much has changed in this regard, but much also remains the same. For example, the role of women as mothers is rhetorically acknowledged from time to time in speeches by politicians and church leaders or at occasions such as Mother's Day.

But the social and cultural value of childhood education is still not very high, as is indicated by the relatively low wages paid to child-care workers and nursery-school teachers.

With the increasing presence of women in the labour force, with changing ideas about the critical role of child care and education, and with the presence of women in public office and on corporate boards, the situation is slowly changing. Yet, as noted earlier, the majority of women in the labour force, about seven out of ten, are in the lowest-paid occupations. There is still a tendency to consider that women make a lesser contribution to society than do men.

In such a context, it is not surprising to find that women are almost twice as likely as men to be dissatisfied with the recognition they receive for their contribution to society: 31 per cent compared to 17 per cent. The higher level of dissatisfaction among women is found at all levels of education, but the difference is particularly strong among the highly educated: 41 per cent of women and 17 per cent of men with a university education are dissatisfied with the recognition of the societal contribution of their gender, a gap of twenty-four percentage points. The gender gap is about half as large at the other levels of education.

In addition, while the sensitivity of women to the degree of recognition received increases steadily with the level of education, among men it does not change beyond the secondary-school level. This also indicates that many women make a distinction between their own personal condition and the status of women as a social category in society. In this instance, at least, individual success does not decrease the concern for the group; on the contrary, it accentuates it. As could be expected, the dissatisfaction with the recognition received for the contribution to society is more frequent among those who feel that they have fewer job opportunities than do members of the other gender (Table 5). This is the case among both women and men, although it is more pronounced among women.

It should be noted, however, that even though their dissatisfaction is more frequent, women are also more likely than men to see that the situation has improved in recent years: 40 per cent of women (compared to 10 per cent of men) consider that they are receiving more recognition of their contribution to society than a few years ago. But the feeling of improvement coexists with dissatisfaction. This is no doubt related to the fact that, in spite of the gains achieved, many women still make less money than men in the same or similar jobs; they are more likely than men to have part-time jobs even though many would prefer full-time employment; they are more likely to be unemployed; they are over-represented in low-paying occupations such as sales and clerical

Table 5   Dissatisfaction with Recognition of Contribution to Society is Related to the Perception of Job Opportunities

	Percent Who Believe Job Opportunities Are		
Gender and Labour-Force Status	Greater	Same	Fewer
MEN			
Total	13	15	35
In Labour Force	14	18	34
Not in Labour Force	11	9	37
WOMEN			
Total	29	13	35
In Labour Force	33	16	45
Not in Labour Force	21	9	47

jobs; and they are still likely to assume the bulk of child-rearing responsibilities and of domestic chores even if they have full-time jobs.

In contrast, men are more likely than women to see a decrease in recognition of their gender's contribution (24 per cent compared to 15 per cent). This suggests that the recent challenges to the "rules of the game" in our society are paying off for women while a certain proportion of men experience them as detrimental to the advantages they previously held. Nevertheless, as noted earlier, even though there have been changes, 40 per cent of male respondents stated that their gender is still advantaged. In fact, although the changes of recent decades have been considerable, men remain dominant in most political, social, and economic institutions, such as governments, political parties, corporations, labour unions, churches, and universities.

HIGHLIGHTS

Our findings in summary:

• Women and men are equally likely to consider that our society is fair for most people (about four out of ten) and to report a very fair personal treatment (about three out of ten).
• One out of two women consider that they have fewer opportunities for jobs and promotions than men and four out of ten men agree that they have *more* opportunities than women; only 15 per cent of men feel they have fewer opportunities than women.
• Women are more likely than men to be dissatisfied with the recognition they receive for their contribution to society, the difference being

particularly pronounced among the highly educated. At the same time, women are more likely than men to find that the situation in this regard is improving.
• There are little or no differences between men and women as far as trust, belonging, and social commitment are concerned.

The fact that women are seen as receiving more recognition of their societal contribution than a few years ago suggests that the women's movement over the last few decades has had positive results. In addition, we have noted that there is a consensus between men and women on social trust and on the trustworthiness of institutional leaders, and that both are equally likely to feel at home in their communities and in our society.

But the level of dissatisfaction with job opportunities and recognition is still quite high: about half in the case of opportunities for jobs and promotions and about one-third in regard to social recognition. Thus, even though gender inequalities are progressively becoming a lesser source of social tension than a number of years ago, they still remain an important social and political problem that could undermine the social fabric.

13

Cultural Diversity
and the Social Fabric

Here in Canada, you are probably trying to discover a distinctive and unique 'Canadian-ness' that takes account of your various ethnic and cultural histories and identities ... How are you to be weld into a coherent community and people, giving due place to what each of the constituent parts regard as absolutely crucial to who they are, without letting that rich diversity overwhelm the unity you want ... The nation or community that succeeds in coming to terms, in coping with difference, is in the end going to be successful, for the clearest characteristic of our day is that we are becoming increasingly diverse, multicultural, multiethnic, multi-faith, multilingual. (Archbishop Desmond Tutu, Bishop Romney Moseley Memorial Lecture, Trinity College, University of Toronto, February, 2000)

The full integration of all ethnocultural groups has always been a matter of social and political concern in our society. All expect to be treated as fully Canadian. All expect full acceptance, respect, fair treatment, trust in dealings with others, and recognition of the contribution made to the community and society. All expect to belong, to feel at home in the society. These have been and still are highly relevant for the strength of the social fabric. Unfairness, lack of recognition, and being made to feel like a stranger are sources of social fragmentation.

In recent decades, the ethnocultural composition of Canadian society was significantly transformed. Some of this transformation took place within the various cultural groups. They changed not only in terms of socio-economic characteristics such as education and income but also in terms of social and political aspirations. This was the case among francophones, especially in Quebec, and among the non-British, non-French groups. The large number of immigrants after the Second World War, the significant increase in the relative size of visible minorities, and the corresponding decline in the demographic weight of the British-origin population were additional factors in changing the ethnocultural matrix of our society. First Nations communities also experienced significant internal social and political change, with serious implications for their relations with the rest of the society.

The public-policy initiatives undertaken in response to new expectations and demands on the part of the various communities were another part of the transformation. To address the discontent about the distribution of advantages, various policies and programs were introduced. Some of their objectives had, directly or indirectly, relevance for the parameters of the social fabric: the promotion of fairness in the treatment of members of the various cultural communities, a greater recognition of their contribution to the society, and their full social integration. These policies were supported by many Canadians but, since they frequently aimed at changing existing socio-economic or political arrangements, they frequently antagonized others. As a result, most of them were the object of intense public debate. This happened, for example, with the policies dealing with language, multiculturalism, employment equity (or affirmative action), and land claims and self-government of Native peoples.

Such a major transformation in the demographic make-up, socio-economic condition, and political status of collectivities can have consequences for the strength of the social fabric. They may have an impact not in and of themselves but in the ways in which they are experienced by the members of different groups. This is so especially because they may or may not correspond to the existing or new cultural values and social expectations of the different groups.

Thus, given all the changes, it is important to ask if the experience of various groups is consistently different along the different dimensions of the social covenant. In other words, to what extent is the social fabric under strain along ethnocultural lines?

FAIRNESS

There is a virtual consensus among Canadians that fairness is essential for the full membership of all ethnocultural and racial groups in our society. This is shown, for instance, by a survey conducted in 1991 which indicated that about nine out of ten of Canadians thought that government policy should aim at eliminating racism in areas such as health care, the justice system, and education, ensuring equal access to jobs regardless of racial or ethnic origin, and promoting equality among all Canadians.[1] These beliefs and values are also embodied in the Charter of Rights and Freedoms, in various pieces of legislation, and in bodies such as human-rights commissions.

Urbanization, the rise in levels of education, and economic growth have facilitated the progressive integration of minorities into the social and economic structure. These factors have also contributed to an increase in the level of tolerance among Canadians. At the same time, constitutional and legal provisions have had an effect in the same direction by affirming the importance of equality for all, regardless of ethnocultural or racial origin and of the value of cultural diversity as a defining characteristic of our society. As a result, the social and institutional rigidities that existed in previous decades have begun to break down. A "quiet revolution" has taken place not only in Quebec but also in English-speaking Canada: "What emerged after the war was a new Canadian society. The educational and industrial institutions that had been blamed for the lack of mobility changed: facilities were expanded at all levels of the educational system, and new and expanding types of business enterprises emerged ... offering opportunities for rapid economic advancement."[2]

Anti-discrimination legislation began to be adopted by provincial legislatures in the mid-1940s. Beginning in the late 1950s and during the 1960s and 1970s, human-rights commissions were established, with the responsibility of enforcing the codes pertaining to fair employment, fair accommodation, and equal pay. In 1971 the federal multiculturalism policy included a reaffirmation of egalitarian principles. One of its objectives was to "assist members of all cultural groups to overcome barriers to full participation in Canadian society."[3] The policy led to the development of programs to combat discrimination.

These policy initiatives facilitated the integration of minorities. If the integration was usually partial in the immigrant generation, by the second and especially the third generation, minorities had reached and sometimes surpassed the level of socio-economic attainment of British-origin Canadians.[4] In recent decades, however, there has been a substantial increase in the size of visible minorities. A number of these minorities have been in Canada for a long time, but their size has increased considerably. As well, new minorities have been added. Whether or not the overall pattern of socio-economic mobility for European-origin minorities will repeat itself for visible minorities is not clear. In some visible minorities, immigrants, especially women, do not reach a level of socio-economic achievement as high as that of other Canadians, but neither was this the case among white immigrants who came in earlier periods.[5] Yet there are variations among visible minorities, with some attaining high levels of occupation and income, even in the immigrant generation.[6]

Given these patterns, we should find little difference in the perceptions and experience of fairness between European-origin minorities

Table 6 Perceptions of Fairness of Society, Fairness of Personal Treatment, and Job Opportunities by Ethnocultural Origin

| | Percentage That Believe | | | |
| | | | Job opportunities | |
Ethnocultural Group	Society Fair for Most	Personally Treated Very Fairly	More	Same
British	42	41	24	52
French	32	26	25	56
Western European	51	45	26	54
Eastern European	41	30	10	66
Southern European	39	26	7	71
Visible minority	32	26	11	39
Other	40	28	9	52
"Canadian"	27	17	17	60

and British-origin Canadians but a higher level of perceived and experienced unfairness among visible minorities than among other groups. Table 6 shows that this is largely the case with regard to the assessment of the fairness of our society: Canadians of western European origin are the most likely to make a positive assessment (51 per cent) and visible minorities the least likely, together with the French and those who declare themselves "Canadian," six out of ten of whom are francophones.

The proportion making a positive assessment reaches 50 per cent only among respondents of western European origin. The case of immigrants from different parts of the world is similar: those from Europe and the United States are more likely to make a positive assessment of the fairness of our society than immigrants from other countries (51 per cent compared to 40 per cent). But the results are somewhat different with fairness of personal treatment. Only among respondents of western European origins do we find the same level of perceived fairness as among those of British origin (45 per cent and 41 per cent). Such an evaluation is significantly less frequent in six of the eight categories, with only between one-fourth and one-third expressing this view. In one category ('Canadian'), the level is even lower: less than one-fifth.

As with the judgment about the fairness of our society, American and European immigrants are again more positive about the way they are treated personally than immigrants from other countries: 44 per cent compared to 31 per cent. Since the perception of fairness is strongly related to social class (see next chapter), these differences may be due to the class-composition of the two categories of respondents. Indeed, 35 per cent of the American and European immigrants, compared to 16 per cent of immigrants from other countries consider themselves as located in the upper-middle or upper classes. Twenty-nine per cent and 45 per cent, respectively, place themselves in the lower or working classes.

In order to explore this further, we can look at the respondents' perceptions of opportunities for jobs and promotions. About one-fourth of all respondents say that people of their own ethnic, cultural, or racial background have *fewer* opportunities than people of other backgrounds. Interestingly, they are almost as likely to think that people of their background have *more* opportunities than others (this is true of about one-fifth of them). The percentage is about the same among men and women and varies little among age, education, and income categories.

In addition, the percentage who feel that members of their group have fewer job opportunities than others does not vary greatly among the various ethnocultural categories: between 19 per cent and 24 per cent (Table 6). But there are two categories that differ markedly from this overall pattern: visible minorities and people classified as "other": 49 per cent of the first and 39 per cent of the second say that they have fewer opportunities than people of other backgrounds. Whether they are immigrants or Canadian-born, and especially if they are immigrants (from non-European countries), they experience a more pronounced disadvantage with regard to job opportunities.[7] Census data on income show the same pattern: "Those who belong to visible minorities have significantly lower incomes than other Canadians at all educational levels," while "for those of European ethnic backgrounds there are virtually no significant differences within educational levels" (except for the French, who earn more than those of British origin).[8]

The persons who perceive that the members of their ethnic, cultural, or racial group are treated unfairly may not feel so themselves. Indeed, while 49 per cent of members of visible minorities feel that members of their group have fewer opportunities than others, only 27 per cent declare that they themselves have not been treated fairly in this society, a difference of twenty-two percentage points. A slightly lower difference, 17 per cent, is found among those classified as "other": 39 per cent feel that their group has fewer opportunities; 22 per cent that they themselves are disadvantaged. These are not inconsistent responses. Simply reading newspaper reports can make one aware that unequal opportunity is a problem. Also, one may know people who experience discrimination. One does not have to feel treated unfairly to make such observations.

The importance that people attach to their ethnic or racial background also makes a difference. Those for whom it is very important are more likely to perceive fewer opportunities for their own group than those for whom it is not important at all – 30 per cent compared to 19 per cent. The uneven distribution of job opportunities is more likely to be attributed to ethnicity or race by those for whom this particular social affiliation matters a lot than by those who attach little importance to it. It is likely, however, that the two phenomena interact with each other: people who attach a lot of importance to their cultural or racial background may, on the one hand, be more sensitive to differential treatment in the labour market or elsewhere, but, on the other hand, the experience of unfair treatment may give a special significance to their background.

RECOGNITION

Beyond the elimination of discrimination, a basic quest of ethnic, cultural, and racial communities is recognition as full participants in the society. Members of these communities resent being defined as a problem, as a burden on society. They want to be seen and appreciated as contributors to the functioning of societal institutions and to the dynamism of economic, social and cultural life. In this study, we do not focus on the recognition of their cultural distinctiveness as such but rather on their contribution to society.

Ethno-cultural groups

Immigrants are frequently seen as an imposition on the rest of society. Frequently, we downplay the fact that we accepted them because we need them for economic or demographic reasons. Rather, we tend to see their presence as a sign of our generosity, of the openness of our country. The mutuality of the exchange is ignored. We prefer to think that they need us, not that we need them. To the extent that this is the case, we fail to recognize their contribution to the society.

Similar observations can be made about established ethnic and racial minorities who feel that their historical and contemporary contribution to the formation and evolution of Canadian society should be adequately recognized. Some claim that they, too, are "founding peoples," because they played a critical role in the building of a particular region of the country and in its institutional development.[9] A newspaper report on a ceremony to honour Black railway porters in 1999 makes a significant statement in this connection: Under the headline 'Railway porters finally get their due: Plaque at Montreal's Windsor Station pays

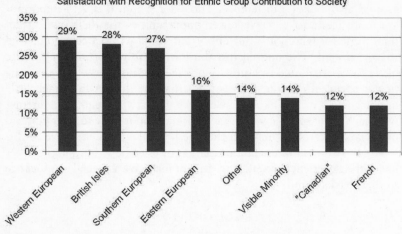

Figure 18
Satisfaction with Recognition for Ethnic Group Contribution to Society

■ Very Satisfied with Recognition of Contribution to Society

homage to *black workers overlooked by history,*' *the newspaper reported that, in a ceremony organized by Canadian Heritage,* "the legions of black men who worked anonymously as Canadian railway porters *will be honoured for their contribution to nation building.*"[10]

Overall, a little more than three-quarters of Canadians are satisfied with the recognition that members of their ethnic, cultural, or racial group receive for their contribution to society. One in five Canadians (21 per cent) are *very* satisfied and about the same proportion (18 per cent) are dissatisfied. There are, however, significant variations among the different ethnic/racial categories (Figure 18).

We find that close to three out of ten respondents of British, western, and southern European origins are *very* satisfied with the recognition their group receives for its contribution to society. This compares with between 12 per cent and 16 per cent among those in the other ethnic categories: visible minority, "Canadian," and "other." There is a difference of about fourteen percentage points between these two sets of ethnocultural categories. As the figure shows, the likelihood of dissatisfaction with recognition of group contribution to society is the opposite for the two categories of groups

Although members of visible minorities are as likely as the French to be *very* satisfied with the recognition received, they are much more likely to be *dis*satisfied. Indeed, one-third express dissatisfaction, the highest percentage of all groups. The next highest is found in the "other" category (28 per cent).

Members of visible minorities and of "other" groups are the most likely to perceive a decline in the recognition for the contribution of their group in the last few years: 34 per cent and 26 per cent, respectively. Such a perception is the lowest among those of western and eastern European origins (13 per cent). The other groups fall in-between. However, it is also members of visible minorities who are the most likely (16 per cent) to feel that the recognition for their societal contribution has *increased* in recent years. This is twice the percentage for the sample as a whole. Thus, the experience of different segments of these minorities seems to be moving in opposite directions. Unfortunately, the number of cases in the sample is too small to allow a more detailed analysis of those different segments.

The linguistic collectivities

The debate over the official recognition of Quebec as a "distinct society" was framed in terms of distinctiveness, but part of this issue is the recognition of the contribution that francophones in Quebec and in the rest of Canada have made and are making to the formation and development of this society. The debate revealed considerable dissatisfaction on the part of francophones in this regard. On the other hand, many Anglophones felt that such official recognition would be to their disadvantage in terms both of status and of other interests.

It is not surprising, then, to find that respondents of French and "Canadian" origins are the least likely to be very satisfied with the recognition received (12 per cent). (The reader should recall that 60 per cent of the "Canadians" are Quebec francophones.) The same results are obtained if we consider home language rather than ethnic origin: 8 per cent of francophones compared to 25 per cent of anglophones (and 16 per cent of "allophones," the term used for those whose ancestral language is neither English or French) are very satisfied with the recognition their group receives for its contribution to Canadian society.

Satisfaction with the recognition of the contribution of one's group is associated with the perception of job opportunities: those who feel that members of their group have fewer opportunities are much more likely to be dissatisfied with the recognition received (35 per cent) than those who perceive more (14 per cent) or the same (13 per cent) amount of job opportunities. A study of Quebec francophones in the labour force found that competition for jobs "has a significant effect on support for separation only when the competition is perceived as unfair."[11] Thus, there seems to be a configuration of experiences and perceptions: unequal job opportunities, the feeling that one's contribution is not appreciated, and resentment against the society that inflicts such treatment.

The same pattern is evident in the respondents' assessment of the evolution of their financial situation.[12] Those who find their financial situation very positive are more likely to be satisfied with the recognition received for the contribution of their ethnic group (35 per cent) than those who see it as negative (13 per cent), a difference of twenty-two percentage points.

TRUST

British and western European respondents are the least likely to be distrustful of others in general. There is little variation across the other ethnocultural categories. As far as trust in specific types of social relationships is concerned, there is no systematic variation across the different ethnocultural categories. This is also the case for trust in institutional authorities. There is one exception: respondents of southern European origins tend to be more distrustful than the average for the sample. This is so with regard to their family, co-workers, fellow ethnic-group members, employers, people with different religious beliefs, and businessmen. In each of these types of relations they are more likely, by ten percentage points, to be distrustful than the total for the sample. However, the number of southern Europeans in the sample is fairly small (seventy-nine) and because of this the findings may not be reliable. There is a pattern here, nevertheless, for this particular ethnocultural category.

BELONGING

Ethno-cultural groups

Multiculturalism as a policy and a social objective introduced a new perspective on cultural diversity and belonging in our society. The objectives of the policy were based on a basically integrative approach, which sought to facilitate the acquisition of at least one of Canada's official languages and to promote creative encounters and interchanges among all Canadian cultural groups. At the same time, however, it rejected the idea that members of cultural groups had to abandon their identity and culture to participate fully in Canadian society. This orientation included the expectation that public institutions of our society should modify their practices so as to accommodate the identity and culture of the diverse cultural groups.

This conception of what constitutes the basic character of Canadian society is probably partly responsible for the fairly high degree of inter-group harmony in our society. It may not be completely accepted in all segments of the population, but it is progressively making its way in our public culture. An indication of this progress is the extent to which members of the different ethnocultural groups feel at home in their community and the society as a whole.

Visible and "other" minorities (who are mostly of non-European origins) are the least likely to *feel very much at home in their local communities*: 44 per cent and 45 per cent, respectively. They are the only two categories in which less than a majority feel very much at home. But this is the only distinction that seems to make a difference. There is little variation among the other categories, the lowest percentages being found among those of eastern European origin (54 per cent) and, paradoxically, among those who declare their origin as "Canadian" (53 per cent). The percentages for the other four ethnic-origin categories range between 58 per cent and 62 per cent.

The distinction between European and non-European origins is also shown when country of birth is considered. The respondents born in Canada do not differ from those born in the United States or in Europe. However, those in both the American and European categories differ from those born in other countries: they are about 10 per cent more likely to feel very much at home in their local community. It is not being an immigrant that matters, but rather being an immigrant from a country other than North America or Europe. These findings point to a social cleavage in Canadian society that is based on a combination of colour, religion, and culture differences that are broadly captured by the European/non-European distinction.

The results are partly different with the *sense of belonging in this society*. A somewhat surprising finding is the absence of difference in the percentage of those who feel very much at home in this society between respondents born in Canada and those born in other countries: 44 per cent among the Canadian-born, 45 per cent among those born in the United States and Europe, and 42 per cent among those born in other countries.

But if the country of origin makes no difference in the sense of belonging to the society, ethnocultural origin does. There appear to be three categories of origins that matter in this regard. Table 7 presents three ethnocultural groupings, the percentage being very much at home in this society shown in order of magnitude. This table shows that there is little variation within each of the three groupings, but a difference of fourteen points between the highest and the lowest category – that is, between the 49 per cent among respondents of western European origins and the 35 per cent among members of visible minorities.

Table 7   The Sense of Belonging Differs for Three Categories of Ethnic Groups

Grouping	Percent Very Much at Home	Grouping	Percent Very Much at Home	Grouping	Percent Very Much at Home
Western European	49	"Canadian"	43	"Other" Origins	37
British	47				
Southern European	47	French	40	Visible Minorities	35
Eastern European	46				

But, in a way, members of the different cultural communities can feel that they have another "home," namely their own cultural, ethnic, or racial community. Respondents were presented with the following statement: "*People have to stay attached to their own cultural, ethnic or racial group because it is only there that they can count on being fully accepted.*" Not surprisingly, respondents who feel that only their ethnic group is really "home" are less likely to feel very much at home in the community where they live: 43 per cent agree with this conception of their group, whereas 64 per cent disagree.

The same is observed with the sense of belonging to the society. Respondents who feel that one's cultural, ethnic, or racial group is the only group in which one can count on being fully accepted are less likely to feel very much at home in this society than those who do not feel this way: 39 per cent compared to 48 per cent. The difference, although not negligible, is not large (nine percentage points).

This relationship, however, can operate both ways. On the one hand, those who are strongly attached to their own ethnic or racial group may feel that, ultimately, it is the only one on which they can count and the only place where they can feel at home. On the other hand, such a feeling about the ethnic or racial group may be a response to experiences of rejection by others. Being made to feel like a stranger by prejudice and social exclusion may well lead people to conclude that their own group is the only socially safe haven. This is especially the case when people perceive a pattern of discrimination or physical assault *and* when, in their view, institutional authorities do not seem to do much about such acts when minorities are the victims.

Consistent with the latter view is the fact that the sense of belonging is related to fairness of treatment. In all ethnocultural categories, the sense of belonging in this society is lower if people feel that members of their group have fewer job opportunities than if they have more or the same as other groups. The difference, however, is more pronounced in some categories than in others. It is generally larger (between seventeen and thirty-one percentage points) in the European-origin groups than in the other categories, where the differences are between six and sixteen points.

Some members of the various cultural groups have positive and others negative experiences in their relationships with others in their local community or in the larger society. In certain circumstances, these differences can generate debates within the communities. Recently, for instance, the murder of a Jewish man in Toronto was analysed differently by different segments of the community. On the one side were those who saw the crime as part of increasing anti-Semitic feeling in Canada and, related to that, as anti-Israel reporting in the media. On the other side were those who sought to reassure the community that there is no epidemic of hate in Canada.[13] The *social* significance of the murder is ambiguous: Is it an indication of a growing threat to the community or the unfortunate result of the action of a psychologically and socially troubled person? The first interpretation can increase the feeling of being a stranger in the society while the second would lead to the perception that many in other groups are equally appalled by the crime. Similar internal debates occur when members of visible minorities are the victims of discrimination or of physical assault.

The linguistic collectivities

For a long time, many Canadians thought of Canada as an English-speaking country. In recent decades, however, various accommodations were made to integrate the French collectivity in the Canadian institutional matrix. The Official Languages Act, adopted in 1969, is one of the initiatives in this regard. Another, which followed from the act, was the recruitment of francophones in the federal civil service – which had been a largely anglophone domain until the Quiet Revolution.

The arrangements are not entirely satisfactory for many on both sides of the linguistic divide. The official definition of Canada as a bilingual country does not command the support of all Canadians. Many francophone Québécois favour independence. They view a bilingual Canada as an impossibility. Others who agree with the objective feel that they are not yet fully accepted as a distinct historical community in this country. On the other hand, many anglophones feel that the policy changes have gone too far or that bilingualism is not an important national objective. A study conducted in 1987 found that only 37 per cent of English-Canadians consider as very important the preservation of French and English as the two official languages of Canada and 27 per cent said that it is not important. The corresponding figures are 80 per cent and 4 per cent among French Canadians.[14] This varies somewhat with age and level of education, but the percentage of support always remains below the majority level. (Even among those with a university education, for example, the figure stands at 45 per cent.) The initial platform of the Reform Party included the repeal of the Official Languages Act. (The revised policy of the new party, the Canadian Alliance, is less extreme. It supports, for instance, the need for key federal institutions to serve Canadians in both English and French but is strongly opposed to measures that would promote bilingualism at the provincial level).[15]

In this climate and in spite of recent accommodations, it is not surprising to find that anglophones are more likely than francophones to feel very much at home in the society. The difference, however, is not as large as could have been expected: 47 per cent and 38 per cent. Perhaps many francophones do not respond to this negative message but choose instead to hear the positive one from those who accept the official definition of Canada as a bilingual country. It could also be that many francophones see themselves as one of the founding peoples of the country. Thus, Canada is home for them, whatever others may think.

It could be assumed that francophones are more likely than anglophones to feel at home in their local community than in the larger society. But this is not the case: anglophones are also more likely than francophones – by a margin of 8 per cent – to feel very much at home in their local community. The result is that the percentage who feel *very much* at home in *both* their local community and in the larger society is again eight points higher among anglophones than among francophones (and the opposite is the case for the percentage who feel somewhat or not at all at home in *both*).

The pattern of differences between anglophones and francophones is not the same when fairness is taken into account. Indeed, among those who feel that members of their cultural group have *more* job opportunities than other groups, francophones are *less* likely than anglophones to have a strong sense of belonging: 39 per cent compared to 56 per cent (Figure 19). If they feel that the job opportunities are the same, the difference remains in the same direction, but reduced (40 per cent and 50 per cent). There is no difference between anglophones and francophones who feel that members of their cultural group have fewer opportunities. Unfairness in the labour market wipes out the difference between the two linguistic collectivities (Figure 19).

Satisfaction or dissatisfaction with the recognition for the cultural group's contribution to society has considerable relevance for the sense of belonging to society. It may be a factor in the difference between francophones and anglophones. Indeed, francophones are less likely

Figure 19
Anglophone Sense of Belonging Related to Perception of Job Opportunities

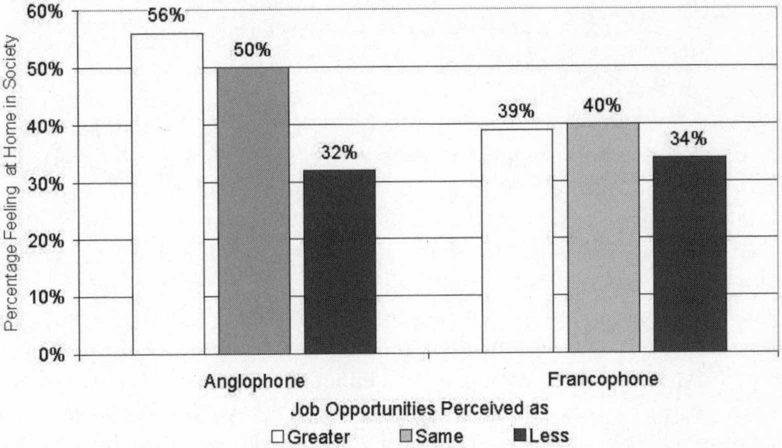

than anglophones to be very satisfied with the recognition received (8 per cent compared to 25 per cent). However, the relationship with the sense of belonging to society is about the same among anglophones as among francophones.[16] Among anglophones who are very satisfied with the recognition received by their cultural group, 70 per cent feel very much at home in this society compared to 31 per cent of those who are dissatisfied. In the case of francophones, the corresponding percentages are not much different: 75 per cent and 24 per cent. In their case, the sense of belonging is even lower if they feel that recognition has decreased in recent years: 16 per cent.

Comparing allophones with anglophones and francophones, we find that they are less likely to feel very much at home in this society. There is a difference of fifteen percentage points between anglophones and those who speak a third language at home (47 per cent compared to 32 per cent). In their case, the lack of familiarity with the language of the majority may be a reason for this relatively low sense of belonging. Whenever they communicate outside their linguistic group, they probably feel (or may even be made to feel) their differentness to a certain degree. This could be due not only to the lack of familiarity with the language but also to the fact of their being immigrants (since a substantial proportion of allophones are first-generation Canadians).

Some francophones could have a similar experience, at least in certain regions of the country. For many francophones, however, the opposite could be the case. To the extent that French is recognized and accepted, a situation that exists in many parts of Canada, the possibility of speaking French would increase the sense that one really belongs.

SOCIAL INDEBTEDNESS, OBLIGATIONS, AND CONTRIBUTIONS

It was seen earlier that visible minorities are more likely than any other group to feel disadvantaged in terms of job and promotion opportunities. The evolution of their economic condition is also more likely to be negative than that of other groups. Yet in spite of this, they are *the most* likely to feel strongly that everyone owes something to society and should try to give something back: 44 per cent compared to between 21 per cent and 34 per cent among members of the various other ethnic categories. In fact, there is little variation among most ethnic categories (between 29 per cent and 34 per cent), except for southern Europeans and "Canadians," who show the lowest level of social indebtedness (24 per cent and 21 per cent, respectively).

This may be so because many members of visible minorities are immigrants. Indeed, immigrants generally and immigrants from non-European countries, in particular, are much more likely to express a strong sense of indebtedness than Canadian-born respondents: 48 per cent of those from non-European countries, 40 per cent of those from Europe, the United States and the United Kingdom, and only 29 per cent of those born in Canada. For visible minorities, the fact of being newcomers may partly override the impact of their relatively more negative experience in the society. Thus, in spite of being disadvantaged, they, hypothetically, would be conscious of the improvement in their lot after migrating to this country and, as a result, would feel socially indebted.[17]

In addition, some members of visible minorities may be among those who say they are treated unfairly and are more disadvantaged in a number of respects but nevertheless think that everyone owes something to society and should try to give something back. The reader is referred to the discussion of these "deviant" cases in a previous chapter.

The greater experience of disadvantage may account for the fact that the strong sense of obligation to help people "in the same boat" and "those from my ethnic, cultural, or racial background" is relatively more common, among visible minorities, among those of "other" origins and among immigrants from countries other than Europe and the United States than among respondents with other cultural backgrounds. That is to say, disadvantage seems to lead people to feel obligated to help others who are experiencing similar

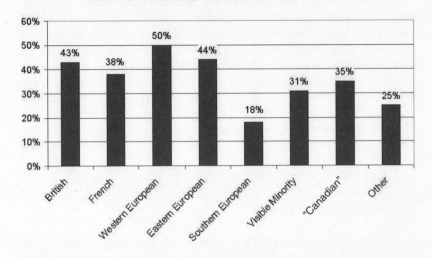

Figure 20a
Ethnic Distribution of High Frequency of Communal Activity

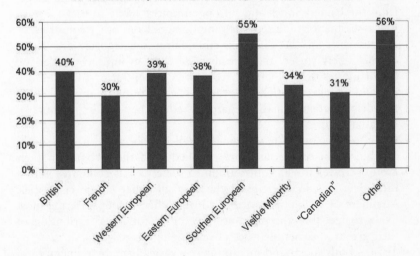

Figure 20b
Do Not Think They Give as Much as They Should by Ethnic Group

conditions. Accordingly, the orientation of their sense of social obligation is less universalistic (that is, feeling obligated to help anyone in need) than it is among other respondents. In contrast, it is among those who are the least likely to be disadvantaged (e.g., respondents of western European origins) that the universalistic orientation is the most common.

The same three categories – visible minorities, respondents of "other" origins, and immigrants from countries other than Europe and the United States – plus those of southern European origin are the least likely to be highly involved in communal activities in comparison with respondents of other cultural backgrounds (Figure 20a). On the other hand, they are the most likely to feel that they do not help or give as much as they should (Figure 20b). Finally, it should be noted that there are substantial variations in the extent of communal contributions across the different ethnocultural categories. Indeed, the percentage of "high" contributors ranges between 50 per cent and 18 per cent, a difference of thirty-two percentage points.

HIGHLIGHTS

We may summarize as follows:

- Canadians of western European origins are the most likely to make a positive assessment of the fairness of our society and of their personal treatment in it. Visible minorities and French-origin respondents are the least likely to make such an assessment. Immigrants from the United States and Europe are more likely to make a positive assessment of fairness than immigrants from other countries.
- Respondents in the different ethnocultural categories are about equally likely to feel that members of their group have fewer job opportunities than others. There are two exceptions: visible minorities and people classified as "other." These groups are more likely to feel disadvantaged in this regard, whether they are immigrants or Canadian-born.
- Close to three out of ten respondents of British, western, and southern European origins are *very* satisfied with the recognition their group receives for its contribution to society. This compares with a little over one in ten among those in all other ethnic categories. Members of visible minorities and of "other" groups are the most likely to feel that the recognition received for the contribution of their group to society has been declining in recent years.
- Trust – both social and institutional – varies little by ethnocultural category.
- Visible and "other" minorities have the lowest feeling of belonging in their *local communities* and in the larger society. More than four out of ten, that is, less than a majority, feel that they belong. There is little variation among the other categories.
- The sense of belonging in *this society* is the strongest among those of British and European origins and the weakest among members of

visible minorities. There is no difference in the likelihood of feeling very much at home in this society between those born in Canada and those born in other countries.

- Anglophones are somewhat more likely than francophones to feel very much at home in this society. The difference, however, exists only if they are dissatisfied with the recognition that their group receives for its contribution. If they are satisfied, they are equally likely to feel a strong sense of belonging. Allophones are less likely than both anglophones and francophones to feel very much at home in this society.
- Even if more disadvantaged than other groups in terms of job opportunities and financial situation, members of visible minorities are the most likely to feel strongly that everyone owes something to society and should try to give something back. There is little variation in this regard among most ethnic categories.
- It is also members of visible minorities as well as those of "other" origins and immigrants from countries other than Europe and the United States who are the most likely to feel a strong sense of obligation to help people "in the same boat" and "those from my ethnic, cultural or racial background."
- On the other hand, the same three categories are also the least likely to be highly involved in communal activities, but at the same time they (except visible minorities) are the most likely to feel that they are not helping or giving as much as they should.

Class and Social Fragmentation

Civil society – citizenship – is incompatible with privilege for the few ... As long as some people are poor, and moreover are condemned to remain poor because they live outside the world market economy altogether, prosperity everywhere remains an unjust advantage. As long as some people have no rights of social and political participation, the rights of the few cannot be describes as legitimate. Systematic inequality – as opposed to comparatively incidental inequality within the same universe of opportunity – is incompatible with the civilized assumptions of the First World. (Ralf Dahrendorf, "A Precarious Balance: Economic Opportunity, Civil Society, and Political Liberty," *The Responsive Community*, Summer 1995, 16)

Social fragmentation along class lines can undermine the social fabric and generate serious problems for the society. The social sciences are replete with studies showing that the position occupied in the class structure (as indicated by such factors as education and income) is related to virtually all aspects of people's life circumstances and to the ways in which they experience community and society. This is so because the resources available to individuals vary considerably across levels of the socio-economic hierarchy. Such resources can be financial, social (social connections, institutional contacts, access to information), and cultural (education, family environment).

Social-class cleavages tend to be less apparent in periods of economic stability. Like many problems and tensions in society, their impact tends to manifest itself in periods of economic change. Macur Olson points out that "economic change entails social dislocation ... [and] that both the gainers and the losers from economic growth can be destabilizing forces ... The fact that there will be some who gain disproportionately from economic growth means that there will be a new distribution of economic power ... and a 'contradiction' between this new distribution of economic power and the old distribution of social prestige and political power."[1] In other words, the social fabric may be subjected to more or less pronounced social and political tension.

A possible source of tension is the widening the gap between income classes, especially between the top fifth and the rest of the society. As indicated in Chapter 1, this phenomenon is in part the result of technological developments and economic restructuring. In an earlier period, average earnings tended to rise in tandem, the rich getting richer but the middle classes and the poor also doing better. In the last few decades, the situation has changed: the incomes at the top of the scale have been increasing, those at the bottom have been decreasing, and those in the middle have tended to remain stagnant. This is a widespread phenomenon taking place in North America and in western, as well as eastern, Europe.

This may be the reason for the feeling among those in the middle of the class structure that they are paying a disproportionate share of the societal burden and suffering at the hands of the "special interest groups." They see the rich as taking care of themselves and the poor as being taken care of by government. They feel relatively deprived in relation to those classes, especially those on welfare, whom they perceive as being better-off even though they have the same or lower educational backgrounds than theirs. Included in this category are those whose economic situation is increasingly precarious: stagnant if not declining wages, the threat of unemployment, underemployment, and part-time work, and the absence of benefits. These are the victims of the measures adopted by employers and governments to increase the flexibility of the labour force.

Social exclusion is another phenomenon attributed to the restructuring of the economy and of the labour force. Ralf Dahrendorf points out that there now appears to be a set of individuals for whom there is no place in the labour market. They are the long-term unemployed. These people become marginalized, existing at the periphery of society. They are not needed; the economy can grow without them; in fact, firms and shareholders prosper as a result of their dismissal. "The rich can get richer without them; governments can even be reelected without them; and GDP can rise and rise."[2]

A manifestation of social exclusion is the fact that the less well-off are increasingly living apart from the rest of the society. This growing social distance is partly shown by the fact that poor families have become more concentrated in high-poverty neighbourhoods in recent years.[3] In 1995 about 18 per cent of poor families lived in 548 such neighbourhoods, a significant increase from 12 per cent in 334 high-poverty neighbourhoods in 1980. Although such neighbourhoods are found in most Canadian cities, they are more numerous in some than in others. Also, in some cities the proportion of low-income families living in such neighbourhoods has increased while in others it has decreased in this fifteen–year period.[4]

Attitudes towards the poor, people on welfare, single mothers, pan-handlers, "squeegee" people, and the homeless also suggest not only social distance between social classes but social exclusion. They are fre-quently blamed for their predicament; they are perceived as a threat rather than as victims; and they are seen as lacking in moral fibre. Mea-sures to make life difficult for them or to make them socially "invisi-ble" and "inoffensive" receive considerable public approval.

These trends underlie the "emerging class structure" in Canada described in a study by Ekos which identifies five classes in our society. At the top are the "insiders," the well-paid, highly skilled, professional knowledge workers. They constitute about 19 per cent of the Canadian public. Next are the "secure" and "insecure middle" classes, which account for about 24 and 16 per cent of the public, respectively. The fourth category consists of people who "are detached from the world of work and rely on government to deliver them from problems such as poverty, unemployment, low skill levels, etc." They are called the "disengaged dependents" and constitute about 22 per cent of the public. Finally, at the bottom, are the "outsiders," (19 per cent), the "angry and alienated ... who operate largely outside the mainstream of the society and at the margin of the economy [and polity]."[5]

All these patterns suggest a considerable amount of dissatisfaction with the ways in which the system functions in our society and, as a consequence, a negative view of its fairness. The existence of a socio-economic hierarchy and social dislocations resulting from economic change are not in themselves sources of tension leading to social frag-mentation. Rather, they are threats to the social fabric to the extent that they are seen as unfair and as depriving people of the social recog-nition they deserve. In addition, some may not trust those responsible for the major changes occurring around them, especially when these leaders deliver little of the help – in adapting to the new circumstances or as compensation for the disruption of lives – that they regularly promise. The result may well be a decreased sense of belonging and of social indebtedness and obligation, as well as declining social involve-ment. This chapter presents results related to these issues.

FAIRNESS

Given such developments, it can be expected that those who are favoured by recent economic and technological changes will express

Figure 21
Perception of Fairness Is Strongly Related to Socio-economic Status

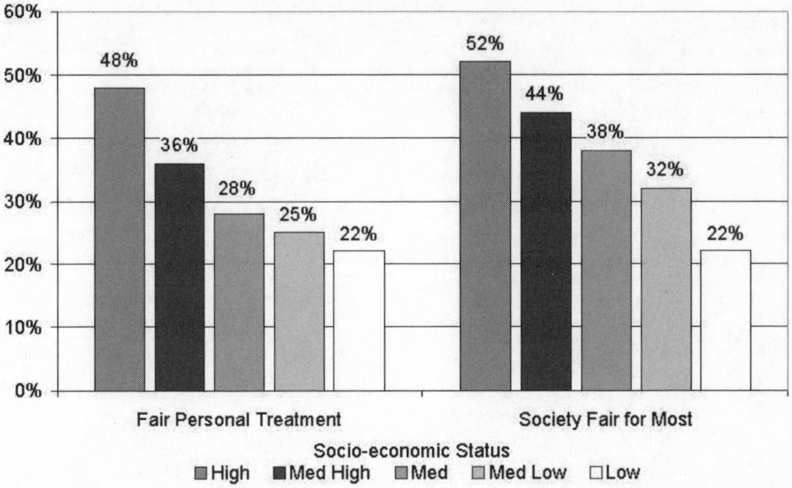

favourable judgments about the fairness of the system in general and of the way they are personally treated in it. Those who do not gain much from these changes or who suffer from them can be expected to judge the situation less favourably or even negatively. In other words, the perceptions and experience of fairness can be expected to be significantly different depending on the position occupied in the socio-economic hierarchy.

This is indeed what we find, whether respondents are located in the hierarchy on the basis of their income and education[6] or whether they locate themselves there on the basis of their own self-identification as lower class, working class, lower-middle class, upper-middle class, or upper class.[7] With both classifications, the variations are substantial: the percentage making a positive evaluation of the fairness of our society and of their personal treatment climbs steadily from a low of about one in five among those at the bottom of the socio-economic hierarchy to about half of those at the top, the differences varying between twenty-six and thirty-four percentage points (Figures 21 and 22).

It should be noted, however, that even among those with high levels of education and income who see themselves in the higher echelons of the social hierarchy, a large proportion *do not* make an entirely positive evaluation either of the system in general or of the way it treats them personally. In other words, unfairness in our society is not only a phenomenon associated with a relatively low position in the social

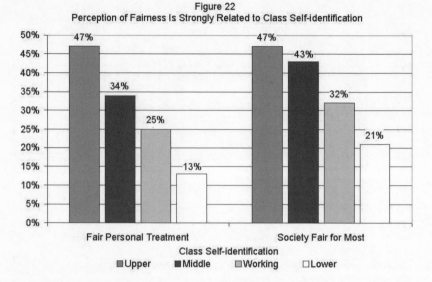

Figure 22
Perception of Fairness Is Strongly Related to Class Self-identification

hierarchy. It is a reality that the relatively better-off also perceive in the society and even experience in their lives.

In addition to asking about the fairness of the society and of personal treatment, we also asked how the class to which the respondent belongs is treated. (Figure 23).[8] Among those who consider themselves in the lower class, two-thirds feel that their class is not treated fairly and one-third say that it is treated somewhat fairly. Few if any (1 per cent) feel that they are treated very fairly. In the working and lower-middle classes, the corresponding percentages are 34, 59, and 7. At the upper end of the class structure, only 15 per cent feel that their class is not treated fairly while 85 per cent consider that it is treated fairly (34 per cent very and 51 per cent somewhat).[9]

The social-class basis of unfairness is also revealed by the reaction to the statement that *"in our society, there are two sets of rules: one for those who have money and one for everyone else."* An imposing 81 per cent agree with this statement, 43 per cent strongly. Not surprisingly, people in the lower echelons of the social hierarchy are more likely to agree with the statement than those at the higher levels: 90 per cent compared to 71 per cent, a nineteen-point difference. However, even among those in the upper echelons, the level of agreement is quite high.

The view that there are two sets of rules is more frequently held by those who feel that our society is basically fair for only a few: among them, 68 per cent think so, compared to 25 per cent among those who

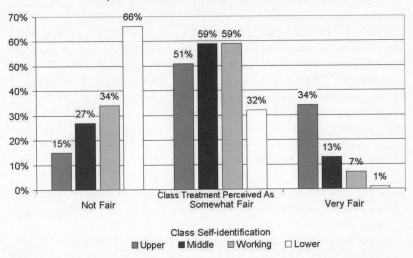

Figure 23
Perception of Fairness Is Related to Class Self-identification

Class Self-identification
■ Upper   ■ Middle   ▨ Working   ☐ Lower

think that it is basically fair for most. Essentially the same result is obtained with regard to fairness of personal treatment: 31 per cent of those treated very fairly and 62 per cent of those treated very unfairly strongly agree with the statement. These two sets of results help to define what people mean by unfairness, namely, that it is, in a significant way, a matter of social class.

These results are consistent with the findings on social inequality in the 1992 International Social Survey Programme. The study included data on the perception of the class structure as it existed 30 years ago and as it exists now, as well as on the public's views on the kind of class structure that is morally preferable. It was found that 56 per cent of Canadians (47 per cent of Australians and 63 per cent of New Zealanders) describe their society today as either "Elite/Mass" or "Pyramid," that is, as consisting of a small elite at the top, few or very few people in the middle, and most or the great mass of people at the bottom. Thus, "with some exceptions respondents seem pessimistic about the society in which they live. They typically characterize it in terms of deep inequalities."[10] They are also pessimistic in the sense that they do not believe that the situation has improved much in recent decades. About half of Canadians (and about half of Australians, too, but only 20 per cent of New Zealanders) describe their society of thirty years ago as "Elite/Mass or "Pyramid," and 56 per cent describe contemporary Canada in the same way.

Finally, less than one out of ten see these two class profiles as the "morally preferred structure." That is to say, the majority of Canadians find that the existing profile of social inequalities in our society does not conform to their expected standards of equity. In fact, in all ten countries studied, the morally preferred society is the middle-class model, that is, that of a society with most people in the middle: from 35 to 62 per cent (49 per cent in Canada) prefer this type of society.[11]

The perceptions and experience of fairness are also related to the respondents' satisfaction with their present financial situation, its comparison with the situation they were in a year ago, and the one they expect to face a year from now. The distribution of respondents in the different financial situations is as follows:

- 28 per cent are in a *very negative* situation: one with which they are very dissatisfied, which has worsened in the last year, and which will not improve;
- 24 per cent are in a *negative* situation: one with which they are dissatisfied, which has not changed in the past year, and which is not expected to change in the coming year;
- 25 per cent are in a *positive* situation: one with which they are satisfied but with no change from the past year and none expected for the coming year; and
- 23 per cent are in a *very positive* situation: one with which they are very satisfied, which is better than in the previous year, and which is expected to improve again in the coming year.

In short, the sample divides about equally between those in a positive and those in a negative financial situation. A recent survey about the assessment of the adequacy of income also reveals a near-equal split between those whose financial circumstances are deteriorating and those whose financial circumstances are stable or improving. Specifically, 56 per cent said that their household income is very adequate in meeting their family's basic needs while 29 per cent said that it was moderately adequate and 13 per cent not very adequate.[12] In a 1998 survey in which people were asked to compare their generation with that of their parents, 40 per cent felt that people in their generation were worse off than those in their parents' generation, 15 per cent about the same, and 44 per cent better-off. A comparison with the responses to the same question about ten years earlier, in 1989, clearly indicates a deteriorating situation.[13] Then, 13 per cent thought that their generation was worse off than their parents' generation, 12 per cent about the same, and 74 per cent better-off.

These findings are reflective of what has in fact been happening in Canadian society. For instance, it has been found that "the earning power of Canadian men has been deteriorating for decades, no matter what their education ... They are earning dramatically less than their predecessors at the same age and there is little reason, based on current trends, to expect them to catch up ... " In contrast, "neither high school or university educated females experienced substantial differences in average weekly earnings across cohorts."[14]

The assessment of one's financial situation and its evolution over time is related to one's judgment about fairness. Those who feel that their economic situation is improving are more likely to say that our society is fair than those who believe that it is uncertain or going downward: 55 per cent compared to 27 per cent, a difference of twenty-eight points. In terms of the way they are treated personally, the difference is even more pronounced: 56 per cent compared to 17 per cent, a difference of thirty-nine points.

Angus Reid also notes that it is especially along class lines that fairness has taken a beating in recent years. Throughout his career as a pollster, he has seen "deep divisions in Canadians' attitudes based on gender, age and geography. But never ... those that have emerged in recent years – divisions based on income." He also observes that social-class differences are the central factor affecting voting preferences and policy attitudes. For example, "in a 1995 year-end poll, 48 per cent of middle-class respondents and 60 per cent of those who defined themselves as 'poor' said they were either 'disappointed' or 'really upset' over the trend in government cutbacks to programs. On the other hand, 72 per cent of wealthy and 61 per cent of upper-middle-class respondents either 'accepted' or 'enthusiastically supported' these cutbacks."[15]

Yet it is not only those in the lower classes who feel that our society is not fair for most people. It is not necessary to be personally subjected to unfairness to see it in the society. There are indeed regular reports in the media about such issues as growing income inequalities, excessive corporate profits, "shareholders versus job holders," outlandish salaries for senior executives, downsizing, and high unemployment. These may make people increasingly aware of and sensitive to social-class realities. As a result, some may perceive that the costs of corporate restructuring and of technological changes are disproportionately borne by particular categories of workers while others are reaping more than their share of the benefits.

Some may believe that government deficits have been reduced (or eliminated) principally on the backs of the less fortunate. The latest

Public Accounts data issued by the Receiver General of Canada indicates that "those who have borne the brunt of Ottawa's transfer-payment reductions are poor people dependent on provincial assistance programs" and people having to pay higher tuition fees for post-secondary education.[16] Recently, a United Nations Report expressed concern about growing poverty, especially among single mothers, homelessness and food banks, the condition of Native peoples, and the level of illiteracy in Canada.[17] Such awareness of the plight of the disadvantaged could be the basis for a perception of unfairness, whether or not one is personally affected.

It is also conceivable that some feel that they are *unfairly advantaged* in society. No study providing evidence on this possibility could be found.[18] However, we have seen that many people in the higher levels of the social hierarchy agree that, in Canada, there are two sets of rules, one for those with money and one for everyone else. (Among those who identify themselves as belonging to the upper-middle or to the upper classes, 26 per cent strongly agree and the same percentage simply agree). It was also found that some men believe that they have more job opportunities than women and that members of some ethnic or racial groups believe that they have more job opportunities than members of other groups.

Some people with relatively high incomes may also draw such a conclusion from the government benefits they receive. Indeed, Bruce Little has recently pointed out that "Canada's income-security programs, you might think, are aimed squarely at the poor. You'd be wrong. As a rule, most transfers from Ottawa and the provinces do go to the poor, but a surprising proportion of the money winds up in the pockets of the rich." (The top 40 per cent of households account for 76 per cent of income and 20 per cent of transfers; those in the middle get about 16 per cent of each; and the bottom two quintiles receive 8 per cent of income and 64 per cent of transfers.)[19]

It is possible that some individuals who are relatively advantaged in general may nevertheless feel unfairly treated in some regard. There are, for instance, people in the middle and upper-middle classes who feel that there are too many special-interest groups getting advantages or privileged treatment from governments and that they are the ones paying a disproportionate share of the resulting costs. This feeling is fairly common among Canadians – and is sometimes exploited by politicians who pit the special-interest groups against the public or the taxpayer. The 1995 Ekos survey found that 77 per cent of Canadians say they are "fed up with interest groups whining about getting their 'fair share' from the federal purse." In our survey, we found 90 per cent agreeing (41 per cent strongly) *"that there are too many people preoc-*

cupied with what they can get out of the system rather than with what they can contribute to the common good."[20]

RECOGNITION OF THE CONTRIBUTION
OF EDUCATIONAL CLASSES

The economic and technological changes of recent years have had a considerable impact on the occupational structure. They have changed the relative importance of different kinds of skills. For instance, there has been much discussion about the "de-skilling" of jobs, that is to say, about the fact that people with certain kinds of training or levels of education have been less and less able to use their skills. In addition, because of the expanding use of computer technology in practically all areas of the economy, the social status of associated skills and occupations has increased considerably, perhaps overshadowing other more traditional skills. At the same time, automation has reduced the importance of different kinds of jobs.

In an occupational structure that is constantly changing, it can be expected that some people will be anxious about their present and future economic security. But they may also be concerned with the importance attached to their role in the economy and in society in general. They may believe that they deserve more recognition than they feel they are given in the society. In other words, besides economic insecurity, they may experience a certain amount of status anxiety.

Indeed, our survey finds that only 11 per cent declare themselves "very satisfied" with the recognition that people with their level of education or training are receiving for their contribution to society. The others are either "somewhat satisfied" (59 per cent) or "dissatisfied" (30 per cent). The dissatisfaction is found in about the same percentage (about 30 per cent) at all levels of education, except among those with an elementary education, where it is lower (22 per cent). On the other hand, the percentage of the "very satisfied" is twice as high among those with a university or post-graduate education as among those with lower levels of education (19 per cent compared to 9 per cent).

The proportion satisfied and dissatisfied with the recognition received is not the same in all fields of socio-economic activity. Generally, we would expect that the fields in which the proportion of those who are very satisfied is high would also be the ones in which there would be a lower proportion of dissatisfied. This is indeed so in the fields of recreation, entertainment, and advertising, which show the highest percentage of dissatisfied (40 per cent) and one of the lowest percentages of very satisfied (7 per cent). Similarly, public administration shows one of the high rates of very satisfied (14 per cent) and the lowest rate of dissatisfied. It is also the case in the domain of personal services (e.g., restaurants, hotels, hair salons, and travel agencies), in which 33 per cent are dissatisfied with the recognition received for the people with their level of education and training (the third-highest) and only 7 per cent are very satisfied (the second-lowest).

Yet there are exceptions. Science and technology, health and social services, and education are fields in which there are relatively high percentages of both very satisfied and dissatisfied workers. In science and technology, we find the highest percentage of very satisfied (18 per cent) but also the second-highest of dissatisfied (37 per cent). In health and social services there is the second-highest of very satisfied (15 per cent) and the fourth-highest (31 per cent) of dissatisfied. In education the percentages are 13 per cent very satisfied and 30 per cent dissatisfied. This suggests that those fields are quite stratified, in the sense that they include both workers whose skills are highly valued and appreciated and ones whose training and contribution is not as recognized as they think it should be. This situation is illustrated by the fundraising campaign recently carried out by a hospital in Toronto. In the television marathon, the public is exposed to the accomplishments of highly trained doctors and technicians yet relatively little, if anything, is said of the other groups of workers who perform the daily work of caring for, monitoring, and rehabilitating patients.

The contribution of administrators and highly skilled professionals and technicians may also have more visibility in some organizations. This may be why, in terms of occupation, it is among them that we observe a relatively high percentage of individuals who are very satisfied (17 per cent), whereas in all other occupational categories the percentage of very satisfied is relatively low (between 6 per cent and 8 per cent).

Given these results, we are not surprised to find that satisfaction with the recognition people receive for their contribution to society is strongly correlated with their society's treatment of their class. This is indeed the case: 38 per cent of those who feel their social class is treated very fairly are highly satisfied, compared to only 1 per cent among those who feel it is not treated fairly.

In addition, dissatisfaction with the recognition received is significantly more frequent among younger people: 40 per cent among those aged eighteen to twenty-four, compared to 20 per cent in the category of fifty-five or older. This may reflect the reality that with age comes experience and with experience more recognition. But it could also be due to the fact that young people frequently obtain work below their

level of training. In other words, dissatisfaction would be more frequent among the young who are not able to find work commensurate
with the educational level they reached.

As seen in Chapter 4, more people are dissatisfied with the recognition received for the contribution to society of their educational category than that of their gender and cultural group: 30 per cent compared to 24 and 18 per cent. It is also in this connection that the
perception of a decline in recent years is the most common, 34 per cent.
A majority see no change and only 8 per cent perceive an improvement.
This perception varies little by region, age, gender, community size,
level of education, and occupational field. It does vary, however, with
the respondent's financial situation. The lower the annual income, the
more frequent the perception of a decrease in recognition: 26 per cent
of those with annual incomes of $80,000 or more feel that their edu-
cational class is receiving less recognition for its contribution to society
than a few years ago, compared to 40 per cent of those with less than
$15,000, a fourteen-point difference. The difference between the 25
per cent of respondents in a favourable financial situation and the 49
per cent of those in a poor and declining one is even more pronounced,
24 per cent.

TRUST

Social trust also varies with social class. As with the perceived fairness
of society, the level of distrust decreases as we go up the socio-economic ladder (measured by education and income). This distrust is
shown by the percentage who strongly[21] agree that people should be
careful about trusting others since there are too many who only seek
to benefit themselves: 44 per cent among those at the lowest echelon
compared to 26 per cent at the highest – a difference of eighteen percentage points. With class self-identification, the difference is a little
less pronounced: from 44 per cent to 32 per cent, that is, twelve percentage points.

Why is trust related to socio-economic class? Why are people in the
upper classes somewhat more trusting than those in the lower echelons
of the social hierarchy?

First, as noted above, the perception of disadvantage stemming
from unfairness is strongly related to social-class affiliation. Thus, it
can be expected that people who experience unfairness will tend to
become somewhat distrustful in their social and economic transactions. And indeed we find that they are more likely to be concerned
that others may take advantage of them: 42 per cent of those who
experience unfairness in three or four areas of their lives (that is,

gender, ethnicity/race, social class, or region of residence) strongly agree with the distrust statement, compared with 27 per cent of those who do not experience unfairness, a difference of fifteen percentage points.

Second, the relevance of social class for trust may also be due to the fact that, at the higher levels of the social hierarchy, people tend to have a sense of control over the way their lives turn out, while, at the lower levels, this sense is lacking. The latter feel that what they do has no real effect on what happens to them. The sense of being more or less vulnerable to external forces leads to a more guarded approach to social life. The view that their condition depends more on the decisions and actions of others than on their own renders people more concerned with others' motives. It increases the likelihood of suspiciousness and distrust. This is what the survey results show: 21 per cent of those who feel they have a great deal of control over the way their lives turn out are trustful of others, compared to only 6 per cent of those who have little or no sense of control.

There is also a relationship between socio-economic status (education and income combined) and sense of control over one's condition: 37 per cent and 55 per cent in the lower and higher echelons, respectively – a difference of eighteen percentage points. With class self-identification, the difference is much larger: thirty-two percentage points. This difference is so pronounced that we could almost say that, to a large extent, the sense of control over one's life is what determines class identification.

Similar results were found in the United States. Francis Fukuyama summarizes an analysis of survey data (carried out at the National Opinion Research Center, associated with the University of Chicago) which found that the lack of trust correlates with, among other factors, low socio-economic status, minority status, and traumatic life events.[22] The latter refers to being a victim of crime and being in poor health. Such experiences can foster a low sense of control over events.

Finally, the occupational field in which people work may be of some importance. The level of trust is 26 per cent in health and social services and 23 per cent in education, compared to about 18 per cent in other fields, except agriculture, fishing, and logging where it is only 8 per cent. The professional training in health, social services, and education may promote a high sense of responsibility, although the differences are not pronounced. Because the lack of expertise of clients makes them vulnerable, there is a need to develop trust in the relationships with them. In addition, the outcome of teaching, of social services, and of health treatments depends in part on the existence of trust in the professional relationship. Thus, nurturing trust becomes a requirement for professional effectiveness. There may be a selection factor as well. People who are more trusting because of their childhood and youth experience may have a somewhat higher propensity to orient themselves in fields involving the socialization and care of others.

It was noted in an earlier chapter that trust does not easily cross religious, political, and moral boundaries. This is so at all levels of education and of class self-identification, which is surprising since the usual stereotype is that more educated people are more tolerant or accepting of ideological and moral differences. They may be more tolerant but, if this is the case, trust does not seem to follow automatically.

The reason may have to do with the difference between the private and public spheres of social life. It may be that tolerance refers to attitudes and behaviour in public life – to the view that public institutions must accommodate the social and cultural differences in the population, and that all have a right to their distinctive identities. Trust, on the other hand, is an element in transactions between groups and individuals. One may accept the presence of others but not be willing to engage in social exchanges with them. Tolerance as a public commitment does not necessarily imply trust in social transactions.

Generally, the level of distrust in vertical relationships tends to decrease with higher positions in the socio-economic hierarchy, as indicated by class self-identification. Those in the upper levels are less distrustful than those who see themselves in the lower echelons. The relationship is quite strong in the case of businessmen: from 59 per cent in the lower class to 41 per cent in the upper and upper-middle classes. In the case of politicians, both federal and provincial, the level of distrust is about equally high in the lower to the middle classes but decreases in the upper and upper-middle classes. That is to say, people who are closer to businessmen and politicians in class position tend to distrust them less than those who are socially distant from them. In short, the level of trust and distrust varies with social class, especially class self-identification, a pattern that suggests *a substantial split between social classes.*

The life circumstances of the different social classes have an important impact on the level of trust. Indeed, the findings indicate that trust is associated with positive, and distrust with negative, life circumstances and experiences. In the words of Trudy Govier, "those who lead a safe, middle-class lifestyle in a relatively affluent and ordered society might benefit by 'trusting more' ... People whose social experience features harshness, poverty, discrimination, abuse, brutality ... are likely to gain an experience of the world that produces increased wariness, fear, a sense of vulnerability ..."[23] This experience also produces

Table 8   The Higher the Social Standing the Greater the Feeling of Being at Home in the Local Community and the Society

Socio-economic Status	Percent Who Feel at Home in		Class Self-identification	Percent Who Feel at Home in	
	Community	Society		Community	Society
Upper	61	51	Upper	67	65
Upper Middle	58	46	Upper Middle	63	55
Lower Middle	59	44	Lower Middle	59	43
Working	56	42	Working	54	42
Lower	51	37	Lower	41	27

a substantial distrust of others and particularly, as seen in chapter 6, institutional leaders.

Certain kinds of labour-market experiences can also undermine trust. The emerging new economy emphasizes the short term, which means that young persons with some college education can expect to change jobs several times during their career. They may have to change their skills as well. Such a situation can undermine trust, loyalty, and commitment. Francis Fukuyama notes that "as a result of downsizing, white-collar managers and blue-collar types no longer trust each other."[24]

BELONGING

Social-class affiliation makes a difference in the feeling of being at home in the community and in the society (Table 8). This is so both with the position in the socio-economic structure, as indicated by the combined level of education and income, and with class self-identification. Those at the top of the social hierarchy are more likely to feel very much at home in both their local communities and in the larger society than those at the lowest echelon. This is especially the case with the subjective measure of social-class affiliation and the sense of being at home in this society: those who see themselves in the higher echelons are particularly less likely to feel alienated from the society than those who perceive themselves at the lower levels: 65 per cent compared to 27 per cent, a difference of thirty-eight percentage points.

It was seen earlier that people at different levels of the socio-economic structure differ in the extent to which they experience fairness of personal treatment and recognition of their contribution to society. They also feel differently about the extent to which they control the way their lives turn out. This, of course, does not mean that none of the high income or well-educated respondents experience unfairness, lack of recognition for the contribution their class makes to society, or a low sense of control. Some do at all levels of the social hierarchy, but more do at the lower levels.

It would seem that these three factors explain in part why social class is related to the sense of belonging. This is because social-class position shapes to a significant degree a person's experience of community and society and this, in turn, affects the sense of belonging.

INDEBTEDNESS TO SOCIETY

The respondents at the lowest and highest echelons of the socio-economic hierarchy are somewhat more likely to feel indebted to society than those in-between, 33 per cent and 37 per cent compared to about 28 per cent. It should be noted, however, that there is no relationship with class self-identification except that those in the highest categories are a little more likely to feel socially indebted than those at all other levels. In short, the sense of social indebtedness is not strongly related to the position occupied in the socio-economic hierarchy.

Fairness, recognition of the contribution to society, and family economic condition seem to make more of a difference. Indeed, those who feel advantaged in these regards are more likely to feel indebted to society than those who experience disadvantage:

- 38 per cent of those who feel that their social class is treated very fairly, compared to 27 per cent of those who feel that it is not treated at all fairly, agree that all owe something to society;
- 43 per cent of those who are very satisfied with the recognition received by their educational class for its contribution to society are more likely to agree that everyone owes something to society compared to 29 per cent of those who are dissatisfied;
- 38 per cent of those whose economic evolution has been very positive are more likely to feel socially indebted in comparison with 28 per cent of those whose financial situation has been negative.

These findings indicate, on the one hand, that the sense of indebtedness to society depends not so much on the position occupied in the social hierarchy as on the way in which one is treated in the society as a member of a particular class. On the other hand, they suggest a certain sense of *noblesse oblige* among some in the upper echelon of the class structure. This second point has been discussed earlier (in Chapter 8).

SOCIAL OBLIGATIONS

Generally, it can be expected that the obligation to help will depend on the extent of personal resources as indicated by the level of education and of income – that is, people who have more resources or means at their disposal will be more likely to have a strong sense of social oblig- ation. This expectation is met in a limited way. First, the data show a positive relationship between socio-economic status and social obliga- tion only with regard to friends: 64 per cent of those of high compared to 52 per cent of those of low socio-economic status feel strongly oblig- ated to help their friends, a difference of twelve percentage points.

Second, there is little variation across socio-economic levels in the propensity to feel very strongly obligated to help family or any person in society who needs help, except that it is slightly lower among those of high status.

Third, in the case of the obligation to help people "in the same boat" in life or people from the same ethnocultural or racial background, the relationship is directly opposite to our expectations: respondents in the *lower* echelons are more likely than those in the higher echelons of the socio-economic ladder to express a strong sense of obligation to help. In the case of people "in the same boat" in life, the difference is 19 per cent; it is 8 per cent in the case of people from the same ethnic, cul- tural, or racial background.

These findings suggest a certain degree of class solidarity. People who are in the less advantaged levels of the socio-economic system are significantly more likely to feel strongly obligated vis-à-vis those who face the same or similar problems or difficulties in life: hence the greater sense of obligation to people "in the same boat" in life among those in the lower than among those in the higher position in the social hierarchy.

But the opposite is the case for the sense of obligation to friends: the higher the social position, the more frequent the sense of obligation. For instance, much useful information about opportunities, useful social contacts, and other matters is obtained from friends. Such exchanges create mutual obligations. Is it possible that such "net- working" and exchanges are more important at the higher than at the lower levels of the socio-economic system? If so, it could, in part, explain the positive relationship between social class and the sense of obligation to friends.[25]

Corresponding to personal resources is the pressure of personal needs. And we do indeed find that those who feel so hard-pressed to take care of their own needs that they worry less about the needs of others are less likely to feel obligated to help others (Table 9). This is

Table 9   The Pressure of Personal Needs Decreases the Sense of Obligation to Help Others

Help Should Be Given to	Percent Who Have Strong Sense of Personal Obligation by Pressure of Personal Needs			
	Very Strongly Pressed	←		Not Pressed at All
Family	83	86	89	92
Friends	56	56	59	71
People in Same Boat in Life	30	27	28	42
People of Same Ethnic/ Cultural/Racial Group	22	17	16	22
Anyone in need	29	29	39	52

what we observe for all types of social relations, except those with people of the same ethnic, cultural, or racial background.

The pressure of personal needs was frequently mentioned in the in-depth interviews by those who felt that compassion was declining in our society:

"It is because of the insecurity that we experience as individuals. We are not sure if we will have work; we are sure of nothing. We are less open to give." (Montreal, Que.)

"Maybe to some extent, as the individuals at the upper end of the socio-economic spectrum are finding themselves less secure. If you know you don't have to worry about your own future then you can spend time worrying about others. If you have to worry about your immediate responsibilities, your family, then you have less time and energy for others. I don't think that means that people care less but they have less to do it with." (Toronto, Ont.)

There are, however, personal needs that are related not to insecurity but to a self-imposed lifestyle: "The more you are involved with people, the more you will let compassion rule, but I think that an increasing number of people are so busy that they don't let themselves get involved. People are so busy going to fitness class, courses, etc ... You don't have the compassion because you don't have the friendships with the people and it is easier to ignore that your neighbour has a need" (Pembroke, Ont.). A number of respondents express the view that the decline of compassion is temporary. Compassion is always there and will eventually resurface: "[Compassion is declining] mainly because these are difficult years due to the economic and world contexts. A lot of unemployment; new technologies also create a lot of unemployment. There is a malaise. I think this is a normal reaction. It is temporary. The idea of mutual help and of sharing is always there" (Rivière-du-Loup, Que.).

COMMUNAL CONTRIBUTIONS

The relationship between position in the socio-economic structure and communal activities is examined separately with education, income, and class self-identification. The reason for this is that only education makes a difference. Among those with the highest level of education 42 per cent engage in communal activities, compared to 31 per cent of those with the lowest level. However, there is little difference between people with different levels of income and those who see themselves as located at different levels in the class hierarchy. Those at a high level of education are also more likely to feel that they are *not* helping as much as they should either through an organization and/or on their own: 42 per cent compared to 26 per cent.

Financial contributions, on the other hand, are strongly related to the level of income, as could be expected. People at the high level of income are *more* likely to donate to an organization or a cause than those at the lowest level – a dfference of twenty-eight percentage points. However, those with high incomes are *less* likely than those with low incomes to feel that they are giving as much as they should. This is so for donations to either religious or non-religious organizations, with differences of fourteen and eighteen percentage points, respectively.

Although those with low incomes donate less than those with high incomes, they are more likely to help others informally. It seems that people with relatively high incomes tend to choose donations while those with less income tend to choose informal help as their form of communal contribution.[26] Thus, the nature of the contribution depends in part on the amount of resources at their disposal – money in one case, time and energy in the other.

People are more or less pressed by their needs and those of their families. Indeed, 46 per cent of the respondents agreed (11 per cent strongly) that *"these days, I am so hard-pressed to take care of my own needs that I worry less about the needs of others."* An indication of this reality is provided by a study by the Vanier Institute of the Family based on 1992 Statistics Canada data. The study reports that "the average family has to work 77 weeks a year just to pay the bills. For the one-third of families with the lowest incomes, it jumps to 83.6

weeks. Since there are only 52 weeks in a year, it means most families have to rely on more than one wage earner."[27]

Not surprisingly, those who feel hard-pressed by their own needs – whose personal resources are exhausted by their own needs and those of their families – are much less likely to be frequent contributors: only 23 per cent of those who feel strongly that they are hard-pressed, compared to 56 per cent who feel the opposite are frequent contributors.

HIGHLIGHTS

We may summarize as follows:

- The perception and experience of fairness are substantially more likely to be positive the higher the position occupied in the socio-economic hierarchy. However, even among those in the higher echelons, a large proportion *do not* make an entirely positive evaluation, either of the system in general or of the way it treats them.
- The view that in our society there are two sets of rules – one for those who have money and one for everyone else – is strongly related to position in the class system. It is much more frequent in the lower than in the higher echelons, but even among the latter the level of agreement is quite high.
- About three out of ten are dissatisfied with the recognition that people with their level of education or training are receiving for their contribution to society, a pattern that is found at all levels of education (except the elementary level). Only one out of ten declare themselves "very satisfied." About one-third feel that the degree of recognition for the contribution of their educational class has declined in recent years.
- The level of distrust, that is, the feeling that people should be careful about trusting others since there are too many who only seek to benefit themselves, decreases as we go up the socio-economic ladder.
- At all levels of education and of class self-identification, there is the same low level of trust of those who differ in their religious, political, and moral beliefs or values. This challenges the stereotype that the more educated people are more tolerant or accepting of ideological and moral differences.
- Generally, the level of distrust in vertical relationships – with employers, businessmen, federal and provincial politicians – tends to decrease as we go up the socio-economic hierarchy.
- Those at the top of the social hierarchy are more likely to feel very much at home in both their local communities and in the larger society than those at the lowest echelon.

- The sense of social indebtedness is not strongly related to the position occupied in the socio-economic hierarchy. What seems to make more of a difference is advantage or disadvantage with regard to fairness, recognition of the contribution to society, and family economic condition.
- There is a positive relationship between socio-economic status and social obligation only with regard to friends. The reverse is observed in the case of the obligation to help people "in the same boat" in life or people from the same ethnocultural or racial background.
- Those in the higher levels of the socio-economic structure are more likely to engage in communal activities than those at the lower levels. Individuals with more personal resources contribute more. They are also more likely to feel that they are *not* helping as much as they should either through an organization or on their own.
- The higher the income, the greater the likelihood of financial donations. However, income level is only weakly related to the other two forms of communal contribution, namely, helping through an organization and informal help. People with relatively high incomes appear more likely to choose donations while those with less income tend to choose informal help as their primary form of communal contribution.

of several publications
of the interview I did with you,
about 1999. It's a pretty mediocre book
but I thought you might find it interesting
nonetheless.

Hope to see you soon.

Paul

15

Inter-provincial Differences

Of the many sources of regional differentiation, the two that are associated with serious and far-reaching inequalities derive from the economic and political situation of regions ... The distributive and redistributive means at the disposal of government can be used to protect regional diversity and to re-channel the allocation of resources and rewards for the equalization of regional opportunities. While the results may still be imperfect ... efforts in this direction are extremely important to prevent building up serious regional grievances. (Mildred A. Schwartz, *Politics and Territory*, 1974, 335)

Provinces differ from one another in many ways, such as in size, natural environment and resources, degree of urbanization, ethnic composition, industrial base, level of unemployment, average income, and political culture. They have access to somewhat different natural resources. They all have a unique history with regard to patterns of settlement, economic development, and political evolution. Their economic and political power in the federation is quite uneven and as a result they have different relations with the central government and with each other.

Over the years, a number of federal government policies have been criticized as restricting or damaging the economic development of a given province or as favouring the development of other provinces, particularly Quebec and Ontario. On the other hand, there have been complaints from the "have" provinces that their contribution to the national institutions and to the regional redistribution of revenues is such that it puts damaging constraints on their own provincial programs.

The differences between regions of the country in the conditions – environmental, socio-economic, demographic, and policy-related – to which they are subjected suggest the possibility of social fragmentation along regional lines. There is also political fragmentation, as indicated by party support in different parts of the country in the recent federal elections. The Canadian Alliance is strong in the west but weak or almost non-existent in the other provinces; the Bloc Québécois exists only in Quebec; the Liberals are very strong in central Canada; the Conservative and New Democratic parties receive relatively little support, mostly from the Maritimes and the western provinces.

Given these circumstances, it is important to explore the possibility of provincial or regional fragmentation along the basic dimensions of the social fabric: fairness, recognition, social and institutional trust, the sense of belonging, social obligations, and contributions. This is the focus of the present chapter.

FAIRNESS

"Have" and "have not" are part of the language used to talk about provinces. Provincial economies do not benefit or suffer in the same ways and to the same extent from global economic changes and technological innovations; the groups and interests that wield political influence are not entirely the same in all provinces; federal policies and programs do not impinge in the same ways on the conditions in all provinces. There are considerable differences among provinces in average income, level of unemployment, and percentage below the poverty line. In the period from 1982 to 1994, there was significantly more inequality in earnings in the Atlantic provinces than in the other provinces. In Alberta and British Columbia, inequality was about at the same as the national average, while in Ontario, Quebec, and Saskatchewan it was slightly below that average. Manitoba had the least inequality, its rate being further below the national average.[1]

This was the situation in 1994. But there are variations in the extent to which inequalities have been growing or declining over time. The inter-provincial differences for *changes* in the degree of inequality are not the same as those for simple inequality. Since 1982, inequality in earnings has grown in four provinces: Newfoundland, Nova Scotia, Alberta, and British Columbia. It has been declining in four other provinces: Prince Edward Island, New Brunswick, Ontario, and Manitoba. And it has remained stable in Quebec and Saskatchewan.

We can thus expect variations in the assessment of fairness across provinces. In fact, our findings reveal some variations on this point, but these variations do not entirely correspond with the above ranking on the basis of inequality in earnings (Figure 24a: the four eastern provinces have been combined because of the small sample sizes in each).

The percentage who think that our society is basically fair for most people varies from 24 percent in Quebec to 55 percent in British Columbia. It is the highest in three of the four western provinces. Manitoba is the exception, which is surprising in view of the fact that it is

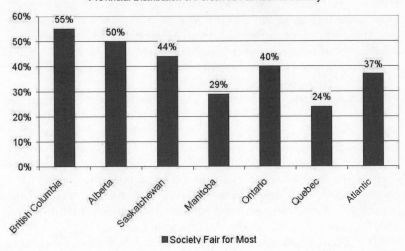

Figure 24a
Provincial Distribution of Perceived Fairness of Society

■ Society Fair for Most

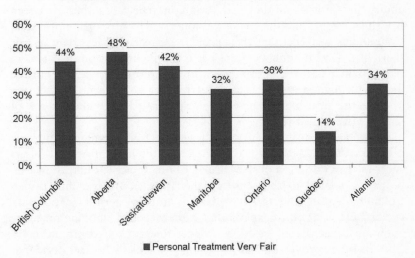

Figure 24b
Provinicial Distribution of Perceived Fairness of Personal Treatment

■ Personal Treatment Very Fair

the province with the lowest level of inequality and, moreover, with decreasing inequality. The Atlantic provinces should have the lowest percentage, but in fact they show the third-highest percentage, close to what is found in Ontario. Quebec has about the same level of inequality as Ontario, yet it shows a much lower percentage.

Similar results obtain with the assessment of the fairness of one's personal treatment in the society (Figure 24b). The favourable judgment is the highest in three of the western provinces: between 42 per cent and 48 per cent in Saskatchewan, Alberta, and British Columbia-believe that they are being treated very fairly. The percentage is the lowest in Quebec (14 per cent) and between 32 per cent and 36 per cent in the other provinces.

If we consider the relationship between the level of income and the judgments about fairness, we find the expected pattern. In each region,[2] except Quebec, the percentage who feel that our society is fair for most increases with the level of income. In Quebec, the percentage who express a positive evaluation of fairness not only starts lower but does not increase as much as in the other parts of the country. The curve is flatter. The same can be observed with the evaluation of the fairness of the treatment received personally. Clearly, in that province, other factors are at play in the assessment of fairness.

The evaluations may be related, for instance, to the perception that one's province is or is not receiving its fair share of federal-government funding.[3] But this does not appear to be the case. Indeed, there is essentially only one important inter-provincial difference in the judgment about the fairness of the distribution of federal funding: between British Columbia and the rest of the country. The proportion of British Columbians who feel that their province is receiving less than its fair share of federal funding is, at 51 per cent, the highest but it is also in that province that the percentage who feel that our society is fair for most is the highest (55 per cent). Alberta, with 46 per cent, is where we observe the next-highest percentage dissatisfied with their share of federal-government funding.

Thus, variations in the proportion who feel disadvantaged in terms of federal funding cannot explain much of the inter-provincial differences in the evaluation of the fairness of our society. It may, however, be partly related to the sense of alienation in Alberta and British Columbia. As an Alberta MP explained, "this Western alienation talk is real." He went on to explain that westerners are "looking for more autonomy, they're looking for a stronger role in Confederation."[4]

In all other provinces, the percentage of those who feel disadvantaged in terms of federal funding varies between 34 and 39. In the country as a whole, almost 40 per cent feel that their province receives *less* than its fair share of federal money. Not quite half (46 per cent) think that their province receives more than or about its fair share.[5] People with different levels of education and of income make essentially the same evaluation.

In addition, there are few sizable inter-provincial variations in the perceptions of fairness with regard to gender, ethnicity, or social class. In all except one province, between 31 per cent and 36 per cent consider that their gender has fewer job opportunities than the other. The exception is Saskatchewan, where the proportion is slightly higher at 39 per cent.

The same can be said about job opportunities for ethnic and racial groups. In all but two provinces, about one in five feel that members of their ethnic or racial group have fewer job opportunities than other groups. The proportions are somewhat higher in Ontario and Manitoba, with 29 per cent and 35 per cent, respectively.

Respondents in Ontario and Quebec (33 per cent and 32 per cent) are the most likely to feel that their social class is not treated fairly. But again the difference with the other provinces is not large: 27 per cent in the Atlantic provinces, 28 per cent in Alberta, and between 21 per cent and 25 per cent in the three other provinces.

RECOGNITION OF CONTRIBUTION TO SOCIETY

The level of satisfaction with the recognition of the contribution to society tends to be lower in Quebec than in most other provinces (Figure 25). Specifically, in Quebec, only one in ten are very satisfied with the recognition of the social contribution of their ethnocultural group. In the other provinces, the percentage varies between 19 and 28, which means that it is twice and sometimes three times as large as in Quebec

The pattern is the same with the satisfaction with the recognition received by one's gender for its social contribution: 9 per cent in Quebec compared to 15 or 16 per cent in the other provinces. Finally, with regard to the contribution of one's educational class, the level of satisfaction is again lower in Quebec than in the other provinces, except Manitoba. The inter-provincial differences, however, are fairly small here: 8 per cent in Quebec and Manitoba compared to between 12 per cent and 14 per cent in the other provinces.

Thus, the difference in the level of satisfaction between Quebec and the other regions is more pronounced with regard to the contribution to society of the cultural group than of the other two social categories (gender and educational level). The differences are of fifteen percentage points in the first case, of four and six in the other two.

The aspiration to be recognized as a contributor rather than as a problem or a burden is also, we believe, partly what underlies the "distinct society" controversy. Indeed, it could be argued that the problem is not that Quebec francophones do not get recognition as a society or as a culturally distinct people, but rather that they do not get the

Figure 25
Satisfaction with Recognition of Group Contribution to Society by Province

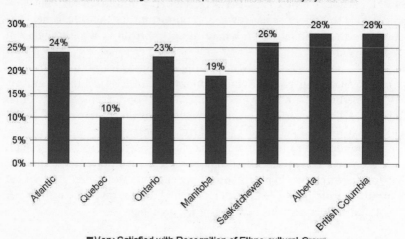

■ Very Satisfied with Recognition of Ethno-cultural Group

appropriate kind of recognition for whatever positive contributions they have made historically and continue to make today to Canadian society. The wish to be recognized as a "founding people" is partly a claim for the recognition of what has been contributed to the building of the society.

Many English-speaking Canadians claim that they do recognize the distinct character of French Quebec. And indeed, the majority probably do. But at the same time, many see that community as "out there" in its own territory, doing its own thing and having little to do with the rest of the country, except making demands on it and failing to acknowledge the support provided. Of course, the regular expressions of dissatisfaction and the regular demands do help to produce that feeling.

As a result, the relationship between Quebec and the "Rest of Canada" has tended to be defined in terms of gains and losses, one side perceiving primarily gains for the other and losses for itself. The recent political discourse has been such as to define Quebec as a burden instead of as a community contributing to the larger society. And the same is true of Quebec's view of the rest of the country. We think that one would be hard-pressed to find much in the public discourse that focuses on the positive contributions each part of the country is making to the society as a whole. The focus is largely on the negative.

It should be noted, however, that if the residents of Quebec tend to be less satisfied with the social recognition received, they are at the

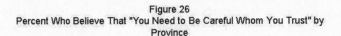

Figure 26
Percent Who Believe That "You Need to Be Careful Whom You Trust" by
Province

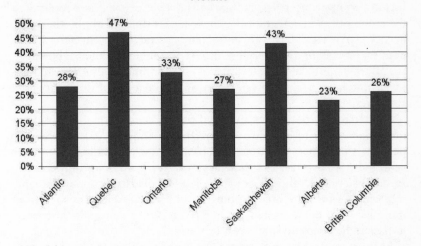

same time more likely to see an improvement in recent years. There is
little variation across the other provinces in the perception of change.
In addition, as with the level of *satisfaction*, the difference in *perceived
improvement* between Quebec and the other regions is more pronounced in the case of the contribution of the ethnocultural group than
of the two other social categories: a difference of ten percentage points
in the first case and of five in the cases of gender and educational level.

HORIZONTAL AND VERTICAL TRUST

Provinces can be grouped in three categories in terms of the level of
general social trust or distrust (see Figure 26). The percentage who
agree that individuals should be careful about trusting others since
there are too many people who seek to benefit only themselves is the
highest in Quebec (47 per cent) and in Saskatchewan (43 per cent); it
is intermediate in Ontario (33 per cent) and much lower in all other
provinces (between 23 per cent and 28 per cent).

As far as the fear of being taken advantage of by family, friends, and
fellow workers is concerned, the distribution is somewhat similar. The
level of trust tends to be lower in Quebec and Ontario than in the other
provinces, among which there is little variation. A possible explanation
for this could be the high level of urbanization in these two provinces.
But this does not seem to be the case since the level of trust is about the
same in large metropolitan areas as it is in smaller communities.

Trust in members of one's own ethnic, cultural, or racial group is about equally low in all provinces: only about one in ten declare a lot of within-group trust. Similarly, the level of trust in people with different political and moral beliefs and values is about the same across provinces. That is to say, it tends to be low in all parts of the country. Trust of people with different religious beliefs, however, tends to be low in Quebec, British Columbia, and Alberta, high in Saskatchewan, and intermediate in Ontario, Manitoba, and the Atlantic provinces.

Similar results obtain with vertical trust. Provincial politicians are a little more likely to be distrusted in Quebec and the Atlantic area (75 per cent and 74 per cent) than they are in Ontario and the west (67 per cent and 68 per cent). But these are not very pronounced differences. In the case of federal politicians, the level of distrust is about the same in all parts of the country. Employers and businessmen are somewhat more likely to be distrusted in Quebec and less likely to be distrusted in Saskatchewan than in the rest of the country.

In short, even though there are some variations in the level of trust, both horizontal and vertical, across provinces, it is difficult to see a systematic pattern of differences, except perhaps in the case of Quebec. Indeed, whenever there are inter-provincial variations, the level of distrust is usually higher in Quebec.

BELONGING

The sense of feeling very much at home in the local community varies across the provinces (Figure 27). It is the lowest in central Canada, that is, Ontario (54 per cent) and Quebec (52 per cent), and is the highest in the Atlantic provinces and Saskatchewan (68 per cent and 67 per cent). The percentage for the other provinces falls in-between (about 60 per cent).

Similar results obtain with the feeling of being at home in this society. It is the lowest in Quebec (38 per cent)[6] which is followed by Manitoba and Ontario (45 per cent and 42 per cent). It is the highest in Saskatchewan (62 per cent) and in the other provinces it is between 48 percent and 52 percent.

SOCIAL INDEBTEDNESS, OBLIGATIONS, AND CONTRIBUTIONS

There are few systematic inter-provincial variations with regard to the sense of indebtedness, social obligations, and communal contributions. Three general observations can be made:

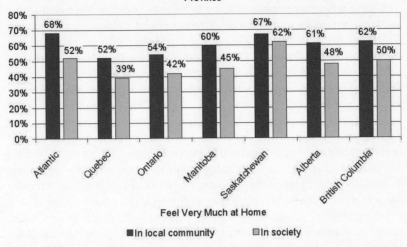

Figure 27
Persons Feeling Very Much at Home in Community and Society by
Province

Feel Very Much at Home

■In local community   ▢In society

- First, as with several of the previous social dimensions considered, the relative frequency of social indebtedness, the obligation to help others, and communal contributions tends to be lower in Quebec than in other parts of the country.
- Second, the sense of obligation to help others tends to be higher in the Atlantic provinces than in the rest of the country, whatever the type of social relationships.
- Third, the high level of communal contributions is the most frequent in the Atlantic region (45 per cent) and in the western provinces (between 45 per cent and 60 per cent). It is the least frequent in Quebec (30 per cent), with Ontario falling in-between (37 per cent).

The regional differences could be due to the fact that the composition of the populations is different. For instance, Protestants are more likely to contribute than Catholics. Is it possible that Quebec is low in communal contributions because there are more Catholics in Quebec?

In order to examine this possibility and similar possibilities for other categories of people, comparisons have been made between people in Quebec and in the western provinces, that is, in the *region with the lowest and the highest* proportion of high contributors. The social categories considered are age, size of community of residence, home language,[7] country of birth, religious affiliation, self-assessed religiosity, socio-economic position, class self-identification, fairness of personal treatment, and whether or not paying taxes is seen as an adequate social contribution.

With a few exceptions, we find a difference between Quebec and the western provinces in all of the different social categories considered. That is to say, Catholics in the west are more likely to be frequent contributors than Catholics in Quebec; similarly for Protestants. The very religious in the west contribute more frequently than those in Quebec. Both anglophones and allophones in the west are more likely to contribute than anglophones and allophones in Quebec; and so on. There are only two exceptions. There is little difference between the two regions among those who identify as lower class and among those who feel that they are not treated fairly in our society.

There are hypotheses as to why the proportion of active contributors is lower in Quebec than in other parts of the country in virtually all social categories. Gary Caldwell, for example, claims that it is a manifestation of a weaker civil society in Quebec, which in turn is the result of economic stagnation, the destabilization of the family as an institution, and the omni-presence of the state bureaucracy.[8] Another theory, specifically with regard to financial donations, is stated by André Verret, president of the Centre québécois de Philantropie. Verret holds that fundraising is less organized and professionalized in Quebec than in other parts of the country: "There are now (1993) 125 fundraising organizations in Quebec compared to 2,500 in Ontario."[9] This may be seen as another manifestation of a less developed civil society.

HIGHLIGHTS

To recapitulate:

- The percentage who think that society is basically fair for most people is the highest in three of the four western provinces (Manitoba being the exception). The percentage is the lowest in Quebec and in-between in the other provinces. Similar results obtain with the assessment of the fairness of one's personal treatment in the society.
- In the country as a whole, almost four out of ten feel that their province receives *less* than its fair share of federal-government funding, which means that many feel that other provinces are getting *more* than their fair share.
- There is essentially only one important inter-provincial difference with regard to the distribution of federal funding: British Columbians are more likely than the residents of other provinces to feel that they are receiving less than their fair share.

- There are few important inter-provincial variations in the perceptions of job opportunities by gender, ethnicity, or race and treatment of one's social class.
- The level of satisfaction with the recognition of the contribution to society tends to be lower in Quebec than in most of the other provinces. The difference between Quebec and the other regions is more pronounced with regard to the contribution of the cultural group than with that of the other two social categories, namely, gender and educational level.
- The percentage who think that individuals should be careful about trusting others since there are too many people who seek only to benefit themselves is the highest in Quebec and in Saskatchewan, intermediate in Ontario, and low in all other provinces.
- Whenever there are inter-provincial variations, the level of distrust is usually higher in Quebec. In some cases it is also high in another province; sometimes not. This is so for general social distrust but also for distrust of family, friends, and fellow workers; people with different religious beliefs; provincial politicians; and employers and businessmen.
- The level of trust is low in all provinces in relation to members of one's own ethnic, cultural, or racial group; people with different political and moral beliefs and values; and federal politicians.
- The sense of feeling very much at home in the local community is the lowest in Ontario and Quebec. It is the highest in the Atlantic provinces and in Saskatchewan, the other provinces falling in-between.
- Similar results obtain with the feeling of being at home in the society. It is the lowest in Quebec and the highest in Saskatchewan; the other provinces rank in-between.
- The relative frequency of social indebtedness, the obligation to help others, and communal contributions tends to be lower in Quebec than in other parts of the country.
- The sense of obligation to help others tends to be higher in the Atlantic provinces than in the rest of the country, whatever the type of social relationships.
- A high level of communal contributions is most frequently observed in the Atlantic and western provinces and the least frequently in Quebec. Ontario falls in-between.

16

Conclusion: The Extent of Social Fragmentation

The second part of the analysis presented in the last four chapters attempted to *identify lines of fragmentation* between groups or social categories in our society. This was done by trying to see if some groups or segments of the population have positive experiences while others have negative experiences along five dimensions of the social fabric. The idea is that such clustering of perceptions and social experiences would reveal the existence of "fault lines" in the social fabric.

In the first section of this chapter, the findings of the previous chapters will be reviewed in order to assess the extent to which there is clustering with regard to gender, ethnicity and race, social class, and province of residence. The existence of more or less extensive clustering along those lines of social differentiation would indicate social fragmentation and thus a fragile social fabric. In addition, findings concerning differences in political, moral, and religious beliefs and values will be discussed from the point of view of fragmentation.

The second section looks into the extent to which the perception of threats to the social fabric – that is, the perception of social fragility – varies along these four lines of social differentiation. Are all respondents about equally likely to perceive the social fabric as fragile or does the diagnosis vary between women and men, social classes, ethnic or racial categories, and provinces?

DO THE PERCEPTIONS AND EXPERIENCES INDICATE FRAGMENTATION?

To address the question of fragmentation along these possible lines of social cleavages, we will proceed somewhat differently for gender and social class than for ethnicity/race and province. The reason is that the first contains only two categories (women and men) and the second a set of ordered groupings (from low to high position in the socio-economic hierarchy). For these, percentage differences provide an indication of the degree of social fragmentation. The larger the differences in percentage points and the larger the number of dimensions along which there are differences, the more pronounced the degree of polarization. Since the other two, namely ethnicity/race and province, contain several non-ordered categories, the extent of fragmentation will be assessed by attempting to identify patterns of differences across the various categories.

Gender Differences

A gap between women and men exists on two dimensions: job opportunities and recognition for the contribution to society (Table 10). On both grounds, women are much more likely than men to feel disadvantaged. When the effects of social class, ethnicity, race, and province of residence are taken into account,[1] the gender difference with regard to both opportunities and recognition persists.[2] As seen earlier, a positive sign is that women are more likely than men to believe that the situation is improving. Thus, although the social fabric is fragmented along gender differences, and there are still grounds for discontent, the situation seems to be on the mend.

Social-class Differences

Table 10 also shows the percentage differences between those at the upper and lower levels of the socio-economic hierarchy for each of these perceptions and social experiences. These differences are quite large across almost all the dimensions considered. And the differences maintain themselves when we control for gender, ethnicity/race, and province of residence. It should also be noted that social class, measured objectively or subjectively, is more consistently related to the components of the social fabric considered than are gender, ethnicity/race, and province of residence.

Table 10   Perceptions and Experiences: Percentage Differences between Women and Men and between Upper and Lower Social Classes

Perception or experience	Gender	Social class[a]	Class self-identification
Our society not fair for most	4	31	26
Not personally treated very fairly	1	27	34
Fewer job opportunities	38	—	—
Unfair treatment of one's social class	—	15	51
Dissatisfied with recognition received for contribution to society	14	8	32
Recognition has declined in recent years	-9	3	22
Distrustful of others	-3	18	12
Distrustful of institutional leaders[b]	5	19	24
Not very much at home in community	2	5	22
Not very much at home in society	1	15	28
Some or a little sense of control	2	17	32
Negative evolution of financial situation	3	16	40

[a] Defined by level of education and of income.

[b] Institutional leaders include federal and provincial politicians and businessmen. Since the level of trust is fairly low for all three, a single index that includes responses to all of them has been constructed for the presentation of a summary of the results.

The largest percentage difference concerns the treatment of one's social class among people who see themselves at different socio-economic levels – fifty-one points. This is higher than what respondents report for their own personal treatment. In other words, a number of people seem to make a distinction between their own situation and that of the collectivities to which they belong.

When we look at the social class to which respondents feel they belong, rather than using an objective measure of class position based on the level of education and income, several of the differences are larger. This is not surprising since one would expect an interaction between what people experience in their social life and where they see themselves in the social hierarchy. However, if the objective and subjective measures of class are simultaneously taken into account, we find that *both* measures make a significant and independent difference with regard to the perceptions and experiences presented in Table 10.

Ethnocultural and Racial Differences

We have seen that respondents of western European origins are the most likely to make a positive assessment of the *fairness of our society* and of their personal treatment in it while members of visible minorities are the least likely to make such an assessment. In addition, we have observed that visible minorities and people classified as "other" are more likely to feel that members of their group have fewer *job opportunities* than others; that respondents of British, western, and southern European origins are more likely than those in any of the other categories to be very satisfied with the *recognition their group receives for its contribution to society*; that British and western European respondents are the least likely to be distrustful of others (as far as *trust* in specific types of social relationships – both social and institutional – is concerned, there are little variations from one ethnocultural category to another); and finally, that members of visible and of "other" minorities have the lowest *feeling of belonging* to their local communities and to the larger society. The sense of belonging in this society is the strongest among those of British and European origins.

These findings – which hold when gender, social class, and province of residence are taken into account – point to two cleavages in our society as far as ethnic or racial background is concerned:

- The deepest is between people of European background, on the one hand, and visible minorities and those of non-European origins, on the other.
- A less pronounced and less consistent one is between people of British and western European origins and all others.

(It should be noted that, given the limitation imposed by the size of the sample, quite broad categories of ethnic and racial affiliation had to be used. Some patterns of differences may have emerged if it had been possible to compare specific groups.)

Other findings, however, suggest a fairly low level of within-group solidarity: only one in ten are *very* confident that members of their own ethnic, cultural, or racial group will not take advantage of them. In addition, less than two out of ten declare a very strong obligation to help people of their own ethnic, cultural, or racial background. Such levels of within-group trust and sense of social obligation are consistent with the absence of social fragmentation along ethnocultural lines. Indeed, fragmentation and the accompanying social tensions would tend to increase the social attachments and commitments to one's group.

Inter-provincial Differences

There is only one important difference as far as the fairness of the distribution of federal funding is concerned: between British Columbia and all other provinces. However, it is significant that, in the country as a whole, almost 40 per cent feel that their province receives *less* than its fair share of federal money, which, in effect, means that many feel that other provinces are getting *more* than their fair share. This suggests a certain degree of inter-regional friction, especially when we note that the two provinces where this percentage is the highest are British Columbia and Alberta. We do not know which provinces *are seen* as getting more than their fair share, but if the same province or provinces tend to be so targeted, it would indicate a potentially serious line (or lines) of fragmentation.

There are inter-provincial variations on the components of the social fabric considered, but there is little clustering of differences along particular provincial lines. The level of distrust is usually higher in Quebec, but, depending on the type of social relation considered, it is also high in other provinces. The distrust of institutional leaders is relatively high in four provinces, moderate in three, and low in two. There are *no* important inter-provincial variations in the perceptions of job opportunities by gender, ethnicity, or race. The same is observed for the perception of the fairness of treatment of the social class to which one belongs. The sense of feeling very much at home in the local community is the lowest in Quebec but also in Ontario; it is the highest in the Atlantic provinces and in Saskatchewan.

The perceived unfairness in the allocation of federal funding suggests a tension between the west and other regions of the country. However, the only *clustering* of differences occurs along the Quebec – "Rest of Canada" divide: the percentage who think that our society is fair for most and who feel that they are personally treated fairly is the lowest in Quebec; the level of satisfaction with the recognition of the contribution to society is lower in Quebec than in most other provinces, especially with regard to the contribution to society of the cultural group; and it is also in Quebec that the feeling of being at home in this society is the lowest.

This clustering is quite similar to the one observed along the linguistic cleavage. Francophones are among those who are the least likely to make a positive assessment of the fairness of our society and of the way they are treated personally. Moreover, francophones are the least likely to be very satisfied with the recognition received for the contribution to society of their cultural group and they are also less likely than anglophones to feel very much at home in this society. This last difference, however, exists only if they are dissatisfied with the recognition that their group receives for its societal contribution. If they are satisfied, they are equally likely to feel a strong sense of belonging.

It should perhaps be emphasized that the three dimensions on which there is clustering are fairness, recognition of the contribution to society, and the sense of belonging. Of all the dimensions considered, it is arguably these three that are the most critical ingredients of the cement that can hold Quebec and the rest of Canada together.

Differences in Beliefs and Values

A result that is quite significant in relation to the strength of the social fabric – and one that we did not anticipate – is the distrust across boundaries of beliefs and values, whether religious, political, or moral. Few Canadians trust those whom they see as ideological – religious or moral – "strangers." Such differences in beliefs and values constitute social boundaries that seem to prevent the emergence of trust and thus represent a possible threat to the social covenant. This is critical given the diversity of the Canadian population in terms of religious affiliation, religious liberalism or fundamentalism, political ideology, life style, moral liberalism or conservatism, and so on. It would be important to find out in future research if these cleavages correspond to other differences considered here.

SOCIAL CLEAVAGES AND
THE PERCEPTION OF FRAGILITY

As noted earlier, Canadians sense a high potential for fragility in the social fabric. Perceived threats to the society, however, appear unrelated to some of the major social cleavages in Canada. Whether one speaks English, French, or another language in the home does not increase the likelihood of more or less concern. Being unemployed does not substantially differentiate people. Although it makes intuitive sense that the ideological positions of our political parties and/or religious groups might shape the world-view of Canadians, political affiliation, party preference, and religious identification make little or no difference. Not even how religious one perceives oneself to be makes a significant difference to the number of potential problems one sees in Canadian society.

Like the general population, at least 60 per cent of the members of most ethnic and racial groups perceive a high level of threat to the Canadian social fabric. There are no significant patterns of relationship between ethnicity, race and/or immigrant status, and perceived threats to the social fabric. The propensity to view society as more fragile is somewhat higher for:

- older Canadians, who are far more likely than those aged eighteen to twenty-four to perceive society as fragile, the progression being steady from younger to older age categories (from 58 per cent to 68 per cent);
- persons living in communities of under 5,000 people – 72 per cent as compared to 58 per cent of those living in communities of 100,000–900,000 and 60 per cent for cities whose population is under 100,000 or over 1,000,000; and
- those who work for others – 66 per cent compared to 57 per cent for the self-employed.

Of the various lines of social differentiation considered in the first part of this chapter, we find that gender and ethnicity or race make little difference: men and women and members of the different ethno-cultural categories are about equally likely to see a low, medium, or high number of potential problems with our society.[3] The strongest relationships are to occupation and to the social class with which respondents are affiliated, as indicated whether by their levels of education and income or by their own self-identification. The association between these variables and the extent to which the social fabric appears to be at risk is clear.

First, the work one does is telling. Unskilled workers, technicians, and tradesmen are far more likely to register a larger number of issues of concern than professionals. Owners and administrators of small businesses are one of the few groups where the majority of respondents (54 per cent) fall into either the low or medium category on the fragility index.

The association between class identification and a high level of concern for the social fabric is practically linear.[4] Just slightly more than half of upper-class respondents rank high in their perception of social fragility. The number rises to nearly three-quarters for those who identify with the lower class. And there are steady increases for middle- and working-class individuals in-between.

CONCLUSION:
THE IMPACT OF STRUCTURED LIFE EXPERIENCE

The findings presented in the first part of this chapter suggest a degree of social fragmentation along lines of class, ethnicity, race, gender, province of residence, and beliefs and values. There are, however, differences in the degree to which this is the case. It seems that it is along class lines that the fragmentation is the most pronounced. Also, it is along class lines that fragmentation is observed for all the components of the social fabric. For the other lines of social differentiation – gender, ethnicity, and province – there is less consistency in the sense that fragmentation exists only along some of the dimensions considered. The second set of findings show that the perceived degree of social fragility – defined as the number of perceived problems faced by our society – also varies depending on the social groups or categories to which people belong.

The ways in which these lines of social differentiation play themselves out on the social stage is, of course, complex. Individuals belong simultaneously to different social categories. For example, there are people of different ethnocultural background at the various levels of the social-class structure. And they do not all live in the same province of the country. Multiple-group affiliations would tend to reduce or prevent social fragmentation since the different social attachments and interests of individuals cut across the lines of social differentiation.

However, we also know that people are not randomly distributed across the different social groupings. Certain ethnic minorities are more frequently found in the lower levels of the socio-economic hierarchy while others are, given their proportion in the population, over-represented in the upper echelons. The same is true for men and women and for residents of different regions of the country. Thus, the more pronounced the overlapping of social boundaries, the more cumulative is the impact of the distribution of social advantages and disadvantages. The clustering of differences observed along the Quebec – "Rest of Canada" divide is partly the result of the cumulative impact of overlapping group affiliations.

Thus, our analysis of the impact of social differentiation shows that, in some regards, it increases and in others it decreases fragmentation. However, what our analysis shows is that, irrespective of these impacts, the social cleavages examined all have an independent import on the strength of the social fabric – independent in the sense that their effect is maintained when the influence of the others is controlled.

Such results are not surprising. Indeed, people differentially located in the social and economic structure face different life conditions, have access to different opportunities, are exposed to different kinds of constraints, and can mobilize different amounts of financial, social, and personal resources in constructing their lives. Thus, the degree of control people believe they have over the outcome of their lives and the feeling that their family's financial status is satisfactory and evolving positively or negatively are strongly related to their reporting of negative experiences or dissatisfaction with regard to fairness, recognition of one's contribution to society, trust, and social belonging. The propensity to claim a greater potential for problems in society is also

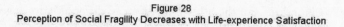

Figure 28
Perception of Social Fragility Decreases with Life-experience Satisfaction

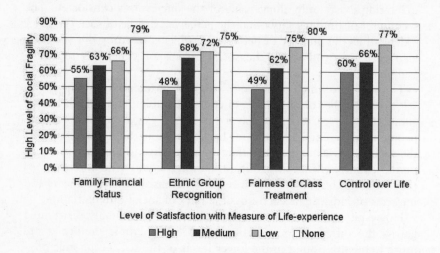

directly related to the sense of control and the assessment of one's financial situation.

For the same reason, perceptions and experiences along the various components of the social fabric are related to the identification of threat to our society. For instance, dissatisfaction with the recognition accorded to the contributions of one's ethnic or racial group to the society and the feeling that one's social class is treated unfairly are more likely to be associated with the perception of social problems. These relationships are graphically represented in Figure 28, which shows, for each of these two measures of life experience, a clear, linear relationship. Similar results are obtained with other factors such as the fairness of personal treatment and sense of belonging.

This study has frequently found that the social-class structure is highly relevant for the state of the social fabric. This is because the position occupied in it (as indicated by levels of education and income) tends to be associated with particular kinds of life experiences, such as fair or unfair treatment or recognition or the lack thereof for one's contribution to society. But everyone in a class category, at whatever level, does not have the same life experience. That is to say, for example, that although the extent of socio-economic advantage increases with class level, people in all classes can experience a loss of control over their lives and unfair treatment or conditions. Thus, both class position and life experience can be associated with the perception of social fragility.

Table 11   Perception of High Level of Social Fragility Varies by How One's Social
Class Is Perceived to Be Treated

	Percent Who Perceive Society Highly Fragile			
Social Class	Class Treated Very Fair	Class Treated Somewhat Fair	Class Treated Not Too Fair	Class Treated Not Fair at All
Lower	50	69	73	75
Working	56	64	79	87
Middle	52	62	69	79
Upper	46	58	79	67

As shown in Table 11, the perception of social fragility is indeed associated with class self-identification and of the perceived fairness of the treatment of one's social class. While there is a class effect on the number of problems one perceives in society, its magnitude is significantly mitigated by how fairly one's class is treated. Indeed, the social-class difference on the fragility index rarely exceeds ten percentage points, whatever the perception of the fairness of treatment of one's class. In addition, the percentages do not increase or decrease consistently from the highest to the lowest class level. In contrast, the perception of social fragility increases steadily with the perception of unfairness at *all* class levels (the upper-class respondents who see their class as treated very unfairly being the only exception). And the increases are quite large: they vary between twenty and thirty-one percentage points, depending on the class level.[5]

This does not mean that the position in the class structure has little relevance. What our finding rather shows is that the assessment of fairness of treatment of one's social class explains, in part, why the position occupied the social-class structure is related to the views of what threatens our society. This is because the assessment of fairness is strongly related to class position. Similar results are obtained when fairness of personal treatment, sense of control over one's life, and satisfaction with one's financial situation are taken into account: these dimensions of experience are also strongly related to position in the socio-economic hierarchy. In fact, when we control for all these experience variables simultaneously, the effect of subjectively defined social-class level is entirely eliminated and the impact of the objective measure is considerably reduced.

In short, the ways in which life is experienced by different social groups or categories have an important impact on the social fabric. Fairness of treatment, recognition of contribution, and control of life chances are powerful determinants of how healthy we perceive our social structures and institutions to be. They explain, in fact, much of the effect of age, gender, region, and social class on perceptions of social fragility. The demographic, social, and cultural fault lines in our society appear rooted in issues of social justice and social commitment.

Diversity is at the heart of the Canadian experiment. Much of our history has been the attempt to come to grips with this complexity. Reconciliation, compromise, accommodation, and care have been our tools. As John Ralston Saul so aptly notes: "If you want to live with complexity in an unusual, even original sort of political arrangement, which Canada clearly [is], the accompanying characteristic [is] care."[6] To a large extent, our experience reflects the finding that societies with a robust social fabric are not necessarily those where difference and conflict are absent, but rather those in which the sense of community is reinforced through policies and processes aimed at the constructive management and resolution of potentially divisive social forces along lines of gender, social class, cultural or racial background, region of residence, religious beliefs, political ideology, and moral values.

17

Strengthening the Social Fabric: Some Final Remarks

Like any society, ours is in a continuing process of reappraisal, reinvention, and renewal. This process, which may be more or less rapid, can be triggered by a variety of events and circumstances, either internal or external. Internal changes may include the growth and increasing diversity of the population, technological innovations, economic restructuring, and shifts in values and aspirations in certain segments of the population. External circumstances can be the growing power of other countries, civil or international wars, the emergence of regional blocs such as the European Union, new or expanded international institutions such as the World Trade Organization and the World Bank, or an increased economic, cultural, and political integration of Canada with the United States.

Change, especially rapid change, can act as a destabilizing force in the sense that it can upset the extent and the character of relations among individuals and groups. Some may be weakened or destroyed and new ones may be created. In addition, change usually challenges the social norms and values previously taken for granted. People are exposed to a multiplicity of new values and world-views. As a result, what people have been accustomed to expect from others and from the society may be undermined. This, in turn, can lead people to reassess whether the evolution of events and circumstances is what they want for their society. As Jane Jenson has well illustrated, the preoccupation with the condition of the social fabric increases significantly in periods of great change.[1]

Reappraisal and reinvention are outcomes of confrontations between different visions of human nature and of a desirable social order. For instance, in today's Canada, some view the social order primarily as the result of an arrangement among interdependent individuals and groups. Others see it as the outcome of the actions of individuals and groups operating independently and in competition with each other. Society is a system either of interdependent or of contending interests. For some, society necessarily involves communal provision; it is, so to speak, a system of mutual help. For others, individuals are expected to fend for themselves and rely on others only in extraordinary circumstances or disasters. For yet others, a society that is culturally and linguistically homogeneous is preferable to one that embodies diversity.

Thus, different people may assess differently the state of our society. In addition, the changes that are taking place affect the life conditions of different categories of people and the ways in which they experience social reality. As noted above, economic, cultural, demographic, and social changes can have an impact on the extent to which ideals and expectations are embodied in the social order and on the ways in which people experience it. For instance, economic restructuring and technological change can have repercussions which may or may not satisfy the expectations of fairness and may bias the allocation of recognition for the contributions to society. Demographic and cultural change may affect the sense of belonging in certain segments of the population. Diversity in culture and values as well as suburbanization may change the patterns of mutual obligations. Competitiveness, downsizing, and, more generally, the market culture may undermine the level of social trust, and the ways in which government institutions function can erode the trust in authorities.

Given this context of change, we felt it useful to investigate the concerns of Canadians and to attempt a diagnosis of the condition of the social fabric in our society, its strength or fragility. As indicated in Chapter 1, central to our diagnosis is the notion that the social fabric is based on a covenant of reciprocal expectations and obligations. The extent to which expectations are met determines the nature and quality of people's *experience* in the society; on the other hand, their *social commitment and contribution* provides an indication of the extent to which they satisfy their part of the covenant. Five types of experience have been considered as fundamental for the strength of the social fabric:

- *fairness* in the functioning of the society and in the way in which its members are treated;

- *recognition* for the contribution made to the society;
- *trust* in relationships with others;
- trust in institutional leaders; and
- a sense of *belonging*.

The sense of social obligation and actual contributions constitute the other side of the social covenant. This reciprocity is fundamental for the vitality of the social fabric. It creates a sense of "social ownership" that goes beyond one's self-interest. Contributing is an investment in the common good. Thus, the following are also critical for the social fabric:

- a sense of *indebtedness*, that is, an appreciation on the part of individuals of what they receive from community and society;
- *mutual obligation*; and
- *contributions* to the functioning of the community and society.

HOW FRAGILE IS OUR SOCIAL FABRIC?

The integrity of the social covenant and the strength of the social fabric depend on, among other things, two major components: a series of social expectations that are shaped by our social values and by our collective experience over time (that is, by the kind of society we have attempted to create over the years and generations); and the recognition of the existing social interdependence and of the requirements it places on individuals. The solidity or fragility of the social fabric rests on the extent to which those expectations are met and are seen to be met in the life experience of citizens and in the functioning of institutions. Measured by these standards, Canada's is a healthy, stable society.

We have a strong sense of belonging to both the communities in which we live and the broader society of which we are a part. Nearly three of every five Canadians feel "very much at home" in their immediate community. Close to half (44 per cent) express a similar sentiment for the country as a whole. Only one in ten of us feels little or no attachment to the contexts in which we carry out our daily lives. Our sense of social integration is relatively robust.

We also have a profound feeling of indebtedness to the society in which we live. More than four of every five Canadians believe that "everyone owes something to society and should try to give something back." It is not our view that society is the outcome of actions taken by individuals pursuing their own goals. In fact, less than 17 per cent of us believe that we do not have obligations to others.

Our belief in mutual dependence is supported by the high value we attach to the obligation to help those with whom we share our personal and social space. Our feeling of obligation extends not only to family and friends but also to members of the groups to which we belong, to others who find themselves in the same life circumstances, and to "anyone who needs help." Despite our highly multicultural society, the obligation to help anyone in need is much stronger than our perceived obligation to the social groups of which we are members. Nearly half of us believe that the norm of beneficence extends beyond particularistic interests. Universalism has strong roots in Canadian society.

These feelings are supported by an abiding commitment to the common good. More than two of every three Canadians believe that upholding our basic values and consideration of the common good in our actions and decisions are among our most important obligations. The single largest source of perceived problems faced by Canadian society are violations of this fundamental value. Lack of commitment to collective interest, whether in the form of the pursuit of self-interest, group interest, or freeloading, are factors to which nine in ten Canadians attribute shortcomings in our relations with each other.

And for the most part "we walk the talk." Our actual contributions to community and society mirror our value commitment. The majority of Canadians are actively involved in helping their neighbours through voluntary organizations, monetary donations, or informal arrangements. In fact, over three-quarters of us demonstrate our commitment through more than one of these ways and a significant proportion believe that we could do even more than we already do. Only a small minority (less than 20 per cent) contend that paying taxes exempts us from our communal responsibilities. Our voluntary activities attest to a vital community life.

Over the years 1996 to 1999, the United Nations ranked Canada as the country with the highest quality of life. The measures in the UN's Human Development Index are based primarily on economic and life-chance factors. Our data, however, suggest that the social, cultural, and moral underpinnings of our communal life definitely need to be taken into account as well.

Disquieting Trends

Despite the underlying strength of Canadian society, a number of our findings should give pause for thought and reflection. Three are particularly worthy of note.

First, some of the elements on which the strength of our social fabric depends are under considerable stress. Fairness, trust, and recognition, which have too often been overlooked in studies of social cohesion, are all under siege.

Canadians do not believe that their society is fair for all its members. Only 38 per cent of us acknowledge that the society we live in is "basically fair for most people." Over two-thirds of our sample claim that they are personally experiencing some form of unfair treatment. More than 60 per cent of Canadians believe that corporations are becoming more irresponsible. Less than half of the population is convinced that their province is receiving a fair share of federal funding.

Trust cannot be routinely assumed. Four of every five Canadians claim that "individuals should be careful about trusting others, since there are too many people who seek to benefit only themselves." We are not confident that others will consider our interests in determining their course of action. And this distrust extends to institutions as well as individuals. Only 18 per cent of Canadians believe that the public interest is the main concern of government. The motives of corporate leaders are viewed with suspicion by three of every five Canadians.

A substantial portion of Canadians express concern with the degree of recognition they receive for what they do or what they contribute. Women and visible minorities are particularly susceptible. The highest degree of dissatisfaction, however, is with the level of recognition granted the educational group of which one is a member. This is occurring at a time when we are actively pursuing the creation of a knowledge economy through the promotion of a more skilled and educated citizenry.

Second, there are indications of social fragmentation. The survey results point to important social cleavages in our sense of community. There are boundaries to our feelings of obligation. Trust, recognition, and perceptions of fairness are not evenly distributed. These cleavages relate to stages in the life cycle, our position in the economic and class hierarchy, and the regions and communities in which we live. We have detailed these in preceding chapters. They include:

- A generation gap in the building blocks of a cohesive society. Younger Canadians (eighteen to thirty-five) feel less at home in both their local community and the broader society. They also exhibit a much lower sense of indebtedness than older Canadians.
- Notable regional and community differences in perceptions of trust, fairness, recognition, and social commitment. The most significant divergence is between Quebec and the rest of the country. It is in Quebec that social and personal fairness and recognition of contributions are perceived to be lowest, and that distrust is highest. The

sense of indebtedness to society is also weaker, and actual levels of voluntary contribution lower, in Quebec than in the country as a whole.

• Significant divisions between social classes. Each of the indicators of a cohesive society are strongly related to the economic situation in which people find themselves and the social class with which they identify. Trust, recognition, the experience of fairness, our sense of belonging, and the obligations we feel towards each other bear an almost linear relationship to class position.

• Boundaries to trust and obligation. There are significant gulfs between elites and the general public. And we are somewhat wary of those whose beliefs and values differ from our own.

These cleavages present important challenges to the creation and maintenance of a cohesive society. While there is a strong basis for a community of shared values, shared challenges, and equality of opportunity, there are undercurrents which suggest that Canadians' ties to each other may be weakening. If the idea that "we are all in this together" is an important source of strength for the social fabric, these fault lines create the potential for "civil society to become less civil."

Finally, many Canadians perceive significant threats to the strength of the social fabric. The chief source of this threat is the pursuit of self-interest rather than the common good. Nine of ten Canadians believe that the sources of our social ills are a preoccupation with what we can get out of the system, an expectation of getting something for nothing, and a concern with special-interest groups rather than with society as a whole. The rewriting of the moral script to self-centred individualism, in fact, far outranks the concern with more material issues such as the decline in the standard of living.

What Happens, Matters

But these challenges also have hopeful undertones. Our data make it clear that life experiences and life conditions strongly affect assessments of the fragility of the social fabric. What happens clearly matters.

The experiences that appear to make the most significant difference are those that structure our conception of fairness and the degree of control we exercise over our life situation. If we believe the social structure and our personal experience to be unfair, perceive little or no recognition for contributions made, or sense little control over our lives, then

- trust in social relations is eroded;
- feeling of belonging to the community is diminished;
- social indebtedness is substantially reduced; and
- actual contributions to communal life decrease.

Furthermore, those who find themselves in such circumstances also believe that the social structure is more fragile. Eight of ten Canadians who experience unfair treatment see society as highly fragile. This drops to one in two for those who have more positive encounters with our social, economic, and cultural institutions.[2]

In many respects Canadians share these characteristics with most advanced industrial democracies. Over the last few decades (at least until 11 September 2001), "such concerns as economic growth, public order, national security [have become] central to a new politics which places more emphasis on individual freedom, social equality and quality of life."[3] As has happened in the United States and Europe, Canadian values have shifted to more "postmaterialistic" concerns. Yet, at the same time, Canada differs from other advanced industrial countries in ways that offer both opportunities and challenges for a healthy, stable social fabric.

Among the opportunities to be harnessed we can include levels of political and racial tolerance and satisfaction with one's financial situation that are higher than those found in Europe and the United States, a keener interest in political affairs (almost twice the European rate) and levels of national pride that are not only among the highest in the world but also based on communal achievement. But the challenges are equally daunting. And most relate to our view of hierarchical institutions in general and governmental institutions in particular. According to the data amassed in the World Values Survey[4]:

- Only 20 per cent of Canadians, as compared to 42 per cent of Americans, trust their government to do what is right most of the time (p.76).
- Nearly half of Canadians, compared to one-third of Americans and 40 per cent of Europeans, believe that government needs to be more open (p.100).
- Support for the idea that greater respect for authority would be desirable in the future decreases with higher levels of education, and the trend is the strongest in Canada (p.39).
- Fully 70 per cent of Canadians feel that our country is run by a few big interests looking out only for themselves (p.76).
- Support for the general principle of deference has declined more, and to lower levels, in Canada than in the United States (p.38).

In addition, trust in elected officials is declining; Canadians have become more inclined to believe that parliamentarians lose touch with those whom they are elected to serve and that government does not much care what people think. Perhaps, and even more significant, the more empowered Canadians feel the less they trust government.

Fairness, recognition of contributions to society, and a sense of control are critical features of an individual's social experience. As we have demonstrated throughout our analysis, much of the differential impact of age, gender, social class, and region, in fact, diminishes or disappears when these factors are taken into account. In other words, what differs in the experience of people in these various social categories is that their social-covenant expectations are more or less respected or violated.

Canadians believe that the actions of the corporate and public elite are among the most significant determinants of social fragility. A large part of this impact results from the fact that variables that affect the degree of fragility are highly susceptible to policy initiatives in both the public and the private sphere. As noted by the Social Cohesion Network: "A large measure of [the impact of fault lines and socio-economic indicators] on the future health, security and well-being of Canadians will be determined by the success of its governance structures – formal, informal, domestic, international, public, private, nongovernmental and voluntary. This is especially the case with respect to strengthening social cohesion. Many of the levers, policies and programs likely to lead to success still lie in the control, responsibility and accountability of Canadians themselves and their leaders."[5]

We can have an impact on the extent of implementation of the social covenant and on the robustness of the social fabric. And a major responsibility for the creation of the conditions that underpin a healthy society rests with those who control its institutions and govern its direction. As Neil Roese notes in his work on Canadians' shrinking trust in government: "Canadians are becoming more interested in the way their government does business and they are directing a keener gaze toward specific government actions."[6]

REINFORCING THE SOCIAL FABRIC

The findings of our study point to several issues our society needs to address. These concern all the dimensions of the social fabric considered in the previous chapters: fairness, recognition of the contribution to society, social trust, trust of institutional leaders, the sense of belonging, social indebtedness, the obligation to help, and communal contributions.

The various issues can be grouped under the following six headings:

1 encouraging countervailing forces to the dominant individualism of
   the market culture;
2 eliminating unfairness in the distribution of opportunities and in and
   institutional practices;
3 achieving fairness in social recognition;
4 bridging social boundaries;
5 narrowing the gap between citizens and institutional leaders; and
6 fostering community entrepreneurship and involvement

1. Encouraging countervailing forces
to the dominant individualism of the market culture

We have seen that a large majority of Canadians are worried that the
pursuit of self-interest is progressively prevailing over a concern for the
common good in our culture. They seem to fear that this tendency is
threatening the delicate balance between the attainment of individual
autonomy, well-being, and self-fulfilment, on the one hand, and the
pursuit of the common good and a quality of life shared by all
members of the community, on the other.

Such a balance is indeed a central issue in the functioning of any
society. Because of this, there is a tension in the choices that individuals and societies have to make: to invest individual and social resources
in such a way as to facilitate the pursuit of the private interests and
goals of individuals, or to assure the economic, social, and cultural
vitality of communities and institutions.

Ideally, there should be some sort of equilibrium between these two
orientations. An overemphasis on one or the other can be damaging for
both individuals and the society. Indeed, pushed to the limit, a collectivity-oriented culture is detrimental to individual freedom and self-fulfilment. On the other hand, a dominating self-oriented culture, as
Alexis de Tocqueville pointed out about one hundred and fifty years
ago, can erode the social fabric by pulling people away from communal concerns and by weakening the sense of responsibility for the
public sphere.

Most Canadians feel that there is now such an overemphasis, that
there is less than an ideal balance between the two requirements for a
vital, cohesive society. In the last few decades, many of the prevailing
tendencies have encouraged the pursuit of private interests. They have
promoted the self-oriented dimension of our culture, which includes a
failure to recognize the interconnection between the quality of personal

and of social life. And it seems that Canadians see these tendencies as threatening the social fabric of our society.

The individualistic system of values that underlie the functioning of a market economy can be a factor in the erosion of some elements of the social and moral infrastructure of society. Indeed, to a large extent, the market culture is based on values that justify the pursuit of individual gain and indifference to the public good. In Albert Hirschman's words, the market as a social system is propelled by a more or less explicit ideology, namely, that "the dogged pursuit of happiness along the private road is not, as we often tend to think, 'what comes naturally'; rather, it is presided over and impelled by an ideology which justifies it, not only in terms of its beneficial results for the individual pursuer, but as the surest and perhaps only way in which the individual can make a contribution to the common good. The ideological claims made for the private life thus sustain the individual's quest with two messages: one, the promise of satisfaction and happiness; and two, the assurance that there is no need for guilt feelings or regrets over the neglect of public life."[7]

The individualistic emphasis also undermines the moral infrastructure by, implicitly if not explicitly, denying the relevance for individual success of a whole range of factors that are largely beyond any one's control. These include one's genetic background and the financial, cultural, and social capital drawn from one's family, from the cultural milieu in which one is integrated, and from the institutions of the larger society. The cultural definition of "success in terms of the outcome of free competition among individuals in an open market" underscores individual effort and "hard work" (and the laziness or lack of motivation of the unsuccessful) and plays down the determining role of advantages inherited from background, family, and publicly provided facilities and supports.

The overemphasis may be the cumulative result of individual decisions and actions. For example, a recent news report on the great commercial success of minivans notes that the success of a more polluting vehicle comes at the same time that Canadians tell pollsters they are concerned about urban smog and global warming. One person interviewed said that the "conversion to more efficient, greener cars ... is the job of governments and the auto industry," not of the consumer.[8] Thus, there may be a concern for the common good but no feeling of personal responsibility for it. To the extent that this is the case, the common good is not pursued and even deteriorates *through* the actions, but *against* the will, of Canadians.

The issue is to bolster the social forces that motivate individuals to be concerned with the public good, to contribute to it, and to consider how their own decisions and actions affect the community and society in which they live. Less emphasis needs to be placed on those forces that incite individuals to pursue their own goals and aspirations and to achieve the maximum well-being for themselves without consideration for their implications for the society and future generations. Rather, what needs to be heightened in the public consciousness is the significance of the public sphere and of collective endeavours in determining the quality of life. Instead of reducing as much as possible the role of public institutions in society, it is important to revitalize them and to redefine their role in the context of globalization and technological change.

It is also imperative to revive the notion of "citizen." The tendency to refer to members of the public as "taxpayers" and, worse, as consumers of public services must be strongly resisted. The idea that part of the year we work for the government and the other part for ourselves destroys the concept of citizen. The symbolic definition of taxes as a usurpation of individual property is a distortion of what taxes are about, namely, a pooling of resources for the provision of public goods. Such a distortion denigrates the public sphere. It erodes the notion that we are members of communities who contribute to the extent of their ability to the common good. It disconnects citizens from their public institutions.

Collective projects that would capture the imagination of Canadians could be identified. Such projects would embody a vision of the kind of society we want for ourselves. In the past, Canadian energies have been driven by such projects. Among these are universal education and health care, human rights, income security, and the accommodation of ethnic minorities. Protecting or enhancing such institutional achievements can still provide a sense of purpose to our society. In *The Canada We Want*, John Godfrey and Rob McLean mention other examples such as the care and nurturing of young children and new energy systems.[9]

Such projects could not only increase the quality of life but also have a powerful impact on the sense of being engaged in a common enterprise, of actively participating in the creation and maintenance of the society. Of course, some of this is already taking place. It needs to be maintained rather than eroded. Its symbolic significance also needs to be kept alive in the minds of citizens so as to strengthen their sense of belonging and commitment to the common good.

2. Eliminating Unfairness in the Distribution of Opportunities and in Institutional Practices

The social fabric of our society is also undermined by the experience of unfairness by a significant proportion of the population, as clearly indicated by the findings of our study. Several members of different social groups or categories see themselves as unfairly treated in one way or another: women, men, ethnic groups, visible minorities, social classes, residents of provinces. In this regard, we found that the division between social classes is most significant basis of social fragmentation. Also, the place occupied in the socio-economic hierarchy is consistently associated with all the components of the strength of the social fabric: the experience of fairness, the trust of others and particularly of institutional leaders, the satisfaction received for the contribution to society, the sense of belonging, and the obligations felt towards fellow citizens.

In addition, inequalities in access to socio-economic resources underlie the other social differences. "In the democracy tradition, socio-economic disparities, not diversities, constitute the focal point. Unequal life chances are viewed as constituting a source of conflict and consequently, as posing a threat to social cohesion."[10] We should add that it is not economic disparities as such that threaten the social fabric, but disparities that are *perceived* as unfair.

In our society, much attention is already given to equality of opportunity for all. Our society is strongly committed to this principle. It is generally accepted and is embodied in the Charter of Rights and Freedoms and in the multiculturalism policy of the federal government. Frequently, the measures adopted take the particular circumstances (history, geography, culture, socio-economic conditions, and so on) of the targeted groups into consideration. The positive results of such efforts are shown in some of our findings: the relatively high percentage of members of different groups who feel that they have the same job opportunities as others; the feeling among a strong proportion of women that the recognition of their contribution to society is increasing; and the relatively small incidence of racial conflicts and violence in our communities.

Generally, such initiatives contribute to the strength of the social fabric. Yet, in some instances, although the policy adopted is designed to achieve greater equity for some segments of the population and thus increase their trust and sense of belonging, it can have the opposite effect for others. That is, the policy can generate social tension. This seems to be the case with "affirmative action," which, while aiming to rectify the historical inequities that have seriously retarded the progress of some groups, is perceived as unfair by others who do not feel responsible for the mistakes of the past. Because of this paradox, the administration of such policies requires as much if not more attention than their design.

Fairness in access to economic opportunity is yet to be achieved. Increases in the number of working poor, homeless, and users of food

banks and "out-of-the-cold" programs are just a few of the manifestations of such unfairness. And the experience unfairness is not a random
phenomenon. It is more likely to occur among women, visible minorities (Native peoples included), and people at the lower echelons of the
social scale.

In recent decades, growing inequalities in the distribution of income
have been seen by many social analysts as reflecting an unfair distribution of the costs of social change. There is also the case of workers
who experience difficulties as a result of globalization and technological change. While some are advantaged by such changes, others pay a
disproportionate share of the costs they bring about. Fairness requires
that those who are advantaged contribute towards defraying the costs
imposed on others. It also requires measures to offset the handicaps
that some experience as a result of the transformations. For instance,
there is a need of programs to help low-skilled, less-educated workers
as well as those whose skills have become redundant make the transi-
tion. To put the matter in terms of fairness, they need to be compensated for the damage that economic and technological change has
inflicted on their socio-economic condition.

Some of the issues need to be dealt with at the international level.
Indeed, the economic environment is increasingly composed of and
dominated by global actors: multinational corporations, financial institutions such as the World Bank and the International Monetary Fund,
and trade bodies such as the World Trade Organization. Equality of
opportunities and socio-economic fairness cannot be pursued adequately without addressing the impact of these global institutions.
What is their impact not only on societies as a whole but also on their
different social segments? To what extent are the global institutions for
the management of the economy responsive to the distributive and
other issues that arise from the promotion of economic development,
trade, and technological change?

In short, fairness must be a basic consideration in the design of
public policies, programs, and administrative arrangements and practices, in addition to such basic questions as costs, efficiency, and technical requirements. This is so at all levels of socio-political organization: local, national, and international. For the quality of life of
individuals and families as well as for the strength of the social fabric,
fairness is as important as the bottom line.

3. Achieving Fairness in Social Recognition

People expect that the contribution they make in their various social
roles and as members of particular groups will be recognized for its

value to others, to the community, and to the society. Recognition is a dimension of fairness. If others do not recognize what an individual or a category of individuals contribute to the community, they are, so to speak, being unfair in the way they see and treat them.

The recognition of *contributions* implies a partial shift from "the politics of identity" to what could be called the "politics of community." The first entails the recognition and acceptance of distinctiveness. Multiculturalism as a policy, as an element of the constitution and as a social value, fosters such recognition. It affirms the value of diversity for our society, indeed portraying it as an essential element of our national character. The constitution requires that diversity be taken into account in the formulation and implementation of public policies.

The second focuses not on identity and distinctiveness but on contribution to society, which, of course, if achieved, constitutes an indirect recognition of identity as well. It emphasizes interdependence by recognizing what is contributed to the common good and to making the society what it is. It could also be called the politics of citizenship since "citizenship is virtually coextensive with 'getting involved' with one's neighbours for the good of the community."[11]

The results of this study show that, although the level of satisfaction with the recognition received is high, the level of dissatisfaction is not negligible: more than two in five express some dissatisfaction with the recognition of the contribution of at least one of the social categories to which they belong: gender, ethnocultural or racial group, and people at the same level of education or training.

It is with regard to their level of education or training that the dissatisfaction with the recognition received for the contribution to society is the most frequent. This may be partly due to the highly promoted view that jobs connected to the knowledge-based economy are more important to the economy than more "traditional" jobs. It may also be related to the technological changes that have brought about the so-called "new economy," in which certain skills based on moderate to high levels of education and training are devalued or become obsolete. Also, some of the new jobs requiring fairly high levels of education may be quite monotonous and entail very little autonomy.

One of the important social boundaries in our society is along linguistic lines and particularly between Quebec and the rest of the country. It was mentioned earlier that there are negative views on both sides of the linguistic divide. One manifestation of this negative reciprocity is the perception by a number of anglophones that claims made by Quebec are simply attempts to gain for itself at the expense of the rest of the country.[12] On the other hand, many fracophones fail to give credit for the measures adopted to rectify at least some of their grievances and simply persist in expressing grievances and making claims. This confirms the perceptions of anglophones and hardens the determination not to give in to Quebec – a reaction that fuels the negative attitudes of francophones. As a way out of such a destructive impasse, an attempt should be made to reorient public attention to what each part of the country is contributing to the common good. If there is concern with the cohesion of the society, this is a good place to begin to address the issue.

Finally, social denigration is the opposite of recognition and is part of the process of social exclusion. Thus, it is critical to avoid any public rhetoric that blames the victim or that focuses on the negative features of the group or category that is the object of a policy or program. Frequently, denigration consists of negative moral judgments such as laziness, self-indulgence, or dishonesty. It is possible to reform the welfare system without denigrating the poor and those who receive social assistance. It is possible to deal with single mothers or the homeless without imputing less than respectable motives to all of them. Rather, attention should be on recognizing the real disadvantages and injuries – physical, social, and psychological – that individuals have to cope with and the efforts they make, individually and collectively, to help themselves.

4. Bridging Social Boundaries

The pursuit of fairness for all categories of citizens will do a lot to bridge social boundaries. Developing and fostering a "community spirit" that encourages mutual help and the willingness to contribute to collective projects will also reinforce the social fabric. However, it can also reinforce social boundaries and, to the extent that this occurs, it erodes the social fabric. The concern for the common good must extend beyond the boundaries of particular social groups, whether these be one's neighbourhood, religious congregation, labour union or professional association, ethnic or racial group, social class, political party, or "lifestyle community."

Our survey results reveal that, for many, the sense of obligation to help others stays within particular social boundaries. However, a cohesive social fabric depends on a willingness to help anyone in need – not only those who think and behave like ourselves, who share the same social or cultural characteristics, or who have the same economic interests as we do. Social concerns must be inclusive rather than exclusive.

Government is the one institution of which all citizens are members. Universalistic programs, that is, programs for all those with particular needs, can help to bridge social boundaries. Of course, a public program does not necessarily reinforce the social fabric. In fact, depending on the way it is designed and administered, it could do the opposite. A two-tier health care system may have financial advantages, but it may also accentuate the cleavage between socio-economic classes.

Public programs can also perform a redistributive function that no other institution can accomplish. They can raise the level of equity in society and thus act as bridges across social boundaries. If properly designed, they can increase solidarity across social classes, ethnic and racial groups, and so on. As Gosta Esping-Andersen points out, "the social rights, income security, equalization, and eradication of poverty that a universalistic welfare state pursues are necessary preconditions for the strength and unity that collective power mobilization demands."[13]

Some urban-development policies accentuate social-class boundaries. They can foster the formation of exclusive communities and a related sense of self-sufficiency in relatively well-off communities. These can become socially and psychologically if not physically "gated." But the way in which urban governance is structured and administered can also sustain the sense of interdependence and solidarity among the different segments of the larger urban agglomeration as well as a sense of responsibility for the different segments of the metropolitan area. For instance, the pooling of social-services costs across an entire metropolitan region can nurture solidarity, in contrast to an administrative segmentation that supports a "we are responsible for ourselves only" attitude and, in so doing, weakens the social fabric.

Some of the issues raised in connection with fairness are also relevant in the present context. For example, Dani Rodrik points out that globalization may "solidify a new set of class divisions – between those who prosper in the globalized economy and those who do not, between those who share its values and those would rather not, and between those who can diversify away its risks and those who cannot ... Globalization reduces the willingness of internationally mobile groups to cooperate with others in resolving disagreements and conflicts ... By reducing the civic engagement of internationally mobile groups, globalization [may] loosen the civic glue that holds societies together and exacerbate social fragmentation."[14]

Earlier, the importance of the rhetoric of institutional leaders was noted. It is also relevant in the present context. It can indeed create bridges across segments of the society or demolish those that already exist. For instance, political campaigning that makes scapegoats of women, minorities, immigrants, welfare recipients, labour unions, or other social groups can be quite damaging for the social fabric. It exploits and encourages social resentments and thus widens the social and psychological gap between groups or categories of citizens.

Some people do feel unjustly treated in comparison to other groups. If they are right, the unfairness they experience can be addressed, as it should, without undermining the social fabric. If they are wrong, it is highly irresponsible to exploit their resentments for political purposes. Indeed, negative public rhetoric may pay off polit-ically but the social costs in terms of fragmentation can be quite high. Such campaigning, aimed at electoral success irrespective of the damage to the social fabric, confirms the judgment of Canadians about too many being concerned with their self-interest rather than with the common good.

Institutional leaders have three interconnected roles in bridging social boundaries. First, their power should be used to generate and mobilize resources to attain common goals, that is, goals that benefit the society as a whole. They are indeed the agents of the community either at the local, regional, or national level. They are public trustees whose function is to manage the affairs of the community in trust for its members.[15] This understanding "exalts politics into the realm of statesmanship in which the high affairs of national life transcend par-ticular interests."[16]

Second, they should respond to the needs of all groups and social categories of citizens, especially those who are in some way disadvan-taged, who frequently do not have the financial and organizational resources to articulate their needs and apply pressure on decision makers, and those who have little or no electoral weight. "Like it or not," writes Bob Rae, "we are all in the same boat, and the flourishing of the commonwealth 'always affords chances of salvation to unfortu-nate individuals.'"[17]

Third, they should act as mediators. Their objective must be accom-modation rather than confrontation. Stephen Dale quotes a politician who sees the challenge of politics as that of "being able to embrace both sides of an issue, being able to broker understandings between competing segments of society ... and to balance competing promises made to different social groups."[18]

5. Narrowing the gap between citizens and institutional leaders

The low level of trust revealed by our survey and by those carried out by other researchers indicates that a serious gap exists between citizens and institutional leaders. Citizens see institutions and their leaders as distant, massive, and complex entities over which they have little control. Governmental leaders are seen as influenced primarily by large corporations and the wealthy rather than by citizens. Large transnational corporations are believed to be beyond the reach of ordinary citizens too. These perceptions are related to the view that there are two sets of rules in our society, one for those with money and one for everyone else.

This is clearly an issue that needs to be addressed if we are concerned with the social fabric. There is a tendency to think of the civic community — from local to national — in "horizontal" terms, that is, in terms of relations between various categories of citizens (e.g., social classes, regions, linguistic, ethnic, or racial groups) and to ignore or pay less attention to its "vertical" dimension, that is, between citizens and their institutional leaders.

It is in the area of policymaking that the main bridge between citizens and institutional leaders can be constructed. Rather than seeking secrecy, citizens should be informed and decision making should be as open as possible. Rather than defining public opinion as something to be manipulated – a process that is, as noted earlier, highly professionalized – citizens should be informed and involved in the political process. As Robert Vipond notes, "unilateral government-by-announcement in which critical citizens, interested associations and elected representatives are derided, marginalized and ignored" may make it possible to cut costs, "but it will also tear at our social solidarity."[19] His observation, made in relation to a particular government, is quite generally applicable. Indeed, one of the structural manifestations of this "imperial" tendency is the increasing centralization of decision making in the hands of the first minister at the federal and provincial levels.

How institutional leaders deal with opposition to their proposed and/or implemented policies is also critical. Indeed, symbolic weapons can be used to exclude critical groups of citizens from the political process. This is done when they are defined as "special-interest" groups rather than as stakeholders with a legitimate interest in a particular public policy, or when public debate over policies is characterized as an obstruction or a nuisance rather than as a necessary element of dealing with issues and problems in a complex society. These negative practices generate distrust of political leaders and, in turn, have a negative impact on the vertical dimension of the social covenant.

The media also shape the relationship between citizens and institutions. To a certain extent, they are responsible for generating distrust, especially of political leaders. First, there is an overemphasis on the negative. A bureau chief for a national network told Hugh Segal that "one of the reasons his network's coverage of most politicians was somewhat negative was because that's what public opinion wanted and his network needed supper-hour audiences to generate revenues." Segal also notes the "solutionist bias" in much of the media: there is frequently the premise that "whatever the problem – high taxes, medical system stress, high prices, unemployment, traffic tie-ups, family violence, the insanity of Serbia and Bosnia – governments ought to, it is deemed ... have a solution ... It is the media industry's manufacturing of the unsustainable expectation that most serious problems have simple answers." But, he adds, "to be fair, politicians often gain by offering 'solutionist' scenarios themselves."[20]

6. Fostering community entrepreneurship and involvement

The survey results show that the majority of Canadians engage in communal activity. Such results suggest that there is also a considerable amount of communal entrepreneurship.

Canadians participate in a wide variety of volunteer activities: community economic development, conflict- or dispute-resolution initiatives, sponsorship of enterprises,[21] victim-offender mediation, assistance to battered women, recreation programs for adults and children, counselling and interpreter services to immigrants, refugee settlement, "out of the cold" programs, food banks, assistance to people with disabilities, and many more.

One of the issues that still needs to be addressed is the extent to which governments should be involved in supporting voluntary communal activity. To what extent can the voluntary sector be a substitute for government-provided services, an argument sometimes used to justify the reduction of such services? But should we think in terms of substitution or of partnerships?

The voluntary sector cannot furnish an adequate *level* of services without government support. Groups or local communities vary widely in their capacity to provide services. They vary in terms of the material resources they can mobilize, in terms of social networks they can use to gain access to information and institutional resources, and in terms of leadership and organizational potential. Government is an essential partner for the equalization of communal potential across various categories of citizens, whether it be along gender, class, ethnic, racial, or other social lines. Also, certain *kinds* of services require specialized skills that volunteers generally do not have. They can provide assistance but trained personnel is needed as well. That is to say, the capacity of civil society to provide a certain range of services is limited. In short, governments definitely have a role to play in sustaining and nurturing the vitality of civil society.

Many Canadians feel an obligation to help others. On the negative side, there is a relatively weak sense of obligation to help people who are not within one's social circles. It is necessary to foster the obligation to help across social boundaries since the vitality of the social fabric is ultimately weakened if communal activity is mostly contained within religious, social-class, linguistic, ethnic, racial, or other kinds of boundaries. Exclusive within-group solidarity strengthens between-group boundaries. "To be modern is to face the consequences of decisions made by complete strangers while making decisions that will affect the lives of people one will never know."[22] In other words, we need to recognize our dependence on strangers and their dependence on us – strangers defined either as people whom we do not know personally or as people who are socially different from us. This interdependence expands the scope of our social obligations.

One way to encourage communal activities and entrepreneurship is through the public recognition of those who make a contribution to society, whether they be individuals, groups, organizations, or communities. Chapter 4 noted that public organizations and programs already exist for such recognition. They no doubt encourage communal involvement and may also provide models for dealing with different kinds of problems. But are there enough such mechanisms? Are they adequately distributed throughout the country? Are they sufficiently sensitive to the contributions of people in all segments of the society? Is the information about the awards widely communicated to the public? These are questions that need to be addressed.

THE CHALLENGE OF GOVERNING

The ties that bind Canadians to each other are strong but they are also tenuous in some regards. How we choose to structure our shared experiences will, to a large extent, determine how fragile those bonds become. As the report of the Senate Committee on Social Affairs, Science and Technology notes, Canada needs intelligent alternatives to "the downward spiral of the polarized society to which we are slowly drifting."

We have choices in how we deal with the fallout of social change. If we are to retain a strong national community, the choices we make must reflect an emphasis on giving people a sense of belonging. In the previous pages, we have indicated some of the ways in which the social fabric can be strengthened. These go well beyond individual initiative and commitment to particular values. Indeed, the effective pursuit of relevant objectives requires appropriate institutions.[23] By design or not, institutions always embody certain values. The challenge is to make sure that they embody values that lead to policies and actions that strengthen rather than weaken the social fabric.

The social fabric "is a societal project which transcends all the institutions in a society. It is the ultimate common property resource. We can all benefit from it if it exists, but it is far too easy to let the social fabric deteriorate as we each pursue our own short-term self-interest."[24] The reference here is clearly to public institutions, although not necessarily governmental. Market institutions may be extremely effective in the economic domain, but if extended to other domains, they may also be detrimental to the social fabric. In this connection, Alan Wolfe notes that "the question is not whether common services can be turned over to private operators; they can. Rather, the question is whether they should be. Privatization is an important trend because it raises the implicit question of whether people have any common stake in the provision of the services that define their society."[25] To judge from the results of our survey, Canadians do feel that they have a common stake in what defines their society.

How we experience society affects all of the building blocks of a strong social fabric. What happens in our everyday lives truly matters! Fairness, recognition for contributions to social life, and trust are the critical building blocks of social commitment. And much of what happens in every day life is structured by institutions through the incentives and opportunities they provide and the requirements they impose on us. Thus, those whom we entrust with the leadership of our institutions bear a large degree of accountability for how successful we are.

The goal of social justice must figure prominently within any strategy to strengthen the social fabric. Indeed, the results of this study indicate quite clearly that the perception and experience of fairness or unfairness is strongly associated with social class. It is therefore important that the focus on social cohesion turn the attention of citizens and policy makers towards social inequalities rather than away from them.[26] Choices that leaders make in policy directions, and in the process by which policies are developed, can have a critical impact on how cohesive our society remains. Ensuring that these choices are the right ones is the ultimate challenge of governing.

APPENDIX

Methodology

The methodological information that follows was supplied by Environics Research, which designed the sample and carried out the interviews for the Canada-wide survey.

The results of this survey are derived from 2,014 interviews carried out in the homes of the respondents between March 11 to 31, 1997: 256 in the Atlantic Provinces, 501 in Quebec, 541 in Ontario and 716 in the Western Provinces.

DATA COLLECTION AND QUALITY CONTROL

The questionnaires are distributed, through regional supervisors, to approximately 150 experienced interviewers across the country. The supervisors are also responsible for training the interviewers and for briefing them on the specific instructions accompanying each survey.

Each interviewer also receives a map of his or her allocated area. On the map, the pre-selected block or blocks in which he or she must carry out his or her interviews are indicated. Starting with a pre-selected address, the interviewer must complete the number of interviews that he or she has been allocated, according to the age and sex quotas indicated on his or her route map. Only one respondent is interviewed per household. The questioning is carried out in the language chosen by the respondent.

In order to check the quality of work completed and the accuracy of the indicated responses, ten percent of each interviewer's respondents are re-contacted by the Field Supervisor. In questionable cases, or when high standards have not been respected, the questionnaires are rejected.

SAMPLE

The sample is drawn in such a way that it represents the Canadian population aged 18 or over with the exception of those Canadians living in the Yukon or Northwest Territories or in institutions (armed forces barracks, hospitals, prisons).

The sampling model relies on stratification of the population by 10 regions (Atlantic, Montreal CMA, the rest of Quebec, Toronto CMA, the rest of Ontario, Manitoba, Saskatchewan, Alberta, Vancouver CMA, the rest of British Columbia) and by four community sizes (1,000,000 inhabitants or more, 100,000 to 1,000,000 inhabitants, 5,000 to 100,000 inhabitants, and under 5,000 inhabitants).

The sample also relies on a gender quota, an age quota, and a working women quota.

Approximately 191 sampling points are used.

The number of cases in each region may not necessarily reflect its actual weight. The samples for some regions have been augmented in order to attain a sufficient number of cases for analysis. The results are then weighted during data processing to give each sampling stratum its proper weight.

MARGIN OF ERROR

The margin of error for a stratified probability sample of this size is estimated to be ± 2.2 percentage points, 19 times in 20. The margin of error increases in the case of a modified probability sample, such as the one used in this survey, and also for results pertaining to regional or socio-demographic sub-groups of the total sample.

Notes

CHAPTER ONE

1 Michael Walzer, *Spheres of Justice* (New York: Basic Books 1983), 64.
2 Hugh Segal, *Beyond Greed* (Toronto: Stoddart 1997), 57, 60.
3 For a detailed analysis of Canadians' diagnosis of the problems facing their society, see the next chapter.
4 Jane Jenson, *Mapping Social Cohesion: The State of Canadian Research* (Ottawa: Canadian Policy Research Networks 1998), 38.
5 The Standing Senate Committee on Social Affairs, Science and Technology, *Report on Social Cohesion* (Ottawa: Senate of Canada 1999).
6 James S. Coleman, "Social Capital in the Creation of Human Capital," *American Journal of Sociology*, 94 (1988): 95–120.
7 Robert D. Putnam, "Civic Disengagement in Contemporary America," *Government and Opposition*, 36 (2001): 135. See also his book *Bowling Alone: The Collapse and Revival of American Community* (New York: Simon and Shuster 2000).
8 Angus Reid, *Shakedown: How the New Economy is Changing Our Lives* (Toronto: Doubleday Canada 1996), 286.
9 Henry Tam, *Communitarianism: A New Agenda for Politics and Citizenship* (Washington Square, N.Y.: New York University Press 1998). See also Robert Bellah et al., *Habits of the Heart: Individualism and Commitment in American Life* (New York: Harper and Row 1985).
10 Charles Taylor, *The Malaise of Modernity* (Concord, Ont.: Anansi 1991), 3–4.
11 John O'Neil, *The Missing Child in Liberal Theory: Towards a Covenant*

Theory of Family, Community, Welfare, and the Civic State (Toronto: University of Toronto Press 1994), 13. See also Robert Kuttner, *The Virtues and Limits of Markets* (New York: Alfred A. Knopf 1997), and R. Keat and N. Abercrombie, *Enterprise Culture* (London: Routledge 1991).

12 See, for example, Jane Jenson, *Mapping Social Cohesion: The State of Canadian Research* (Ottawa: Canadian Policy Research Networks 1998).

13 These percentages may not be entirely comparable. In 1941 the census asked about the ancestry on the male side only and did not accept multiple origins. In 1996, multiple origins were counted (e.g., British and 'other'; French and 'other,' etc.). Thus, of the 42 per cent with non-British, non-French, non-aboriginal origins, 26 per cent declared one and 16 per cent two or more origins.

14 The results of the 1996 census on ethnic origin and visible minorities are presented in Ravi Pendakur and Jenna Hennebry, *Multicultural Canada: A Demographic Overview* (Ottawa: Multiculturalism, Department of Canadian Heritage 1998).

15 The non-white population was still largely foreign born: between 72 and 94 per cent for all visible minority groups in 1991, except the Japanese (23 per cent) and the Pacific Islanders (63 per cent). See Karen Kelly, "Visible Minorities: A Diverse Group," *Canadian Social Trends*, 37 (summer 1995): 4.

16 Lester C. Thurow, "Building Wealth," *Atlantic Monthly*, June 1999, 60.

17 Donald Savoie, *Governing from the Centre: The Concentration of Power in Canadian Politics* (Toronto: University of Toronto Press 1999).

18 The results of a survey quoted by Alan C. Cairns in *Disruptions* (Toronto: McClelland and Stewart 1991), 20.

19 Guy Crittenden, "Flack Attack," *Globe and Mail*, 31 October 1998, D1.

20 Neil Nevitte, *The Decline of Deference* (Peterborough, Ont.: Broadview Press 1996), 301–6.

21 An analysis of the impact of structural and value changes in our society is provided in Neil Nevitte, "Value Change and Re-orientations in Citizen-State Relations" *Canadian Public Policy*, 26 (supplement, 2000), S73–S94.

22 Francis Fukuyama, *Trust: The Social Virtues and Creation of Prosperity* (London: Hamish Hamilton 1995).

23 The World Values Survey is a worldwide investigation of socio-cultural and political change. It has carried out representative national surveys of the basic values and beliefs of publics in more than sixty-five societies in all six inhabited continents, containing almost 80 per cent of the world's population. It builds on the European Values Surveys, first carried out in 1981. A second wave of surveys, designed for global use, was completed in 1990–91, a third wave was carried out in 1995–96, and a fourth wave

took place in 1999–2001. This project is being carried out by an international network of social scientists, with local funding for each survey (though in some cases, it has been possible to raise supplementary funds from outside sources). See the website vws.isr.umich.edu.

24 The survey involved in-home interviews with a randomly selected sample of 2,014 adult respondents (eighteen years of age and older). They were carried out in the spring of 1997 by Environics Research, Toronto. For more details on the sample, see Appendix.

25 Initially, the grant from the Social Sciences and Humanities Research Council of Canada stipulated that the study be limited to Quebec and Ontario. It was only after the first phase of in-depth interviews was completed that additional funding was obtained from the Kahanoff Foundation to extend the survey to the entire country. For a description of the sample and of the way in which it was selected, see Appendix.

26 The approach is similar to that adopted by Nevitte in *The Decline of Deference*. While tests of statistical significance are not presented in the text, they are an integral part of our analysis. The overall margin of error in our sample is ± 2.2 percentage point, nineteen times out of twenty. Where differences between subgroups are noted, most are significant at a 0.01 per cent level of significance. All that are attributed substantive significance reflect at least a 0.05 per cent. Where the significance level is lower, the data is noted as supporting trends or directions.

CHAPTER TWO

1 Respondents were asked the following question: *"People have different views about the problems faced by our society. Do you strongly agree, agree, disagree or strongly disagree that the trouble with our society is ...?"*

2 Over 66 per cent of upper-class respondents perceived this to be an important problem and ranked it ninth out of twelve items. Among the lower class, the values were 85 per cent and sixth place respectively.

3 This occurs among Canadians aged eighteen to twenty-four, of whom only 46 per cent saw it as a threat, and among Québécois, where the figure stands at 49 per cent.

4 John Ralston Saul, *Reflections of a Siamese Twin: Canada at the End of the Twentieth Century* (Toronto: Viking 1997), 438–9.

5 Neil Nevitte, *The Decline of Deference* (Peterborough, Ont.: Broadview Press 1996), 230.

6 Ibid., 95–7.

7 Jim Coyle, "A civil city is nothing to sneer at," Toronto Star, 20 July 1999, B1.

CHAPTER THREE

1   Jane Coutts, "Ontario civil service in crisis situation, Ombudsman warns," *Globe and Mail*, 17 June 1999,

2   Patricia Orwen, "Disabled workers cut off by new benefits," Toronto Star, 4 December 1999, A27.

3   As part of our study we conducted in-depth interviews with a sample of Canadians in two small towns and two large cities in Ontario and Quebec. The location of the respondent is indicated in parenthesis.

4   Angus Reid Group, *Canada and the World: An International Perspective on Canada and Canadians* (Winnipeg: Angus Reid Group 1992), 125.

5   This compares with 81 per cent in France, 71 per cent in the United States and Australia, and 61 per cent in Britain.

6   René Morissette, John Myles, and Garnett Picot, "Earnings Polarization in Canada, 1969–1991," in Keith G. Banting and Charles M. Beach, ed., *Labour Market Polarization and Social Policy Reform* (Kingston, Ont.: Queen's University, School of Policy Studies 1995), 31.

7   Clarence Lochhead and Vivian Shalla, "Delivering the Goods: Income Distribution and the Precarious Middle Class," (Canadian Council on Social Development), *Perception*, 20 (1996): 15–19.

8   Statistics Canada, *Income after Tax, Distributions by Size in Canada* (Ottawa, 1997, Cat. # 13–210–XPB). The measure used is the Gini coefficient. It varies from zero, which would mean perfect equality of incomes, and one, which represents perfect inequality.

9   Sarah Bélanger and Maurice Pinard, "Ethnic Movements and the Competition Model: Some Missing Links." *American Sociological Review*, 56 (1991): 453.

10 The question asked is: *"Do you think the society we live in is basically fair for most people, for some, or for only a few?"*

11 The question asked is: *"What about you personally: how fairly do you feel you are being treated in this society: very fairly, somewhat fairly, not too fairly, or not at all fairly?"*

12 The three questions asked are the following:

      "Let me ask you about opportunities for jobs and promotions. Do you think that people of your own ethnic, cultural, or racial background have more, the same, or fewer opportunities for jobs and promotions as people of other ethnic, cultural, or racial backgrounds?"

      "What about men and women: do you think that [men/women – select according to gender of respondent] have more, the same, or fewer opportunities for jobs and promotions than (men/women)?"

      "How fairly would you say that the class you belong to is treated in our society today: very fairly, somewhat fairly, not too fairly, or not at all fairly?"

13 There is very little difference in the likelihood of multiple jeopardy among people with different levels of education. Education may protect individuals against certain kinds of unfairness but not against exposure to more than one. For instance, a well-educated person may be unlikely to feel unfairness on the basis of class but nevertheless experience it on the basis of ethnicity and gender.

14 Paul Sniderman et al., *The Clash of Rights: Liberty, Equality and Legitimacy in Pluralist Democracy* (New Haven, Conn.: Yale University Press 1996), 84–5.

15 Angus Reid Group, *Canada and the World*, 147. For Canada the number was 67 per cent. A similar proportion thought this to be the case in the United States (68 per cent), and in Britain (69 per cent), while a slightly lower proportion was recorded in France (62 per cent) and Australia (61 per cent).

16 Angus Reid, *Shakedown: How the New Economy Is Changing Our Lives* (Toronto: Doubleday Canada 1996), 289. The actual figure for Canada was 60 per cent.

CHAPTER FOUR

1 Virginia Galt, "Fighting 'poor' label earns Parkdale kids special recognition," *Globe and Mail*, 15 November 1999, A7. Emphasis added.

2 On the different types of fairness, see James Q. Wilson: *The Moral Sense* (New York: The Free Press, 1993), Ch.3.

3 Virginia Galt, "Fighting 'poor' label," A7.

4 Erma Collins, "Don't blame me; work with me," *Toronto Star*, 19 April 1994. Emphasis added.

5 The following questions were asked:
"This country is made up of many different kinds of people. Although each one makes a contribution to our society, that contribution may not be recognized to the same degree."

"I would like to ask you about the contribution to society of people of your own ethnic, cultural, or racial background. How satisfied are you with the recognition people of your background are receiving for their contribution to society: very satisfied, somewhat satisfied, somewhat dissatisfied, or very dissatisfied?"

"What about people with your level of education or training? How satisfied are you with the recognition that they are receiving for their contribution to society: very satisfied, somewhat satisfied, somewhat dissatisfied, or very dissatisfied?"

"And what about (women) (men)? [Ask about gender of respondent] How satisfied are you with the recognition that (men) (women) are

receiving for their contribution to society: very satisfied, somewhat satisfied, somewhat dissatisfied, or very dissatisfied?"

6 The following questions were asked:

"Would you say that people of your ethnic, cultural or racial background are receiving more, less or about the same recognition for their contribution to society as they did a few years ago?"

"Do you feel that people with your level of education and training are receiving more, less, or about the same recognition for their contribution to society as they were a few years ago?"

"Do you feel that (men) (women) are receiving more, less, or about the same recognition for their contribution to society as they were a few years ago?"

7 Reginald Bibby, *Social Trends Canadian Style* (Toronto: Stoddart 1995), 82.

CHAPTER FIVE

1 Trudy Govier, *Social Trust and Human Communities* (Montreal: McGill-Queen's University Press 1997), 4.

2 Reginald Bibby, *Social Trends Canadian Style* (Toronto: Stoddart 1995), 59.

3 This and other problems faced by our society are discussed in Chapter 9.

4 Allan R. Gregg, "A Confident Nation," *Maclean's*, 29 December 1997, 45.

5 Frank Graves and Paul Reed, *Canadians and Their Public Institutions* (Ottawa: Canadian Centre for Management Development 1998), 17.

6 The following question was asked:

"Some people place different amounts of trust in others; they may be concerned that others may take advantage of them. How much do you trust the following people to not take advantage of you: a lot, some, not very much, or not at all? a) Your fellow workers; b) your friends; c) people who have different political beliefs; d) members of your ethnic, cultural, or racial background; e) people who have different moral values; f) your family; and g) people who have different religious beliefs?"

CHAPTER SIX

1 Neil Roese, "Canadians' Shrinking Trust in Government: Causes and Consequences," in Neil Nevitte, ed., *Value Change and Governance in Canada* (Toronto: University of Toronto Press, 2002).

2 Allan Gregg and Michael Posner, *The Big Picture* (Toronto: Macfarlane Walter and Ross 1990), 54.

3 Ibid.,58.

4 The interconnections among institutions would be an important object of analysis. It is, however, beyond the scope of the present study.

5 The question is the same as for horizontal trust, expect that it is asked about the following: *"a) politicians in the federal government; b) businessmen; c) politicians in your province; and d) your employer."*

6 Tom Tyler et al., "The Influence of Perceived Injustice on the Endorsement of Political Leaders," *Journal of Applied Social Psychology*, 15 (1985): 717. Emphasis added.

7 Ekos Research Associates, *Rethinking Government '94. An Overview and Synthesis* (Ottawa: Ekos Research Associates 1995), Table 3.

8 Frank Graves and Paul Reed, "Canadians and Their Public Institutions" (Ottawa: Canadian Centre for Management Development, mimeograph, 1988), 14–15.

9 Angus Reid Group, *Canada and the World: An International Perspective on Canada and Canadians* (Winnipeg: Angus Reid Group 1992), 150. The percentages are lower in other Western societies: United States, Britain and Australia, 69 per cent; France, 62 per cent; and Italy, 53 per cent.

10 Lisa Young, "Civic Engagement, Trust and Democracy: Evidence from Alberta," in Neil Nevitte, ed., *Value Change and Governance in Canada*.

11 Jeffrey Simpson, "How can there be accountability without responsibility," *Globe and Mail*, 8 January 1997, A19.

12 Neil Nevitte, "Value Change and Reorientations in Citizen-State Relations," *Canadian Public Policy*, 26 (supplement) (2000): S79.

13 Neil Nevitte, *The Decline of Deference* (Peterborough, Ont.: Broadview Press 1996), 301–6.

14 Angus Reid, *Shakedown: How the New Economy Is Changing Our Lives* (Toronto: Doubleday Canada 1996), 289.

15 Peter C. Newman, *The Canadian Revolution 1985–1995: From Deference to Deviance* (Toronto: Viking 1995), 69–70.

16 Graves and Reed, "Canadians and Their Public Institutions."

CHAPTER SEVEN

1 Stephen Dale, *Lost in the Suburbs* (Toronto: Stoddart 1999), 29.

2 The following questions were addressed to the respondents:
"How much do you feel at home in the community where you live: very much, somewhat, a little, or not at all?"
"How much do you feel at home in this society as a whole: very much, somewhat, a little, or not at all?"

3 In the remainder of the chapter, only the sense of being at home in the society will be considered, since we believe this issue to be more important for society as a whole than the sense of belonging to the local community.

4 Subsequent chapters will explore how the sense of being at home varies according to gender, social class, ethnic and racial background, and province of residence.

5 The respondents were asked the following: *Some people feel they have control over the way their lives turn out, and other people feel that what they themselves do has no real effect on what happens to them. What about you: do you feel you have a great deal of control, some, not very much, or none at all over the way your life turns out?"*

CHAPTER EIGHT

1 These will be dealt with in subsequent chapters.

2 Among the very religious, 43 per cent of Catholics and 46 per cent of Protestants express a strong sense of social indebtedness.

CHAPTER NINE

1 Alvin W. Gouldner, "The Importance of Something for Nothing," in *For Sociology: Renewal and Critique in Sociology Today* (New York: Basic Books 1973), 263–6.

2 Robert D. Putnam, "The Prosperous Community: Social Capital and Public Life," *The American Prospect*, 13 (spring 1993): 37. See also James S. Coleman, "Social Capital and the Creation of Human Capital," *American Journal of Sociology*, 94 (Supplement) (1988): S95–S120.

3 Michael Walzer, *Spheres of Justice: A Defense of Pluralism and Equality* (New York: Basic Books 1983), 64, 68.

4 The question is as follows:
  "How strong an obligation do you feel towards helping the follow-ing kinds of people: Very strong, moderately strong, not too strong, or not strong at all? a) Family; b) close friends; c) people in the same boat as I am in life; d) people from my ethnic, cultural, or racial back-ground; e) any person in society who needs help."

5 The orientation is also related to the degree of importance that respon-dents attach to their own ethnic, cultural, or ethnic background.

6 In this case, the difference is between those who consider the background as very important and those who see it as not at all important. The ques-tion asked is as follows: *"How important is your ethnic, cultural, or racial background to you: very important, somewhat important, not very important, or not at all important?"*

CHAPTER TEN

1 The question asked in the survey is as follows: *"In the past twelve*

months, did you help some organization or group by doing such things as canvassing, organizing activities, coaching, providing care, delivering food, doing clerical or administrative work, or other kinds of activities?" Another question asked about the frequency of such activities.

2 The question asked here was: *"Some people also help others on their own, not through an organization or a group. Please try to recall any unpaid help you may have given to others in the past year, including friends, neighbours and relatives, but not people in your own household. In the past twelve months, did you help with such things as cooking, shopping, babysitting, writing letters, shovelling snow, mowing the lawn, or any other way?"* This question was also followed by one about the frequency of such help.

3 The question here was: *"In the past twelve months, have you made a donation to an organization or to a cause of one kind or another?"* It was also followed by a question pertaining to the frequency of such donations.

4 Michael Walzer, "Toward a Theory of Social Assignments," in Winthrop Knowlton and Richard Zeckhauser, ed., *American Society: Public and Private Responsibilities* (Cambridge, Mass.: Ballinger Publications 1986), 90–3.

5 Alexis de Tocqueville, *Democracy in America* (New York: Vintage Book, 1954), vol. 2, 109 (initially published in Paris in 1835).

6 Andras Kelen, "Making Pledges and Requirements: Historical Variants of 'Voluntary Labor,'" *International journal of Comparative Sociology*, 26 (1985): 210.

7 The correlation is +.36 between helping an organization and informal help; +.34 between helping an organization and donations; and +.17 between informal help and donations.

8 Only 22 per cent of our sample believe that paying taxes exempts them from making voluntary contributions to their community

9 Alvin W. Gouldner, "The Importance of Something for Nothing," in *For Sociology: Renewal and Critique in Sociology Today* (New York: Basic Books 1973), 280.

10 Almost seven out of ten (68 per cent) of those who are involved in an organization feel very much at home in the community, compared to 52 per cent of those who are not at all involved. About two-thirds (65 per cent) of the very religious and 54 per cent of the not very religious feel very much at home in their local community.

11 Michael Hall et al., *Caring Canadians, Involved Canadians: Highlights from the 1997 National Survey of Giving, Volunteering and Participating* (Ottawa: Statistics Canada 1998), 33, 37.

12 James S. Coleman, "Social Capital and the Creation of Human Capital," *American Journal of Sociology* 94 (supplement) (1988): S104.

CHAPTER TWELVE

1 Pat Armstrong and Hugh Armstrong, *The Double Ghetto: Canadian Women and Their Segregated Work*, 3ʳᵈ ed. (Toronto: McClelland and Stewart 1994).
2 Angus Reid Group, *Canada and the World: An International Perspective on Canada and Canadians* (Winnipeg: Angus Reid Group 1992), 138. The percentage of women who make this assessment is about the same in the United States, higher in Britain and Australia (about 55 per cent), and lower in France (about 30 per cent). If all levels of agreement are considered, a strong majority of both men and women agree in fifteen of sixteen countries included in the survey.
3 Paul Beaudry and David Green, "Cohort Patterns in Canadian Earnings: Assessing the Role of Skill Premia in Inequality Trends," The Canadian Institute for Advanced Research, Working Paper 96, 1997. See also René Morissette, "Declining Earnings of Young Men," *Canadian Social Trends*, 46 (autumn 1997): 8–12.

CHAPTER THIRTEEN

1 The national survey with a sample size of 3,325 was sponsored by Multiculturalism and Citizenship Canada and conducted by Angus Reid.
2 S.D. Clark, "The Post Second World War Canadian Society." *Canadian Review of Sociology and Anthropology*, 12 (1975): 29.
3 Canada, House of Commons *Debates*, 1971, 8546. Initially, the implementation focused on another component of the policy, namely, to assist "all cultural groups that have demonstrated a desire and effort to continue to grow and contribute to Canada." As a result, many Canadians got the impression that the policy was only about cultural maintenance. The focus on overcoming barriers came later.
4 Monica Boyd, "Gender, Visible Minority and Immigrant Earnings Inequality: Reassessing an Employment Equity Premise," in Vic Satzewich, ed., *Deconstructing a Nation: Immigration, Multiculturalism and Racism in the 1990s in Canada* (Toronto: Fernwood Press 1992).
5 Ibid. See also Jeffrey G. Reitz and Raymond Breton, *The Illusion of Difference: Realities of Ethnicity in Canada and the United States* (Toronto: C.D. Howe Institute 1994), 97.
6 Karen Kelly, "Visible Minorities: A Diverse Group," *Canadian Social Trends*, 37 (summer 1995): 2–8.
7 The members of these minorities are also the most likely to experience unfairness on more than one basis (such as gender and class).
8 Jason Z. Lian and David R. Matthews, "Does the Vertical Mosaic Still

Exist? Ethnicity and Income in Canada, 1991," *Canadian Review of Sociology and Anthropology*, 35 (1998): 461–2.

9 An illustration is the title of a book on the history of the Finnish Organization of Canada: William Eklund, *Builders of Canada: History of the Finnish Organization of Canada, 1911–1971* (Toronto: Finnish Organization of Canada 1987).

10 Ingrid Peritz, "Railway porters finally get their due," *Globe and Mail*, 15 February 1999, A3. Emphasis added.

11 Sarah Bélanger and Maurice Pinard, "Ethnic Movements and the Competition Model: Some Missing Links," *American Sociological Review*, 56 (1991): 453.

12 Respondents were asked three questions with regard to their financial situation and its evolution. First, they were asked how satisfied they were with the way they and their family were getting along financially. They were also asked if they were better off, worse off, or about the same financially as a year ago. Finally, they were queried about their financial prospects a year hence. Their financial situation was classified as follows: a) negative if they were very dissatisfied and if their financial situation had worsened in the last year and would not be improving in the future; b) poor if they were dissatisfied and if their situation had not changed in the past year and would not be changing in the coming year; c) positive if they were satisfied and if there had been no change in their situation from the past year and none was expected for the coming year; and d) very positive if they were very satisfied and their financial situation was better than in the previous year and was expected to improve again in the coming year.

13 Marvin Kurz, "The Canadian Jewish divide," *Globe and Mail*, 26 July 2002.

14 Paul M. Sniderman et al., *The Clash of Rights: Liberty, Equality, and Legitimacy in Pluralist Democracy* (New Haven, Conn.: Yale University Press 1996), 196–7. The survey included 2,084 respondents.

15 Recently, the leader of the Canadian Alliance declared that "the federal government should not cajole a course or impose a regime [of official bilingualism] on a province." *Globe and Mail*, 6 August 2002, A1.

16 The number of respondents whose home language is neither English nor French is too small to give reliable results here.

17 Since the number of cases in our sample is small, it is not possible to explore this hypothesis by comparing immigrant and Canadian-born respondents who belong to visible minorities.

CHAPTER FOURTEEN

1 Mancur Olson, "Rapid Growth As a Destabilizing Force," in Jason L.

Finkle and Richard W. Gable, ed., *Political Development and Social Change* (New York: John Wiley and Sons 1966), 560.

2 Ralf Dahrendorf, "A Precarious Balance: Economic Opportunity, Civil Society, and Political Liberty," *The Responsive Community* (summer 1995): 27–8.

3 Kevin K. Lee, *Urban Poverty in Canada: A Statistical Profile* (Ottawa: Canadian Council on Social Development 2000), 21–4.

4 Between 1980 and 1995, the number of low-income families living in poor neighbourhoods increased by 10 per cent or more in Toronto, Montreal, Winnipeg, Saskatoon, and Edmonton; it decreased by 10 per cent or more in London, Sherbrooke, Trois-Rivières, Windsor, Chicoutimi-Jonquière, and St Catharines-Niagara (Lee, *Urban Poverty in Canada*, 24).

5 Ekos Research Associates, *Rethinking Government '94* (Ottawa: Ekos Research Associates 1995), 5–6.

6 Position in the socio-economic hierarchy is measured by combining the educational and income levels of the respondents. Thus, a person at the bottom is at the lowest level on both scales, a person at the top is high on both scales, and so on.

7 Respondents were asked to identify the social class to which they belong. The resulting distribution is as follows: lower class: 7 per cent, working class: 37 per cent, lower middle-class: 33 per cent, upper middle-class: 22 per cent, upper class: 1 per cent. In this analysis, the two higher levels have been combined because of the small number of cases in the upper class.

8 The question asked was the following: *"How fairly would you say that the class you belong to is treated in our society today: very fairly, somewhat fairly, not too fairly, or not at all fairly?"*

9 Similar but less pronounced results are obtained with the measure based on income and education: 77 per cent of those in the upper echelons (25 per cent very and 52 per cent somewhat fairly) and 62 per cent in the lower echelons (9 per cent very and 53 per cent somewhat fairly) declare that their class is treated fairly.

10 Carl J. Cuneo, "International Images of Social Inequality: A ten-Country Comparison," in Alan Frizzell and Jon H. Pammett, ed., *Social Inequality in Canada* (Ottawa: Carleton University Press, 1996), 31–66. The International Social Survey Programme (ISSP) is a voluntary grouping of study teams in twenty-five nations, each of which carry out a short, annual self-completion survey containing an agreed set of questions asked of a probability-based, nation-wide sample of adults. The topics change from year to year by agreement, with a view to replication every five years or so. The questions themselves are developed by subgroups and then thrashed out at an annual meeting attended by representatives of each national

team ... The ISSP's "official" data archive, the Zentralarchiv, is located at the University of Cologne. See the website www.issp.org/info.htm.

11 Ibid, 39.

12 Murray Campbell, "Lives are improving but many Canadians feel insecure: Study," *Globe and Mail*, 26 April 1999, A6. The findings are from a report prepared by the Canadian Council on Social Development.

13 Richard Mackie, "Seem harder to make ends meet? You're not alone, survey says," *Globe and Mail*, 4 August 1998, A7.

14 Paul Beaudry and David Green, "Cohort Patterns in Canadian Earnings: Assessing the Role of Skill Premia in Inequality Trends" (Toronto: Canadian Institute for Advanced Research 1997), 21.

15 Angus Reid, *Shakedown: How the New Economy Is Changing Our Lives* (Toronto: Doubleday Canada 1996), 307, 319.

16 Edward Greenspon, "Health care not the only casualty of federal cutbacks," *Globe and Mail*, 19 December 1998, A9.

17 Valerie Lawton, "U.N. condemns Canadian poverty," Toronto Star, 5 December 1998, A11.

18 An American study found that some people do feel that they are overpaid, given their qualifications and/or the nature of their work. However, considering the nature of the study – an in-depth analysis of a small number of cases – an estimate of the proportion of such cases in the United States population cannot be made. Jennifer Hochschild, *What's Fair? American Beliefs about Distributive Justice* (Cambridge, Mass.: Harvard University Press 1981).

19 Bruce Little, "Why the rich get benefit payments," *Globe and Mail*, 4 May 1998, A7.

20 Ekos Research Associates, *Rethinking Government '94. An Overview and Synthesis* (Ottawa: Ekos Research Associates 1995).

21 Those who strongly agree are more clearly distrustful than the others. The relationship with other variables, when there is one, is more compelling.

22 Francis Fukuyama, "The Great Disruption: Human Nature and the Reconstruction of Social Order," *Atlantic Monthly*, May 1999, 70.

23 Trudy Govier, *Social Trust and Human Communities* (Montreal: McGill-Queen's University Press 1997), 44.

24 Quoted by Stephen Handelman, "Moral crisis," *The Sunday Star* [Toronto], 19 November 1995, F7.

25 Along the same line, it was seen in the previous chapter that the very strong sense of obligation to help people "in the same boat" and from the same ethnic, cultural, or racial background is the highest among visible minorities, those of "other" origins, and immigrants from countries other than Europe and the United States.

26 Although weak, these correlations are statistically significant.
27 Elaine Carey, "Average family works 77 weeks to pay bills," Toronto Star, 7 February 1998, A7.

CHAPTER FIFTEEN

1 Ross Finnie, "Differences in Earnings Inequality by Province, 1982–1994," *Canadian Economic Observer* (Ottawa: Statistics Canada, February 1998).
2 For an analysis that involves a third variable, the western provinces have to be combined, because there are not enough cases in the sample to treat each one separately.
3 The respondents were asked: *"I would like to ask you about federal government programs: Is the province you live in getting more than its fair share of these programs, about its fair share, or less than its fair share?"*
4 Paul Adams,"What does Alberta really want?" *Globe and Mail*, 5 February 2001, A9.
5 Fifteen per cent do not know.
6 The language factor, as it relates to the sense of belonging, is discussed in Chapter 13.
7 No comparison could be made involving those who speak French since there are too few cases of western francophones in the sample.
8 Gary Caldwell,"The decay of civil society in contemporary Quebec," *Inroads*, 7 (1998): 176–84.
9 He is quoted in Jean Benoît Nadeau, "La Charité, Ça S'organise," *L'Actualité*, 15 May 1993, 35–6.

CHAPTER SIXTEEN

1 Multiple regression is the statistical technique used for this kind of analysis. Its general purpose is to study the relationship between several independent variables and a dependent variable. For example, in this case, we wish to find out if each of the independent variables (gender, social class objectively or subjectively defined, ethnicity or race, and region of residence) have an independent impact on the perceptions and experiences related to our specified components of the social fabric when the other three are taken into account, that is to say, are controlled for. The technique also provides a measure of the relative impact of each on the dependent variables.
2 The explanatory input of gender is both high and statistically significant. Beta coefficients provide a measure for the relative strength of the relationship of each variable with the behaviour or attitude under study, when other factors are controlled. For gender, they are .430 with per-

ceived differences in job opportunities and .195 with recognition of contributions of one's gender to society. Both are significant at the highest
possible level (p=.000). In fact, gender explains almost all of the variation
in the perceptions studied.

3 Respondents of southern European origin are a little less likely than the
others to see a large number of problems facing our society.

4 The results with social-class affiliation defined by level of education and
income are the same. For instance, the difference in percentage points
between high and low is the same: sixteen.

5 Similar results obtain with social class level defined by levels of education
and income.

6 John Ralston Saul, *Reflections of a Siamese Twin: Canada at the End of
the Twentieth Century* (Toronto: Viking 1997), 385.

CHAPTER SEVENTEEN

1 Jane Jenson, *Mapping Social Cohesion: The State of Canadian Research*
(Ottawa: Canadian Policy Research Network 1998).

2 For a more detailed discussion of relevant social experiences, see Neil
Nevitte, *The Decline of Deference: Canadian Value Change in Cross-
national Perspective* (Peterborough, Ont.: Broadview Press 1996). The
analysis of tolerance is found on pages 223–36; satisfaction with one's
financial situation on pages 160–62;interest in political participation on
pages 75–106; and national pride on pages 63–4.

3 Ibid., 11

4 Ibid.

5 Social Cohesion Network, "Rekindling Hope and Investing in the
Future," in Policy Research Initiative, ed., "Sustaining Growth, Human
Development and Social Cohesion in a Global World" (Ottawa: Mimeo-
graph 1999), 33.

6 Neil Roese, "Canadians' Shrinking Trust in Governance in Canada," in
Neil Nevitte, ed., *Value Change and Governance in Canada* (Toronto:
University of Toronto Press, forthcoming).

7 Albert O. Hirschman, *Shifting Involvements: Private Interest and Public
Action* (Princeton, N.J.: Princeton University Press 1982), 67.

8 Rosemary Spiers, "For boomers, minivans are still a big gas," Toronto
Star, 11 March 2000, A1 and A24.

9 John Godfrey and Rob McLean, *The Canada We Want* (Toronto: Stoddart 1999).

10 Danielle Juteau, "Patterns of Social Differentiation in Canada: Understanding Their Dynamics and Bridging the Gaps," *Canadian Public
Policy*, 26 (2000): S104.

11 Robert N. Bellah et al., *Habits of the Heart: Individualism and*

Commitment in American Life (New York: Harper and Row 1985), 200.

12 More generally, we think that one would be hard pressed to find much in the public discourse that focuses on the positive contributions that each part of the country is making to the society as a whole. The focus is largely on the negative.

13 Gosta Esping-Andersen, *The Three Worlds of Welfare Capitalism* (Princeton, N.J.: Princeton University Press 1990), 16.

14 Dani Rodrik, *Has Globalization Gone Too Far?* (Washington, D.C.: Institute for International Economics 1997), 6–7, 70.

15 Daniel J. Elazar, *Community and Polity: The Organizational Dynamics of American Jewry* (Philadelphia: Jewish Publication Society of America 1976), 336.

16 Bellah et al., *Habits of the Heart*, 201.

17 Bob Rae, *The Three Questions: Prosperity and the Public Good* (Toronto: Viking 1998), 166. The author quoted is Thucydides, *The Peloponnesian War*, revised in Robert B. Strassler, ed., *The Landmark Thucydides* (New York: Free Press 1996), 148.

18 Stephen Dale, *Lost in the Suburbs* (Toronto: Stoddart 1999), 79–80.

19 Robert Vipond, "Mike Harris, imperial premier," *Globe and Mail*, 11 December 1995, A15.

20 Hugh Segal, *Beyond Greed* (Toronto: Stoddart 1997), 73–5.

21 These involve experienced owners or employees of successful enterprises helping individuals who want to start a business. For a report on such an initiative in Quebec, see *L'Actualité*, 1 October 1994, 31–40.

22 Alan Wolfe, *Whose Keeper? Social Science and Moral Obligation* (Berkeley, Calif.: University of California Press, 1989), 3.

23 On the importance of institutions, see Raymond Breton et al., *Cultural Boundaries*, 5–14 and Jane Jenson, *Mapping Social Cohesion*, 30–2.

24 The Standing Senate Committee on Social Affairs, Science and Technology, "Final Report on Social Cohesion" (Ottawa: mimeograph), 5.

25 Alan Wolfe, *Whose Keeper?* 75.

26 Danielle Juteau, "Patterns of Social Differentiation," S96

Selected References

These are some of the publications that have informed our own thinking and that readers might consult.

Barber, Bernard. *The Logic and Limits of Trust*. New Brunswick, N.J.: Rutgers University Press, 1983.

Bellah, Robert N., et al. *Habits of the Heart: Individualism and Commitment in American Life*. New York: Harper and Row 1985.

Breton, Raymond, Jeffrey G. Reitz, and Victor Valentine. *Cultural Boundaries and the Cohesion of Canada*. Montreal: Institute for Research on Public Policy 1980.

Coleman, James. "Social Capital and the Creation of Human Capital." *American Journal of Sociology*, 94 (supplement) (1988): S95–S120.

Dale, Stephen. *Lost in the Suburbs*. Toronto: Stoddart 1999.

Govier, Trudy. *Social Trust and Human Communities*. Montreal: McGill-Queen's University Press 1997.

Hewitt, John. *Dilemmas of the American Self*. Philadelphia: Temple University Press 1989.

Ignatieff, Michael. *The Needs of Strangers*. New York: Viking Press 1985.

Jenson, Jane. *Mapping Social Cohesion: The State of Canadian Research*. Ottawa: Canadian Policy Research Network 1998.

Nevitte, Neil. *The Decline of Deference: Canadian Value Change in Cross-national Perspective*. Peterborough, Ont.: Broadview Press 1996.

– ed. *Value Change and Governance in Canada*. Toronto: University of Toronto Press, 2002.

– "Value Change and Reorientations in Citizen-State Relations." *Canadian Public Policy*, 26 (supplement, 2000): S73–S94.

Putnam, Robert. "The Prosperous Community: Social Capital and Public Life." *The American Prospect*, 13 (spring 1993): 35–42.

Rae, Bob. *The Three Questions: Prosperity and the Public Good*. Toronto: Viking 1998.

Reid, Angus. *Shakedown: How the New Economy is Changing Our Lives*. Toronto: Doubleday 1996.

Saul, John Ralston. *Reflections of a Siamese Twin. Canada at the End of the Twentieth Century*. Toronto: Viking 1997.

– *The Unconscious Civilization*. Concord: House of Anansi Press 1995.

Segal, Hugh. *Beyond Greed: A Traditional Conservative Confronts Neoconservative Excess*. Toronto: Stoddart 1997.

Sniderman, Paul, et.al. *The Clash of Rights: Liberty, Equality, and Legitimacy in Pluralist Democracy*. New Haven, Conn.: Yale University Press 1996.

Taylor, Charles. *The Malaise of Modernity*. Concord: House of Anansi Press 1991.

Walzer, Michael. *Spheres of Justice: A Defense of Pluralism and Equality*. New York: Basic Books 1983.

Wolfe, Alan. *Whose Keeper? Social Science and Moral Obligations*. Berkeley, Calif.: University of California Press 1989.

Index

Abercrombie, N., 200n11
Adams, Paul, 156, 212n4
alienation. *See* estrangement
Armstrong, Hugh, 208n1(ch.12)
Armstrong, Pat, 208n1(ch.12)

Beaudry, Paul, 139, 208n3(ch.12), 211n14
Bélanger, Sarah, 33, 121, 202n9, 209n11
Bellah, Robert, 73, 191, 213n11, 214n16
belonging
– and authentic membership, 65; and psychological well-being, 65; regional differences, 160; and tolerance of diversity, 65–6; sense of, 15; social-class differences, 146
– to local community: anglophone-francophone comparisons, 126–7; by community size, 67; and ethnocultural origin, 123; by marital status, 67; respondents' sense of, 66–7, 72, 99
– to society: among allophones, 128; anglophone-francophone differences, 125–6; and country of birth, 123; and cumulative disadvantages, 71; and ethnocultural origin, 123–4; and perceived fairness, 69, 124; and satisfaction with recognition of contribution, 70–2; sense of, 68, 72, 99; and sense of control, 71, 72; and social diversity, 66, 68, 72; and trust, 71, 72
beneficence, norm of, 83, 95, 178
Bibby, Reginald, 45, 49, 204n2
Boyd, Monica, 208n4
Breton, Raymond, 208n5, 214n23

Cairns, Alan C., 12, 200n18
Caldwell, Gary, 162; 212n8
Campbell, Murray, 211n12
Canadian Senate, Standing Committee on Social Affairs, Science and Technology, 7
Carey, Elaine, 150–1, 212n27
census data, comparability of, 200n13

tion, 136; and ethnocultural origin, 117–18; gender differences,
108; and perceived fairness of distribution of federal funding, 156–7;
perception of, 34, 38, 99; regional
differences, 154; social-class differences, 118, 135–6
feeling at home. *See* belonging, sense
of
financial contribution. *See* donations
financial situation, satisfaction with:
and perceived fairness of society,
139; trends in, 138
Finnie, Ross, 212n1(ch.15)
Fukuyama, Francis, 3, 17, 144, 146,
211n22

Galt, Virginia, 41, 42, 203nn1,3
gender: as a line of social fragmentation, 108; and perceived fairness,
108
globalization, 11; and social cohesion, 190
Godfrey, John, 185, 213n9
good society, 22; dimensions valued
in, 22; perceived threats to, 24–6
Gouldner, Alvin W., 83, 89,
205n1(ch.9), 207n9
governmental institutions, changes
in, 12
Govier, Trudy, 47, 145, 204n1,
211n23
Graves, Frank, 50, 60, 63, 204n5
Green, David, 208n3(ch.12),
211n14
Greenspoon, Edward, 140, 211n16
Gregg, Allan R., 49, 56, 203n4,
204nn2,3(ch.6)
group self-image and recognition of
social contribution, 42

Hall, Michael, 96, 207n11

Handleman, Stephen, 211n24
helping others, obligation regarding,
15–16, 81–8, 98; and class solidarity, 148; and personal needs,
148–9; and social boundaries, 83,
85–7; by socio-economic status
148; and strength of social fabric,
87, 99; and universalistic versus
particularistic orientations, 86, 87,
88, 98
Hennebry, Jenna, 10, 200n14
Hirshman, Albert, 184, 213n7
Hochschild, Jennifer, 211n18
horizontal trust. *See* trust in social
relations

indebtedness to society, 15; among
disadvantaged, 78; and life experiences, 76, 79, 147; and perceived
fairness, 76–9; regional variations,
161–2; and self versus collective
orientations, 74–6, 79; sense of,
73–80, 89; social-class differences,
147; and social interdependence,
73–4; in visible minorities, 128
individualism, culture of, 74. *See
also* market culture
infrastructure
– material and technical, 4
– social and normative, 4; and
social covenant, 4
institutional leaders: citizens views
of, 192; role in bridging social
boundaries, 191, 192; and special-
interest groups, 192
International Monetary Fund, 187
International Social Survey Program,
137
Isaacs, Harold R., 64

Jenson, Jane, 7, 9, 176, 199n4,
200n12, 213n1
jeopardy, multiple, 36–8, 203n13